The Prose Poem in France
Theory and Practice

The Prose Poem in France
Theory and Practice

edited by MARY ANN CAWS
and HERMINE RIFFATERRE

COLUMBIA UNIVERSITY PRESS

NEW YORK

1983

Library of Congress Cataloging in Publication Data
Main entry under title:

The Prose poem in France.

Includes index.
1. Prose poems, French—History and criticism—
Addresses, essays, lectures.   2. French poetry—
History and criticism—Addresses, essays, lectures.
I. Caws, Mary Ann.   II. Riffaterre, Hermine B.
PQ491.P76   1983   841'.009   82-20691
ISBN 0-231-05434-3
ISBN 0-231-05435-1 (pbk)

Columbia University Press
New York   Guildford, Surrey

Clothbound editions of Columbia University Press books are
Smyth-sewn and printed on permanent and durable acid-free
paper.

Contents

Preface

The essays assembled here in no way represent an attempt to set limits upon a genre as complex and controversial as that of the prose poem, but rather the presentation of a number of views and their confrontation with the prose poem as center. The interest generated by the prose poem, particularly in France, has been perhaps in recent years more enthusiastic than productive: thus the continued reference to Suzanne Bernard's massive tome of 1962, to which there has been no noticeable sequel. It may well be that the topic calls for multiple approaches: this volume is a response of many minds and hands to a single question and a specific subject.

With a genre so clearly situated at a crossroads or at an especially problematic locus, the question is less one of inclusion (all the possible angles of and on the prose poem or all the great practitioners of it) than of the representation or sampling of a number of related topics requiring present attention and of their cross-linkings, and of an equal number of appreciations of the various types of such poems. Instead of trying to gloss over the differences of treatment or of opinion among the essayists included here, or to flatten out the discrepancies into some homogeneity—at the risk of making the subject into an object—we have left each author free for a personal response. The overlappings, contradictions, and disagreements, some apparent, some implied, are more properly to be cherished than to be deplored: the variousness of style and of sight bears witness to the present passion about the genre.

Ideally, this collection would have just the traditional qualities recognized in the prose poem itself at its best: brevity, intensity, and self-containment or integrity; it would be limited in length but unlimited in application, in forms, and in substance. In fact, it is determined by the individual reactions of the authors called upon here.

It scarcely needs to be said that we were unable to cover all the topics or invite all the opinions we would have liked to, and that we express our warmest thanks to all those who helped with their counsel, their interest, and their concern. To all the contributors, our lively appreciation, and to the readers, our hope that they will find the essays stimulating, including any dark patches or difficult passages which may appear, and take to heart Ruskin's saying about paintings: "Excellence of the highest kind, without obscurity, cannot exist" (*Modern Painters*, vol. 4). The painting we would make of the prose poem, full of light and shade ("of shadow mingled with its surface"), of partial order and ironic passion, is not meant in any sense to arrest the subject as a static thing, but above all to open it out and up to reflection, as it is held, successively, in different lights and before different eyes.

MARY ANN CAWS

Introduction

The essays that make up this volume have been arranged according to their emphasis: history, theory, or textual analysis. But whatever their bent, all are founded upon close reading of the text.

The first two pieces, historical in perspective, offer answers to the question of why the prose poem developed in the first place, and why, to this day, it remains a genre practised chiefly in France. Leroy C. Breunig finds its roots in poets' impatience with the straitjacket of traditional French versification. He compares the two possible ways of escaping conventional metrics: you could liberate verse from prosodic constraints—Apollinaire's solution; or you could repudiate verse—Rimbaud's more radical departure. Roger Shattuck, likewise, shows how Baudelaire's prose poems fit into the overall scheme of nineteenth-century French theory and practice of the arts: Baudelaire's art criticism rests upon a concept of beauty the poet envisioned as a new esthetic gospel. It is on the basis of these principles—later to inspire French impressionism—that he creates his prose poems.

Five essays on the theory of the genre attempt, in different ways, to find out which formal and semantic features are constant, minimal components of the prose poem and can therefore help us define it as a literary entity. Michel Beaujour proposes two constants, formal and ontological: the poem must be short and mimetic (e.g., the city as analogical model for poetic consciousness, in Baudelaire's *Spleen de Paris*). He further suggests that the elimination of verse as an agent of differentiation becomes conceivable where

the poet sees poetic language as ontologically different from ordinary language and giving access through visionary experience
to a universe that so to speak inhabits the obverse of language.
Images no longer refer to signifieds: images only signify themselves.

Like Beaujour, Tzvetan Todorov recognizes brevity as a req-
uisite, but only as an additional restraint upon the basic mixture
of prose and the poetic (rather than poetry) defined as a purely
thematic category. Casting an eye over *Illuminations,* however, he
is prompted to insist that poetry cannot be compassed by one single
definition, and that in Rimbaud's case presentation is at work
rather than representation. Meaning is not mimetic; the work of
art and its object are one.

Barbara Johnson locates the specificity of the prose poem in
figural deconstruction. On the one hand, equivalences between
mutually exclusive metaphors confer their unity upon poems of
Baudelaire. On the other hand, erasure of the contradiction between literal and figurative meanings begets poeticity, entails erasure of the difference between subject and object. It is from the
figure, from its violation of the logic of contradiction, that the poem
derives its own language or poetic quality. To me, a textually motivated closure looks characteristic of the prose poem's poeticity: I
show how parallel textual constants (two or more image sequences,
for instance) first appear unrelated, then combine into a lexical or
thematic clausula that melds the morphological and semantic features of the sequential constants. Michael Riffaterre discovers a
constrast between verse poetry and prose poem in their differing
modes of text production: in verse, form is imposed upon content
by an arbitrary, preestablished convention—metre. In a prose
poem form is not arbitrary, it is motivated by content, follows an
ad hoc rule: intertextuality. For example, in the texts of Francis
Ponge he discusses, images look gratuitous or absurd or, more
generally, ungrammatical in context until the reader realizes that
they make sense in an intertext; this perception restores grammaticality. The consistency of the intertextual relationship makes
for the unity we expect in a poem.

Under "Practice" we have grouped three essays centered less
on theory than on empirical readings. Robert Greer Cohn tests his

tetrapolarity model on texts from Baudelaire and Mallarmé: the vertical and horizontal axes of the model account for the oxymoric linkage of "prose" and "poem" in the genre's name. He finds the axes aptly symbolized in the recurrent image of *croisée* (French window). James Lawler analyzes a collection of Paul Valéry's prose poems and decides that the very features (mostly auditory or musical, like repetition and symmetry) distinguishing this prose from ordinary discourse are also figures of content ("mystical"), which reflect the personal crisis that drove Valéry to forsake verse: he identified verse too closely with the kind of man he had once been. Mary Ann Caws takes a similar approach: in Claudel's *Connaissance de l'Est* she points out poetic forms that also have a metapoetic function. Thus recurring images (here, water imagery) have their intrinsic value but also guide our reading of the text (e.g., the mirroring of the landscape, or its dissolving in the seascape, demand of the reader "an intense participation in sight as in text"). The edges of Reverdy's prose poems lend their own kind of knowledge to the metapoetic landscape.

Albert Sonnenfeld draws out and develops to the full the implications of poetic closure. Methodologically his paper belongs in the second section, but its topic makes it "metapoetically" a tempting conclusion to the collection—we could not resist. Sonnenfeld underscores how exactly the breakdown of traditional formal constraints coincides with the renewed emphasis upon the poem's boundaries. Significantly, this emphasis is all the stronger, as is syntactical coherence, in extreme cases of semantic incoherence such as Rimbaud's texts and the dream poems of the surrealists.

Despite the diversity of approaches evident in this volume, or perhaps because of that very diversity, a clear consensus emerges as to what traits will define a genre too often thought undefinable: brevity, closure, inner "deconventionalized" motivation of forms, relationship between representation-space and the poem's spatial features, one shaping the other, and so forth. All lead to the inescapable conclusion that the prose poem, as Mary Ann Caws puts it, "having no necessary exterior framework, no meter or essential form, must organize itself from within."

HERMINE RIFFATERRE

The Prose Poem in France
Theory and Practice

Prose is not to be read aloud but to one's self at night, but it is not quick as poetry but rather a gathering web of insinuations which go further than names however shared ever go. Prose should be a long intimacy between strangers with no direct appeal to what both may have known. It should slowly appeal to feelings unexpressed, it should in the end draw tears out of the stone.

—HENRY GREEN, *PACK MY BAG*

PART I Situation

1. Why France?

LeRoy C. Breunig

A recently published international anthology of the prose poem gives the biggest slice to the French and restates the generally accepted fact that for the West at least the genre originated in nineteenth-century France.[1] Born of Aloysius Bertrand in his *Gaspard de la nuit*, it came into bloom in Baudelaire's *Petits Poèmes en prose* and achieved what may well be its masterpiece in Rimbaud's *Illuminations*.

But why France? In its own way this question demands as complex an answer as "Why did the French make the French Revolution?" And without presuming in the least to become the Michelet or the Carlyle of the prose poem—Suzanne Bernard has already aspired to that honor—we can in these several pages examine what I believe to be one of the major reasons: the revolt of one poet in particular, Arthur Rimbaud, against the yoke of French prosody. This revolt was his own Bastille Day. Baudelaire, acknowledging the originality of Bertrand, wrote his prose poems as a kind of sideline, an experiment; they were not meant to outshine the verse of *Les Fleurs du mal*. And few readers would claim to find the prose version of "L'Invitation au voyage," for example, more beautiful than the harmonious lines of the verse poem. Baudelaire was classical to the extent that he never rejected the constraints of

THROUGHOUT THIS BOOK, unless another source is given, all translations of quotes from the French are by the author of the article or by Mary Ann Caws.

French prosody; indeed he profited from them. For Rimbaud, on the contrary, the prose poem became a necessity, a kind of Copernican step, the only form of expression that remained after the rejection of the conformities imposed by the meter and rhyme of the French poetic language.

It is often difficult for one whose native language is the same as Shakespeare's to appreciate the stringent rules of classical French versification. "France where poets were never born!" the Victorians would say; and some of the most sensitive English-language critics have been baffled by what they consider the monotony of French verse, particularly the alexandrine. Dryden's commentator, Edmond Malone, disparaged it by claiming that it "runs exactly like our ballad measure: 'A cobbler there was and he lived in a stall.'" Émile Legouis in his *Défense de la poésie française* has shown how Malone's remark is typical of most English criticism of the eighteenth and nineteenth centuries.[2]

The misunderstanding comes from thinking of French meter in terms of feet. Unlike iambic pentameter, for example, where the basic unit is the iamb, a French alexandrine is not a piling up of feet but is itself the basic unit, a dodecasyllabic line, which may be subdivided in a great variety of ways. An English line is synthetic, a French line analytic. Racine's couplet from *Phèdre* is customarily cited in English manuals as the finest example of the French alexandrine:

> Ce n'est plus une ardeur dans mes veines cachée:
> C'est Vénus toute entière à sa proie attachée . . .

(It is no longer mere ardor hidden in my veins: It is Venus herself attached to her prey . . .)

Now it is true that these two lines may be read as anapestic tetrameter ("ballad measure"), but if we see each as a unit, subdivided first into two symmetrical hemistichs of six syllables—like the peruke of Louis XIV, where the caesura is the part in the hair—and again divided into a 3–3 rhythm (*Ce n'est plús une ardeúr*, etc.), we can then appreciate the variation in the opening line of this same speech of *Phèdre* (act 1, scene 3), which is not anapestic at all:

Mon mal vient de plus loin. À peine au fils d'Égée . . .

(My suffering goes further back. Scarcely to Aegeus' son . . .)

Here the meter is 2–4 / 2–4 with the secondary stress in each hemistich most appropriately falling upon the words *mal* and *peine*. The
accent on the word *mal* in particular conveys both the depth of
Phèdre's suffering and the sense of evil of her illicit love for Hippolyte. If the next line

Sous les lois de l'hymen je m'étais engagée

(Had I consented to be wed)

reverts to a 3–3 / 3–3 rhythm (anapestic tetrameter), the very regularity of the meter reflects the illusion of order and harmony in
the marriage vows with Thésée. Granted that the anapest may
dominate the French alexandrine in purely statistical terms, the
possibility of twenty-one other combinations within the tetrameter
(2–4 / 4–2; 2–4 / 5–1; 4–2 / 3–3; etc.) allows nonetheless for a great
variety of rhythms.

　　Thus Racine, willingly accepting the dodecasyllabic mold, created rhymed couplets in which the harmonious fusion of sense
and sound was to produce the most subtle and haunting effects.
He brought to a state of perfection a form that had already been
richly illustrated by the poets of the Pléiade, the baroque poets,
Malherbe, and Corneille.

　　The eighteenth century, however, was to justify much of the
English scepticism about French poetry. The mold was still there,
but it became hollow. The rules were all dutifully observed. As
long as the caesura divided the two hemistichs, as long as hiatus
was carefully avoided—a proper French poet could not say "Tu
es" to his beloved—as long as the twelve-syllable count included
mute *e*'s (but not at the end or before a vowel or mute *h*), so long
as masculine and feminine rhymes or pairs of rhymes alternated
and certain types of rhymes were eschewed, the most prosaic
thoughts became "verse," and "verse" and "poetry" became synonymous.

Voltaire's contemporaries considered him the best poet of the age and applauded such lines as the following from his anticlerical tragedy *Oedipe*:

Nos prêtres ne sont pas ce qu'un vain peuple pense;
Notre crédulité fait toute leur science.[3]

(Our priests are not what a vain people think; our credulity accounts for all their skill.)

Victor Hugo and his fellow romantics made a sizable dent in the classical armor, and the trimetric alexandrine (4 / 4/ 4) represents a significant victory against the Academy. But in his very attack on the alexandrine, as in the "Réponse à un acte d'accusation" (*Les Contemplations*, Hugo uses none other than the alexandrine, and a fairly conservative one at that, in which, except for line 7 below with its very apt stress on the third syllable followed by the caesura, the hemistichs are carefully observed:

Nous faisons basculer la balance hémistiche.
C'est vrai, maudissez-nous. Le vers, qui sur son front
Jadis portait toujours douze plumes en rond,
Et sans cesse sautait sur la double raquette
Qu'on nomme prosodie et qu'on nomme étiquette,
Rompt désormais la règle et trompe le ciseau,
Et s'échappe, volant qui se change en oiseau,
De la cage césure, et fuit vers la ravine,
Et vole dans les cieux, alouette divine.

(We throw the hemistich scales off balance. It's true, curse us. The line of verse, which on its brow used to wear twelve feathers in a ring and kept hopping on the double racquet called prosody and etiquette, now breaks the rule and fools the chisel, and escapes, a shuttlecock become a bird, from the caesura cage and flees toward the ravine, and flies in the skies, a lark divine.)

The Parnassian movement in the middle of the nineteenth century came as a reaction to the excesses of romantic freedom. This meant both a tightening and a further codification of the rules. Rhymes were categorized not only according to their position as *rimes plates, croisées,* and *embrassées* but also according to their degree of homophony as *rimes pauvres, suffisantes,* and *riches,* with poets like Banville and Coppée vying for richness. Again the poets welcomed the yoke, even though the alexandrines that emerged could be as flat as the bosom of the beloved in the following couplet, which comes, I believe, from Maupassant:

Qu'importent tes seins maigres, Ô ma douce chatte;
On est plus près du coeur quand la poitrine est plate.

(Never mind your tiny breasts, oh my kitty-cat; one is closer to the heart when the bust is flat.)

In his earliest verses Rimbaud showed himself to be as docile as any of the Parnassians. Here are the opening lines of "Les Étrennes des orphelins," his first poem in French (he had already written in Latin):

La chambre est pleine d'ombre; on entend vaguement
De deux enfants le triste et doux chuchotement.

(The room is full of shade; vaguely is heard the sad and gentle whispering of two children.)

In the first line the caesura follows *ombre* at the end of the first hemistich. The twelve-syllable count includes the mute *e*'s of *pleine* and *vaguement* but not of *ombre*. In the second line the caesura after *triste* is considerably attenuated; in fact, the hemistichs give way to a trimeter which was for the most part acceptable to the Parnassians. The twelve-syllable count includes the mute *e* of *chuchotement* but not of *triste*. For English ears the couplet could read as iambic hexameters were it not for the definite anapestic beat of the second hemistich of the first line: *on enténd vaguemént*. The rhyme is "rich," comprising as it does the three sounds [ə], [m], [ã]. The poem in its entirety is made up of *rimes plates* with alternating pairs of masculine and feminine rhymes.

There is certainly nothing very seditious in the form of this first work of *Poésies*; and in fact, except for two octosyllabic quatrains in "Bal des pendus," the first ten pieces of the volume contain nothing but alexandrines, some 600 lines of them, arranged in rhymed couplets or *rimes croisées*. These include three sonnets in which while observing the classical mold Rimbaud perversely fills it with the most unseemly content ("Le Châtiment de Tar-tuffe," "Morts de Quatre-vingt-douze . . . ," and "Vénus anad-yomène.")

Beginning with the alternating eight- and four-syllable qua-trains of "Les Reparties de Nina," Rimbaud tries a great variety of different rhythms, not only mastering each in a seemingly effort-less manner but experimenting in numerous combinations of even- and odd-numbered syllables. By the time he gives up verse poetry he will have tried either singly or in combinations not only the two-, four-, six-, eight-, ten-, and of course twelve-syllable line, but the five-, seven-, and nine-syllable line as well. The *Album zutique* even has a monosyllabic sonnet!

It is not enough for Rimbaud to fit in to the set forms; he sets out to destroy the molds themselves. Beginning with "Le Dormeur du val" he undertakes to "dismember" the alexandrine.[4] This son-net has so many enjambements causing misplaced caesuras that the dodecasyllabic meter breaks down completely. In "Oraison du soir" the regularity of the hemistichal pattern gives way to an asy-metrical 7 / 5 rhythm as in the line:

Je pisse vers les cieux bruns très haut et très loin.

(I piss toward the brown skies very high and very far.)

And in "Voyelles" the use of the comma to separate each vowel named from the rest of the line produces a syncopated effect. In the following line from "Le Bateau ivre" no trace remains of the classical caesura:

Et dès lors, je me suis baigné dans le Poème . . .

(And from then on I bathed in the Poem . . .)

In a comment on "Mémoire" Richard Vernier has suggested that one of the reasons for the unexpected semicolon in the first line

L'eau claire; comme le sel des larmes d'enfance . . .

(Clear water; like the salt of the tears of childhood . . .)

may be to "imposer le mutisme à un *e* atone, et faire boiter l'al-
exandrin" ("make an unstressed *e* mute so as to cripple the alexandrine").[5] All in all the variety of split rhythms would tempt one
to call Rimbaud the Gerard Manley Hopkins of French verse, except
that the very rigidity of French prosody makes his innovations all
the more defiant. Why should he be tradition-bound? In "Les Pauvres à l'église" a lone decasyllabic line (p. 17) turns up among the
alexandrines, causing French critics to label it "un vers faux." Why
false? If Rimbaud wants to break the regularity of the twelve-syllable meter and increase the staccato effect of the jottings in this
particular stanza, why shouldn't he feel free to do so? A generation
later when Apollinaire introduced a single alexandrine among the
octosyllabic lines of "Marie" (*Alcools*) or more recently when Yves
Bonnefoy introduced two decasyllabic lines within the alexandrine
quatrains of "Aux arbres" (*Du mouvement et de l'immobilité de Douve*)
there was no hue and cry, perhaps for the very reason that Rimbaud had paved the way.

In his rhymes Rimbaud was equally bold. At an early stage
he showed that he could be as ingenious as a Victor Hugo or the
Parnassians with such pairs as *couacs / cornacs, voyous / pioupious*
("À la musique"); *dada / papa* ("L'Éclatante Victoire de Sarrebruck");
Grand Truc / aqueduc ("Chant de guerre parisien") *Vénus / anus*
("Vénus anadyomène"); *latrines / narines* ("Le Poète de sept ans");
tanna / Juana ("Les Mains de Jeane-Marie"); etc. It is not impossible
that the surrealist heroine Rrose Selavy was born from the glint in
the eye of Rimbaud when he juxtaposed *Eros* and *roses* in the alternation of masculine and feminine rhymes in "Soleil et chair."

It was not long before Rimbaud was not only breaking the
rules of rhyme but doing away with it altogether. Contrary to ap-
proved practice he ends some lines with prepositions and articles,
producing such pairs as *avec la / éclat* ("Ce qu'on dit au poète à
propos des fleurs") and *jusqu'à / Sahara* ("Bruxelles"). In the *Derniers vers*, along with some of the songs which Rimbaud called
"romances" and which are remarkable for the euphony of the
rhyme—one thinks of the "Chanson de la plus haute tour" and
"Ô saisons, ô châteaux"—one finds others containing end-words
which cannot even be justified as assonant since the homophony

is based on consonants rather than vowels: *tour / flore, facile / elle* ("Âge d'or"); *sentinelle / nulle, élans / selon* ("L'Éternité). Long before Apollinaire and the innovation which Louis Aragon called the "rime apollinarienne," Rimbaud muddled the age-old distinction between masculine and feminine rhymes by simply ignoring the mute *e*, as in *bruyère / vert* of "Larme." Finally the octosyllabic lines of "Bannière de mai" dispense completely with rhyme, be it *riche, suffisante,* or *pauvre.* This poem is quite frankly in blank verse.

In a word, when Rimbaud came to the moment of renouncing verse he had stretched the rules as far as possible without actually turning his poems into prose. How did he justify these transgressions? Already in the "Lettre du voyant" to Paul Demeny he had claimed in one of those magnificently sweeping generalizations which only adolescence can inspire that since the Greeks and down to the romantics, from Ennius to Casimir Delavigne, all poetry had been rhymed prose, the work of "versificateurs." On the one hand he condemns "la forme vieille" of Lamartine, "mesquine" of Baudelaire; on the other hand he praises *Les Misérables,* calling this vast prose work "un vrai poème." This blurring of the distinction between prose and poetry and the insistence upon new forms ("demandons aux *poètes* du *nouveau*") combine with the notion of poetry as "voyance" ("les inventions d'inconnu réclament des formes nouvelles" ["inventions of the unknown require new forms"] to produce a style that is completely liberated from the shackles of meter and rhyme. In the remark "si ce que [le poète] rapporte de *là-bas* a forme, il donne forme; si c'est informe il donne de l'informe" ("if what [the poet] brings back from *beyond* has form, he gives form; if it is formless he gives the formlessness"), if "forme" denotes verse, "informe" can mean only the prose poem.

We have no documentation on exactly when or how the leap took place. There is no reason to suppose that simply because "Après le déluge" is the liminary piece of *Illuminations* it was the first to be composed. If one wished to view the change as a gradual evolution it would be plausible to see "Marine" and "Mouvement," which predate the *vers libre* of the symbolists, as the bridge between verse and prose. The combination of anaphora and a *verset* that seems to announce Claudel and Saint-John Perse in "Enfance," "Départ," "Vieillesse," "Solde," and "Dévotion" would make another bridge. But this is pure supposition. Lacking any evidence we can only imagine a moment when, like "le cuivre [qui] s'éveille clairon" ("the brass that wakes up as a bugle") ("Lettre du voyant"), a kind of Ovidean metamorphosis takes place with Rimbaud fascinated looking on. The lines, centered in the middle of the page, begin to lengthen in both directions. The capital letters on the left start to wither, losing their neat ladder-like formation, to become insignificantly lower case. Words shift about and reshape themselves into the thick blocks of paragraphs which would be completely rectangular were it not for the tiny indentation top left and the longer blank lower right. Rhyming words either disappear or like the meter on occasion hide themselves snugly within these blocks. A brief title, usually a single word in large caps, tops it off and, presto, the metamorphosis is complete. The form (or the "informe"?) of *Illuminations* has come into being.

Rimbaud was of course not the only poet of the period to break the hallowed rules of French prosody. Cros, Corbière, Laforgue succeeded as well in limbering up the stiff lines of the Parnassian heritage and indeed the greatest technical victory of the symbolist movement was that of the *vers libre*. The point, however, is that having been driven inexorably by his own infractions to make the leap into prose Rimbaud produced a volume which more than any other collection in the nineteenth century—Mallarmé for example never published his prose poems separately—was to sire the numerous offspring of our own century. There are of course many reasons for the prevalence of this genre in modern poetry, one of the most obvious being the shift, as Elaine Marks puts it, "from rhetoric to metaphor."[6] But that the prose poem should have emerged from French soil is due in large measure—and so paradoxically—to the very tyranny of French verse. Had it not been for Rimbaud's battle with the alexandrine, the *poème en prose* as we know it would probably not have been born.

Geoffrey Brereton has stated quite categorically: "The most striking development in French poetry in the twentieth century has been the breakdown of regular versification."[7] Already at the beginning of the century the avant-garde poets felt free to choose whatever form of verse or prose they wished. It is conceivable that this very freedom might have impeded any further development

of the prose poem. Presumably the relative absence of the genre
in English until the recent efforts of a number of American poets
can be traced to the traditional freedom of English verse. There
was no strait jacket to pull out of. If the French poet was now just
as unfettered as his English confreres why not celebrate this newly
won freedom by composing in any combination of free as well as
regular verse that the occasion demanded? The answer seems to
be that the nineteenth-century prose poem models were there waiting to be emulated, particularly *Illuminations*. Claudel's *Connaissance de l'Est* (1900), Reverdy's *Poèmes en prose* (1915), Max Jacob's
Cornet à dés (1916) all take a bow to Rimbaud and like *Illuminations*
consist almost entirely of short pieces of rarely more than a page
or two. Among the surrealists the master of the genre was probably
Breton but, as in *Clair de terre*, for example, he generally preferred
in any single volume to mix free verse and prose texts. Most of
the surrealists followed him in this practice. It is in fact difficult to
find a major French poet today who has remained immune to the
genre. One would have been tempted to cite Yves Bonnefoy but
for the recent appearance of his volume *Rue traversière* (1977).

And yet few are the writers whose reputation rests primarily
upon the prose poem. Max Jacob? Possibly, but most of his readers,
I dare say, would be loathe to sacrifice the rhythms of *Le Laboratoire
central* despite their esteem for *Le Cornet à dés*. The one name that
comes most persistently to mind is Francis Ponge. For all his rich
production since the war it is still the little volume *Le Parti pris des
choses* (1942) which receives the most accolades.

The style of Ponge is in sharp contrast with that of another
poet some twenty years his senior, the only major poet of the
century in France who chose to ignore the prose poem almost completely, Apollinaire.[8] Apparently the author of *Alcools* and *Calligrammes* felt so completely at home with the *vers libre*, which he
succeeded in emancipating even further, not to mention his pen-
chant in his more traditional moments for regular meters, especially the octosyllabic line, that if the thought of writing a collection
of prose pieces like those of his friends Jacob and Reverdy ever
occurred to him he quickly put it out of his mind.

It might be fruitful to compare two texts, one of Apollinaire
and one of Ponge, as evidence of the tremendous range in poetic

forms that has emerged in modern France. Both poets have written on a theme that is quite prevalent today, the theme of language itself. The century that has witnessed the spread of linguistics and semiotics was bound to find among its poets a preoccupation with the one thing of which they are the practitioners supreme. Of course there is hardly a poet since antiquity who has not written his ars poetica in one form or another, but the poem that has as its central theme the frustrations, the inadequacies, the infidelities—and the grandeur—of language in general seems to be if not a new phenomenon at least one that has appealed in our time to the spiritual offspring of Rimbaud and Mallarmé.

In "La Victoire" (*Calligrammes*), composed during the First World War, Apollinaire claims that the old languages we are used to have become so moribund that it is only through habit and lack of daring that we go on speaking them. And he exclaims somewhat grandiloquently:

Ô bouches l'homme est à la recherche d'un nouveau language

(O mouths mankind is in search of a new language.)

There follows as a momentary anticlimax a series of suggestions for increasing the phonetic range of language:

On veut de nouveaux sons de nouveaux sons de nouveaux sons

(We want new sounds new sounds new sounds)

sounds such as spitting sounds, more plosives, consonants without vowels, the noise of a spinning top, belches, finger snapping, cheek drumming. Beneath all this dissonance there seems to lie the serious notion that newness, which for Apollinaire is in itself a virtue, entails multiplicity, profusion, just as in the poem "La Jolie Rousse," which immediately follows "La Victoire," the poet speaks of the "couleurs jamais vues" ("colors never seen") the "mille phantasmes impondérables" ("thousand imponderable phantasms"), the vastness of the mysterious domain to which the poet, through language of course, will give reality.

And in fact at the end of the catalogue of "new sounds" in "La Victoire" we suddenly leap from the phonetic to the semantic with an apostrophe:

Ô paroles

(O words)

The words of the new language are then evoked in such a way as to enhance, as in "La Jolie Rousse," the mystery of their meanings. The poet sees them, the words, in a myrtle garden following Eros and Anteros. He associates them with the treacherous language of the sea, and speech itself becomes a "trembling god." Interwoven with these enigmatic evocations is a series of rather messianic proclamations on the poet's own role in the propagation of the new language. One would assume that Apollinaire has now shifted from a consideration of language in general to the language of poetry alone, but for him the distinction does not really exist. The "victory" of the poem's title, more than simply prophesying the end of the war, seems to announce the fusion of the two types of language. And the poem concludes with the exhortation:

Et que tout ait un nom nouveau.

(And may all have a new name.)

"La Victoire" is a verse poem but of the freest kind, with lines ranging from one to seventeen syllables and with no apparent informing principle in their succession. The poem is divided into stanzas in which couplets and tercets predominate, reminding one of the short paragraphs that characterize Apollinaire's prose. But there are also stanzas (one each) of eleven, twelve, and thirteen lines. Some of the stanzas such as the following could have been printed in prose with no great loss:

Et ces vieilles langues sont tellement près de mourir
Que c'est vraiment par habitude et manque d'audace
Qu'on les fait encore servir à la poésie . . .

(And these old languages are so close to death that it is really out
of habit and lack of daring that they go on being used for poetry
. . .)

If one ignores in the last line the mute *e* of *encore*—and with Apollinaire as with other practitioners of the *vers libre* a mute *e* before
a consonant may or may not count in the scansion—this line becomes dodecasyllabic, but it has none of the resonance of an alexandrine.

One finds such stanzas interspersed with octosyllabic and alexandrine quatrains which please the ear with the regularity of
their meter and rhyme. These alternations seem to reflect a conflict
within the poet between the old and the new, nostalgia and prophecy, tradition and adventure, a conflict similar to that between
"poetry and antipoetry" which Marcel Raymond discerned in
"Zone,"[9] and which runs through much of Apollinaire's work,
finding its formal expression in this alternation of irregular and
regular verse.

In the case of "La Victoire" Apollinaire's ambivalences revolve
around the theme of language. Like his friends the Dadaists although somewhat more fitfully than they, he yearns for a complete
renovation of language. But almost immediately doubts and contradictions begin to assail the poet. Implicit in the list of "nouveaux
sons" is their cacophony, so sharply in contrast with the gentle
sounds of the words that walk the myrtle grove. The new language
will be god-given, it seems, but haven't the gods all drowned and
in that same treacherous sea to which the language is compared?
The poet who claims he speaks this language knows nonetheless
that he can command only existing words and gropes in his effort
to evoke the new. Indeed throughout, the voice of the poet fluc-
tuates so much that beneath the optimism of the last line, "Et que
tout ait un nom nouveau," one detects an underlying note of despair and futility.

The verse molds itself to these fluctuations and indecisions,
now irregular to express the élan toward the new, now regular to
evoke the traditional, but also vice versa, depending upon the
mood of the poet. It is clear that Apollinaire's realization for his

own lyric voice of the justness of this combination with all its variations precluded any temptation to turn to the prose poem.

Francis Ponge, on the contrary, writing a generation later, found in the prose poem the perfect instrument for his antilyrical style. *Le Parti pris des choses*, published during the Second World War, is composed of thirty-two pieces, the majority covering less than a page, and bearing such titles as "La Bougie," "La Cigarette," "L'Orange," "L'Huître," "Le Pain," "Escargots," etc. As the title of the collection implies Ponge is taking up the cause of simple objects against the language of abstraction, philosophical disquisition, rhetoric. Through the "thickness of language" Ponge seeks to evoke the "thickness of things" and thanks to a subtle combination of an objective, concrete prose style and the devices of analogy, metaphor, and word play he creates not a textbook description of an oyster, let us say, but the poetic characterization, its linguistic equivalent.

There is one piece, somewhat less typical than the others, "Le Cycle des saisons," which ostensibly treats the succession of the four seasons but actually deals with the same theme that we noted in "La Victoire," the renovation of language. It is short enough to quote in its entirety:

Le Cycle des saisons
Las de s'être contractés tout l'hiver les arbres tout à coup se flattent d'être dupes. Ils ne peuvent plus y tenir: ils lâchent leurs paroles, un flot, un vomissement de vert. Ils tâchent d'aboutir à une feuillaison complète de paroles. Tant pis! Cela s'ordonnera comme cela pourra! Mais, en réalité, cela s'ordonne! Aucune liberté dans la feuillaison . . . Ils lancent, du moins le croient-ils, n'importe quelles paroles, lancent des tiges pour y suspendre encore des paroles: nos troncs, pensent-ils, sont là pour tout assumer. Ils s'efforcent à se cacher, à se confondre les uns dans les autres. Ils croient pouvoir dire tout, recouvrir entièrement le monde de paroles variées; ils ne disent que "les arbres." Incapables même de retenir les oiseaux qui repartent d'eux, alors qu'ils se réjouissaient d'avoir produit de si étranges fleurs. Toujours la même feuille, toujours le même mode de dépliement, et la même limite, toujours des feuilles symétriques à elles-mêmes, symétriquement suspendues! Tente encore une feuille!—La même! Encore une autre! La même! Rien en somme ne saurait les arrêter que soudain cette remarque: "L'on ne sort pas des arbres par des moyens d'arbres."

Une nouvelle lassitude, et un nouveau retournement moral. "Laissons tout ça jaunir, et tomber. Vienne le taciturne état, le dépouillement, l'AUTOMME."[10]

(*The Cycle of the Seasons*

Tired of contracting all winter the trees suddenly flatter themselves on being dupes. They can no longer hold it: they let their words go, a flood, a vomiting of green. They try to work for a complete foliation of words. Too bad! It will have to arrange itself as it can! But actually it *is* getting arranged! No freedom at all in the leafing. . . They come out, at least that's what they think, with any words at all, they shoot forth stems for hanging more words: our trunks, they think, are there to take everything on. They try to hide, to mingle in each other. They think they can cover the whole world with varied words; all they say is "trees." Incapable even of holding on to the birds that leave them, when they were so pleased to have produced such strange flowers. Always the same leaf, always the same way of unfolding, and the same limit, leaves that are always symmetrical to themselves, symmetrically hanging! Try another leaf! The same! Still another! The same! Nothing in fact could stop them except suddenly this remark: "One cannot get away from trees by means of trees." A new kind of lassitude, a new turning of the spirit. "Let's let all of that get yellow and fall. Let the taciturn state come in, the stripping, the AUTUMN.)

This is actually one of the more exclamatory poems of *Le Parti pris des choses* and for that very reason it lends itself perhaps more aptly to a comparison with "La Victoire." Note first of all the great difference in attitude of the two poets, the optimism (on the surface at least) of Apollinaire as against the dejected determinism of Ponge, reflecting incidentally the different states of mind that mark the two world wars. Where the poet of "La Victoire" in his moments of enthusiasm sees the multitudinousness of sounds and words as a desirable enrichment of language, the narrator of *Le Cycle des saisons* sees it as a kind of absurd proliferation that reaches a point of saturation. Words cloy. Apparently there can be no renewal except through silence, "le taciturne état," but in fact language thus reborn will be identical to its self, just as the new spring will be part of the same old cycle.

One could easily give a linguistic interpretation of Ponge's text, stressing the notion that language limits the freedom of its speakers to the extent that it predetermines their thought patterns. Our purpose, somewhat more modest, is simply to examine the text as a prose poem. In this particular piece the author's intention, unlike that in most of the other prose poems in the volume, is not to imitate poetically the sober descriptive style of a scientific handbook. The central analogy between word and leaf, based on the dual qualities of proliferation and uniformity, allows the development of an extended metaphor which expresses a strong emotion on the part of the narrator, a mixture of tedium and disgust, a kind of Sartrian nausea. Thanks to the transferral of *parole* to *feuille* the trees acquire the gift of speech and engage in a dialogue, both directly and indirectly, with the narrator, a dialogue that dramatizes the conflict between the naïve partisans of renewal and those for whom such a hope is futile.

If then the style of "Le Cycle des saisons" lacks the objectivity and sobriety that characterize the other pieces, would it not have been more appropriate to compose it in free verse on the assumption that for Ponge at least—as indeed for Apollinaire—the more lyrical a style the more it tends to shape itself into verse? Is there any *necessity* for the prose form here, other than the fact, hardly justifiable in itself, the the poem is included in a volume where all the other texts are in prose?[11]

As a young man Ponge wrote the following apostrophe:

. . . CARACTÈRES, objets mystérieux perceptibles par deux sens seulement et cependant plus réels, plus sympathiques que des signes,—je veux vous rapprocher de la substance et vous éloigner de la qualité. Je veux vous faire aimer pour vous-mêmes plutôt que pour votre signification. Enfin vous élever à une condition plus noble que celle de simples désignations.[12]

> (. . . CHARACTERS, mysterious objects perceived by two senses only and yet more real, more congenial than signs—I want to bring you closer to substance, alway from quality. I want to make you loved for yourselves rather than for your meanings. In a word, raise you to a more noble condition than that of simple designations.)

This fascination with the elements of language was never to leave him, and need it be said that the exasperation which such pieces as "Le Cycle des saisons" express derives directly from Ponge's passion for language and his chagrin at its abuse? For Ponge then the typographical arrangement of letters and the words they compose is of paramount importance. And what better way to print a poem on the proliferation of words than to present it in all its typographical "thickness" as a single, compact paragraph with both sides as close as possible to the two margins and totally bereft of the indentations, the breathing spaces that would accompany verses or brief paragraphs or *versets*? And within this rectangle, as an imitation of the leaves, a profusion of monosyllabic words such as *las, dupes, flots, vert*, and especially the alliterations in *t* (*tâchent, tant, tente, tout*, along with the two-syllable words *toujours, tenir*), all of which by association with *tronc* and *tige* tighten the central analogy and prepare the dénouement of silence, the season of bare trunks and branches which the same plosive *t*—as if to stress the inadequacy of language—announces: "le *taciturne état* . . . l'AU-TOMNE."

Now all this monosyllabic and alliterative word play could of course have been contained in a series of *vers libres*, but it is thanks to its presence in the block of prose that *forme* and *fond* are most successfully fused. Ponge has shown us here how to fight words with words, and in a sense the creation of the poem in itself represents a victory over the nausea that he had set out to express.

One should beware of generalizations from the two texts we have examined. I have simply wanted to show not only the range of poetic form in French as illustrated by two majors poets but the manner in which individual poets select the form that most properly suits them. Today among the younger poets the prose poem has by no means gained the ascendancy; on the contrary the *vers libre* in its many forms seems to be considerably more prevalent, and the alexandrine, no longer the enemy, has recovered its appeal along with the other regular meters, rhymed or unrhymed. At best one can affirm merely that the frontiers between verse and prose poetry no longer block the writer, who can shuttle back and forth without a visa and in fact often does so within the framework of a single poem.

When Matthew Arnold pronounced the following judgment in the mid-nineteenth century he was, with his usual touch of Victorian smugness, thinking of French poets as versifiers: "Set [a

Frenchman] to write poetry, he is limited, artificial, and impotent; set him to write prose, he is free, natural, and effective. The power of French literature is in its prose writers, the power of English literature is in its poets."[13] Arnold was a contemporary without knowing it of Baudelaire, Rimbaud, and Mallarmé. He would have been amazed by their inventions. And it is a vindication of French literature today (assuming for the moment that Arnold's half-truth is a truth) that thanks in large measure to the *poème en prose* its "poets" and "prose writers" have become equally "free, natural, and effective."

Notes

1. Michael Benedikt, ed., *The Prose Poem: An International Anthology* (New York: Dell, 1976).

2. Émile Legouis, *Défense de la poésie française* (London: Constable, 1912) pp. 78ff.

3. Othon Guerlac, in his *Citations françaises* (Paris: Armand Colin, 1933), cites this as a familiar quotation.

4. See Louis Forestier's comment in the *Poésie*/Gallimard edition of Rimbaud: *Poésies, Une Saison en Enfer, Illuminations*, Louis Forestier, ed. (Paris, 1965), p. 245.

5. Richard Vernier, "De la poésie objective à la vénération de la matière: Francis Ponge," *Stanford French Review* (Spring 1978), 2:5.

6. Elaine Marks, *French Poetry from Baudelaire to the Present* (New York: Dell, 1962), p. 11.

7. Geoffrey Brereton, *An Introduction to the French Poets* (London: Methuen, 1960), p. 236.

8. In addition to "Onirocritique," which Apollinaire included in *L'Enchanteur pourrissant* in 1909, one finds in the section *Poèmes retrouvés* in the Pléiade edition of the *Oeuvres poétiques* (Paris, 1962) two pieces entitled "Un Matin" and "Table." It could be argued that certain calligrammes of Apollinaire if typographically rearranged as regular prose texts would fit into the category, but does this not destroy the very essence of the calligrammes as such?

9. Marcel Raymond, *De Baudelaire au surréalisme* (Paris: Corti, 1974), p. 235.

10. Francis Ponge, "Le Cycle des saisons," in *Le Parti pris des choses* (Paris: *Poésie*/Gallimard, 1967). Copyright © 1967, Gallimard. Reprinted by permission.

11. A poem in unrhymed alexandrines, "Le Tronc d'arbre," on the same theme as "Le Cycle des saisons" and using the same central metaphor is in fact excluded from *Le Parti pris des choses*; it appears in *Proêmes*, published in 1948, a volume made up of notations and miscellaneous texts.

12. Francis Ponge, *Proêmes*, in *Tome Premier* (Paris: Gallimard, 1965), p. 146.

13. Matthew Arnold, "The Literary Influence of Academies," in *Essays in Criticism*.

2. Vibratory Organism: *crise de prose*

ROGER SHATTUCK

We rarely read a text "cold." Only literary editors and participants in experiments like those of I. A. Richards face a poem or a passage without some equivalent of program notes.[1] The author's name, or even a century number, is enough to prepare our reactions. Such information sets the work in context and fits it into a system of interlocking classifications that direct, or prejudice, the reading. The scholar virtually encases himself in such tendentious data before venturing out onto the frontiers of knowledge. Yet it is those of us who live with and by literature who most need to come back to the written word "cold turkey," without props and habits and protective garments.

I say all this in order to adjure my readers to peruse the following quotation "naïvely and sincerely," as its author would have said. For this purpose the best method is to read aloud. Some scholars will recognize the words immediately; they might try feigning ignorance. I shall ask the others not to worry over the question of attribution. For heuristic purposes we can hold off the recognition scene as long as possible.

[a] Supposons un bel espace de nature où tout verdoie, rougeoie, poudroie et chatoie en pleine liberté, où toutes choses, diversement colorées suivant leur constitution moléculaire, changées de seconde en seconde par le dé-

From Marcel Tetel, ed., *Symbolism and Modern Literature: Studies in Honor of Wallace Fowlie* (Durham, N.C.: Duke University Press, 1978). Copyright © 1978, Duke University Press. Reprinted by permission.

21

placement de l'ombre et de la lumière, et agitées par le travail intérieur du calorique, se trouvent en perpétuelle vibration, laquelle fait trembler les lignes et complète la loi du mouvement éternel et universel.   [b]—Une immensité, bleue quelquefois et verte souvent, s'étend jusqu 'aux confins du ciel: c'est la mer.   [c] Les arbres sont verts, les gazons verts, les mousses vertes; le vert serpente dans les troncs, les tiges non mûres sont vertes; le vert est le fond de la nature, parce que le vert se marie facilement à tous les autres tons.*   [d] Ce qui me frappe d'abord, c'est que partout,—coquelicots dans les gazons, pavots, perroquets, etc.,—le rouge chante la gloire du vert; le noir,—quand il y en a,—zéro solitaire et insignifiant, intercède le secours du bleu ou du rouge.   [e] Le bleu, c'est-à-dire le ciel, est coupé de légers flocons blancs ou de masses grises qui trempent heureusement sa morne crudité,—et, comme la vapeur de la saison,—hiver ou été,—baigne, adoucit, ou engloutit les contours, la nature ressemble à un toton qui, mû par une vitesse accélérée, nous apparaît gris, bien qu'il résume en lui toutes les couleurs.

[f] La sève monte et, mélange de principes, elle s'épanouit en *tons mélangés*; les arbres, les rochers, les granits se mirent dans les eaux et y déposent leurs *reflets*; tous les objets transparents accrochent au passage lumières et couleurs voisines et lointaines.   [g] A mesure que l'astre du jour se dérange, les tons changent de valeur, mais, respectant toujours leurs sympathies et leurs haines naturelles, continuent à vivre en harmonie par des concessions réciproques.   [h] Les ombres se déplacent lentement, et font fuir devant elles ou éteignent les tons à mesure que la lumière, déplacée elle-même, en veut faire résonner de nouveau.   [i] Ceux-ci se renvoient leurs reflets, et, modifiant leurs qualités en les *glaçant* de qualités transparentes et empruntées, multiplient à l'infini leurs mariages mélodieux et les rendent plus faciles.   [j] Quand le grand foyer descend dans les eaux, de rouges fanfares s'élancent de tous côtés; une sanglante harmonie éclate à l'horizon, et le vert s'empourpre richement.   [k] Mais bientôt de vastes ombres bleues chassent en cadence devant elles la foule des tons orangés et rose tendre qui sont comme l'écho lointain et affaibli de la lumière.   [l] Cette grande symphonie du jour, qui est l'éternelle variation de la symphonie d'hier, cette succession de mélodies, où la variété sort toujours de l'infini, cet hymme compliqué s'appelle la couleur.

* [m] Excepté à ses générateurs le jaune et le bleu; cependant je ne parle ici que des tons purs.   [n] Car cette règle n'est pas applicable aux coloristes transcendants qui connaissent à fond la science du contre-point.

(Let us imagine a beautiful expanse of nature where the prevailing greens and reds shimmer and modulate in complete freedom, where all objects, variously colored according to their molecular structure, changing from second to second by the interplay of heat, exhibit a perpetual vibration that makes their outlines tremble and fulfils the universal law of external movement.—An immense area, sometimes blue and more often green, extends to the furthest limits of the sky: it is the ocean. The trees are green, the grass is green, the moss is green; green weaves along the tree trunks; the unripe shoots are green; green is nature's basic color, combining easily with all other tones. What strikes me first is that everywhere—dandelions in the lawn, poppies, parrots, etc.—red sings the praises of green; black—where there is any—an insignificant solitary vacancy, borrows heavily from the blue or the red. The blue, that is the sky, is broken by light white puffs or gray masses that relieve its raw uniformity; and, since a seasonal mist, winter and summer, bathes, softens, and blurs all contours, nature comes to resemble a great spinning top which, turning very fast, looks grey to us even though it contains in itself all colors.

The sap rises, and its blend of elements spreads out everywhere in mixed tones; trees, rocks, granite formations are mirrored in the water that receives their image; anything transparent absorbs flecks of light and color as they pass through, from close by or far off. As the daystar moves overhead, the tones change in value but, always observing their natural sympathies and repulsions, continue to live in harmony through reciprocal concessions. The shadows shift slowly and chase certain colors out ahead or extinguish them, while the lighting itself changes and starts other tones quivering again. These tones reflect one another and, modifying their textures with borrowed transparent glazes, endlessly multiply their melodious and fluid marriages. When the great ember descends into the water, scarlet fanfares burst forth on every side; a blood-red harmony fills the horizon, and the green deepens to a rich purple. But soon huge shadows begin rhythmically chasing away the scattering of orange and rose tones that act like the remote muted echoes of the lost light. This great symphony of daylight, which is the eternal variation of yesterday's symphony, this succession of varied melodies welling forth directly from the infinite, this commodious hymn is called color.

* Except with its two generating colors, yellow and blue; however I'm speaking only of pure shades. For this rule does not trouble transcendental colorists, who have mastered the science of contrast and counterpoint.)

If we found this passage as an anonymous fragment in an obscure provincial collection, would we pause to examine it closely? Does this unitive vision seem excessive, or does it project a powerful sensibility in command of its medium? Does it immediately reveal its provenance? I shall assume that an inner voice, literary conscience or unconscious, has prompted us to look again.

The text opens with the phrasing of a mathematical demonstration. After the first clause, the style veers sharply toward sensuous-scientific description of a strange landscape. The scene appears both abstract and visionary, like a painting that combines full-blown impressionism with Magritte's petrified space. The only objects in the picture are either conventional (sea, sky, trees) or seemingly emblematic (poppies, parrots, rising sap). The first sentence focuses on the intense Brownian movement that animates everything within the encompassing stillness. The expanded scale of events forces us to confront molecules and seconds. This palpitating closeness gives way to a composition of vivid colors which, by an accelerating momentum carried over from the opening, fuses into the grey blur of a spinning top (sentences b–e). Meanwhile we learn that a correspondingly fleeting consciousness—"me" (d); "nous" (e)—is beholding the scene. In the second paragraph solar time enters the picture (f–i) and shifts the pattern of tones inexorably toward the violence of sunset (j). Twilight (k) restores the hush shattered by the dynamic movement of the opening sentence, and the closing sentence reinserts the composition into a vast cyclical pattern of time and change.

A few words project out of this carefully developed passage: "vibration" (a), "mouvement universel" (a), "toton" (e), "reflets" (f, i), "harmonie" (g, j), "réciproque" (g), "résonner" (h), "mariages" (i), "variation" (l), "générateurs" (m), and "contre-point" (n). They all depict some form of self-contained or reciprocating motion. Several verbs are made reflexive at key points. The beholding consciousness does not appear to stand outside the scene but rather to join the dance with a minimum of syntactic separation. Because of these devices the entire composition develops as self-reflexive, self-beholding, and gradually takes on an all-inclusive wheeling motion. The initial "vibration" becomes the rotation of an enormous top. As readers we are drawn into the elemental turning of the scene, of the earth itself as the sun "goes down," of the whole natural cosmos, and of the tiny human consciousness here appended to it, creating and observing it. The vocabulary and subtly circular style of the passage carry us to the edge of vertigo, the great grey blur of natural process.

One could say much more, about the imagery and the rhythm and the sonority. Does it add up to a text of any literary significance? Is this a page out of a journal by Van Gogh? or Kandinsky? Is it some third-rate romantic foisting off on us an overwritten account of a howling drug experience? Why so much semiscientific color theory? Is this a fragment out of a larger work? In any case, the last line seems weak. The crescendo of visual display and intense feeling will not finally balance on the head of the word *couleur*. For by the end, the color theme has been overworked. Yet these confident effusions cannot be the work of a third-rater. The author has assembled a vivid and convincing sensibility.

No, not a third-rater. Baudelaire *fecit*—as many of you may have divined. The passage represents not typical but quintessential Baudelaire. This self-contained text appears at the opening of the third chapter, "De la couleur," of the *Salon de 1846*.[2] Read beside the other 130 pages of his first important published work, it appears very much like a separate piece of writing intercalated into the assemblage of notes Baudelaire must have pulled out of his drawers in order to meet his deadline. He claimed he composed the *Salon* in a week. It appeared as a printed book eight weeks after the vernissage. He was in top form.

Yet 1846 was a desperate year for Baudelaire, who at twenty-five was better known as a bohemian and dandy than as a poet. Two years earlier his family had put his inheritance into a trust from which he received an allowance. Financial need drove him to write the *Salon de 1845*, an ineffective pamphlet that earned him practically nothing. A month later he melodramatically and feebly attempted suicide. Meanwhile he seems to have been reading widely, particularly in the works of Swedenborg, Hoffman, and probably Fourier. The historical significance of the text I have quoted can be succinctly conveyed by listing the various ways in which it represents a "first."

1. These opening paragraphs from "De la couleur" represent

Baudelaire's first *poème en prose*.[3] He ends the previous chapter by saying, "Je veux écrire sur la couleur une série de réflexions qui ne seront pas inutiles pour l'intelligence complète de ce petit livre" (p. 230). After the two initial paragraphs, the rest of the chapter on color breaks down into short paragraphs mostly of one sentence and of a discursive nature. Therefore the passage quoted even looks like a shaped fragment of heightened experience, and its style generally conforms to Baudelaire's major statement in the 1862 dedication of *Petits poèmes en prose* to Arsène Houssaye:

Quel est celui de nous qui n'a pas, dans ses jours d'ambition, rêvé le miracle d'une prose poétique, musicale sans rythme et sans rime, assez souple et assez heurtée pour s'adapter aux mouvements lyriques de l'âme, aux ondulations de la rêverie, aux soubresauts de la conscience? (p. 146)

> (Which of us has not, on his ambitious days, dreamed up the miracle of a poetic prose, musical without rhythm or rhyme, both supple and rough enough to adapt itself to the lyric movements of the soul, to the undulations of reverie, to the jolts of consciousness.)

Baudelaire made a first unsuccessful attempt to write a prose poem in the opening pages of *Salon de 1845*. Delacroix' painting, *Les Dernières Paroles de Marc-Aurèle*, is seen as a "harmonie de vert et du rouge," and the whole composition gives "l'effet d'un object monochrome et tournant" (p. 205). The following year Baudelaire dispensed with Delacroix and composed his own visionary landscape saturated with shrill colors. This 1846 text is well described by the title he proposed sixteen years later for his collection of prose poems. In the letter Baudelaire sent to Houssaye in 1862 with the manuscript, he proposed the general title "La Lueur et la fumée."

Even though he may not have articulated and named the genre of *poème en prose*, all these circumstances permit us to see the color passage as a nearly conscious attempt to write and publish such a work. Two comparisons reinforce the association. The second of the prose poems actually published as such, "Le *Confiteor* de l'artiste," employs a setting and a state of mind so similar to that of the color poem that they both seem to express the same vibratory response to a scene: "le *moi* se perd vite" (p. 149). The later text expresses a more self-affirming and combative attitude toward nature, and also replaces most of the color imagery with the concentrated point of a sail contrasting with the vastness of the seascape. Yet it is recognizably the same imagination at work.[4]

The other work of Baudelaire's that comes to mind in reading the 1846 color passage is a poem whose date of composition is uncertain and which might be contemporary. "Harmonie du soir" embodies in its pantoum form a powerful turning movement that encompasses all the elements of the poem—rhyme, rhythm, air, sunset, and the poet's state of mind. Only the somewhat arbitrary last line gives the composition a different direction. These two works deserve the kind of joint reading we accord to other associated poems and prose poems.

For all these reasons I propose that the color passage is not merely "like" a prose poem found in a critical essay. It actually is Baudelaire's first such text, explicitly set off as a separate whole, and reaffirming the early onset of Baudelaire's desire to develop a form of writing distinct from both formal verse and expository prose.[5]

2. The intensity of Baudelaire's writing in the color poem, as well as repeated terms like "harmonie" and "loi du mouvement éternel et universel" attest to the fact that this is his first treatment of the theme of *correspondances*. Though the word itself does not appear, the rest of the chapter concerns nothing else and leads into the famous passage quoted from Hoffmann's *Kreisleriana*: "je trouve une analogie et une réunion intime entre les couleurs, les sons et les parfums" (p. 232). Several details suggest that Baudelaire intended in this chapter to make his contribution to the reigning dispute over the relative importance of *ligne* (Ingres) and *couleur* (Delacroix). What came from his pen instead was a manifesto on universal analogy. There should be no need to belabor this point. In 1846 Baudelaire had already advanced a long way into his "forêts de symboles."

3. Because of the way he transposed his personal experience of seascape and color—as he had seen them either in the tropics, or in Delacroix's paintings, or in hashish-induced hallucinations— Baudelaire created in the *Salon de 1846* a word tableau which we could call the first impressionist painting. The text quoted speaks for itself. Everything is there to describe a Monet or a Renoir.[6] On

the next page Baudelaire sets down a whole series of statements that open the way for impressionist theory.

La couleur est donc l'accord de deux tons . . . ils n'existent que relativement.

L'air joue un si grand rôle dans la théorie de la couleur que, si un paysagiste peignait les feuilles des arbres telles qu'il les voit, il obtiendrait un ton faux . . . (p. 231)

> (Color is therefore the consonance of two tones . . . they exist only relatively. . . . Air plays so important a role in color theory that, if a landscape artist were to paint trees as he sees them, he would obtain a false tone. . . .)

He imagines himself a painter, and it is in this role that he makes the final affirmation of the chapter: "Les coloristes sont les poètes épiques" (p. 232). Like the most extreme of the impressionists at the height of their scientific experiments, Baudelaire yearns to obliterate the contours of objects in order to convey the pervasive vibration of molecules and light.

It is possible, moreover, that Baudelaire derived some of his color theory and vocabulary from Chevreul, the director of the Gobelins tapestry workshop, a meticulous experimental scientist with an artist's eye. His magisterial illustrated work, *De la loi du contraste simultané des couleurs*, had appeared in 1839. Directly, or indirectly through accounts in *L'Artiste* and elsewhere, Baudelaire probably became familiar with Chevreul's ideas. The "coloristes transcendants" in the footnote (n) probably refer not only to painters but also to Hoffman and Chevreul.[7] To a degree not yet fully explored, the impressionists (particularly Seurat, who had a strong scientific and optical bent) found verification and support for their practice in Chevreul's theories. After all, he was thinking in terms of juxtaposing colored threads in a tapestry in order to form a harmony of tones; the optical mixing of colors in the observer's eye is the implication that lies behind whole sections of his experiments and his account of them.[8]

4. I shall propose lastly that the quoted passage by Baudelaire instituted a line of thinking and looking that would eventually lead to nonfigurative or abstract painting. On the following page he

states that "l'art n'étant qu'une abstraction et un sacrifice du détail à l'ensemble, il est important de s'occuper surtout des masses" (p. 231; "art being only an abstraction and a sacrifice of detail to the whole, it is important to concern oneself primarily with masses"). Of course he is using the word *abstraction* analytically more than esthetically or historically, yet one cannot ignore the drift of his thought. A little later in the same chapter on color, he makes himself clearer: "La bonne manière de savoir si un tableau est mélodieux est de le regarder d'assez loin pour n'en comprendre ni le sujet ni les lignes" (p. 232; "the right way of knowing whether a painting is melodious is to look at it from far enough away so as to understand neither its subject nor its lines"). He is asking us to consider the pure play of color. Veronese and Delacroix are both in his mind. He returned to the same idea seven years later in a famous passage about Delacroix in the *Exposition Universelle de 1855*: "On dirait que cette peinture . . . projette sa pensée à distance. . . . Il semble que cette couleur pense par elle-même, indépendamment des objets qu'elle habille" (p. 369; "It seems as though this painting . . . projects its thought at a distance. . . . It appears that this color thinks by itself, independently of the objects it clothes"). What Baudelaire later begins to call "l'art pur" in the unfinished essay "L'Art philosophique" is probably a further exploration of the non-representational possibilities of painting. In a phrase reminiscent of Coleridge and anticipating Mallarmé, he defines pure art as "une magie suggestive contenant à la fois objet et sujet . . ." (p. 424). Faint echoes of pure art survive in the *Salon de 1859*) in the discussions of photography and the imagination. After that, in the last essays on Delacroix and Guys, this strand of critical thought gives way before the doctrines of modernity and spontaneity. Nevertheless, the evolution of the idea of "abstraction" can be followed as far as 1859 from its beginnings in the 1846 prose poem on color. The theory is very tentative, but we learn what Baudelaire actually saw.

These last two "firsts"—that is, a prose poem straining to transform itself into an impressionist painting, and the same prose poem projecting out of its swirling movement the possibility of an "abstract" color composition without identifiable objects—lead to the not unexpected conclusion that in the 1846 color passage Baudelaire was practicing a kind of imaginary *ekphrasis*. In highly rhetorical language he describes a work of art that can be attributed only to his own hand and that looks prophetically forward toward two major developments in European painting of the next hundred years.

With a little perseverance therefore, one can place Baudelaire's early prose poem on color in a rich historical context that arrays his career as a writer beside the development of painting and art criticism in the nineteenth century. The two intensely written paragraphs begin to look like a remarkable anticipation of things to come. But once again I find myself impelled to ask the question with which I began. Without the historical and literary context, does one receive a direct impression of the literary significance and merit of this text?

When I try to put aside the rich associations evoked in the preceding pages and come back to it "cold," the color passage from the *Salon de 1846* leaves me with two principal impressions. The first is of the hortatory tone propelling the entire exposition, even the most personal responses. The text exceeds the bounds both of description and of meditation. The second impression is of the author's sustained effort to affirm a single principle that will embrace all the elements of his experience—physical and spiritual, moral and esthetic.

Read aloud, the two paragraphs take on the sonorities of a sermon. Bossuet's periods move like a groundswell beneath the surface rhythms. In this light I believe we can begin to understand better the oddly addressed opening chapter, "Aux bourgeois." You have taken over the government and the city, Baudelaire tells them boldly; now in order to reach "cette suprême harmonie" you must learn to appreciate beauty. One sentence leads me to doubt the possibility that irony undercuts the words here: "Jouir est une science, et l'exercice des cinq sens veut une initiation particulière, qui ne se fait que par la bonne volonté et le besoin" (p. 227; "Pleasure is a science, and the exercise of the five senses requires a special initiation, which is reached only through inclination and need"). This helps us. For it suggests that the two paragraphs we have been discussing belong to a "special initiation." In his mid-twenties, Baudelaire still wanted to believe that he could convert the middle class to see and feel as he did. The initiation he proposed, encountered in its most concentrated form in the color passage, consists in a direct presentation of what Baudelaire perceived under certain circumstances. The natural bent of his sensibility included a strong urge toward insight, clairvoyance, hallucination, distortion, abstraction. He was conscious of it and cultivated it deliberately and far longer than Rimbaud. The words *étrange, bizarre, dédoublement*, and the like stud his prose even when he is not concerned with drugs. And hashish can be seen as belonging to the systematic exercise of his heightened powers of vision. We can hear his resolute visionary intent, and the same hortatory tone, in the fragment on realism he wrote in 1855: "La Poésie est ce qu'il y a de plus réel, c'est ce qui n'est complètement vrai que dans *un autre monde*" (p. 448; "Poetry is what is most real, it is what is completely true only in *another world*"). When, in 1862, Baudelaire states, "J'ai cultivé mon hystérie avec jouissance et terreur" (p. 640), he feels the approach of madness because the process has gone on for fifteen years—since 1846 at least. The vision into which Baudelaire sought to initiate the bourgeois begins to sound like the "hallucination vraie" which Taine derived in part from his highly revealing correspondence with Flaubert about the imagination.[9]

Because of the special nature of his sensibility, Baudelaire was not content to cast his initiatory message entirely in words. He painted a picture; he directly depicted what he saw and what he implied we too can see. "Goût permanent depuis l'enfance de toutes les représentations plastiques" (p. 617; "a permanent taste since childhood for all plastic representations"), he states in a biographical note. His fundamentally didactic purpose in writing about the arts is probably best expressed in the late essay on Guys: "peu d'hommes sont doués de la faculté de voir; il y en a moins qui possèdent la puissance d'exprimer" (p. 553; "few men are endowed with the faculty of seeing; fewer possess the power of expression"). He began in 1846 with the idealistic goal of converting the bourgeois; gradually he restricted himself to writing for fellow artists and poets. But until the very end the evangelistic manner continues.

One of the most apt terms to identify what Baudelaire saw and what he wanted others to see is the word he introduces force- fully at the very end of the *Salon de 1846*: "Le merveilleux nous enveloppe et nous abreuve comme l'atmosphère; mais nous ne le voyons pas (p. 261; "the marvellous envelops us and nourishes us like the atmosphere; but we don't notice it"). He uses the word also in the essay on laughter (p. 377) written at about the same period. It conveys Baudelaire's sense of wonder that so many parts of the world carry meaning, connect with one another, and speak to us. I believe it is a strong sense of the marvelous that radiates from his early undeclared prose poem—even if we know nothing about its provenance and circumstances. Eighty years later the sur- realists elected *le merveilleux* as their ideal. But by then the word had come to mean not so much *relation* as *rupture* with conventional modes of living and feeling. *Le merveilleux* testifies to the shifting ideology of modernism across two centuries.

The title of the chapter and the vocabulary of Baudelaire's in- itiatory prose poem appear to present color as the key to his vision. He probably thought so himself, in great part because of Delacroix's influence.[10] Samuel Cramer, the highly autobiographical hero of *La Fanfarlo* written the same year, consoles himself by composing a book on color symbolism (p. 287). Yet closer inspection of the piece under consideration will show that the key is not so much the distribution and relation of tones as a deep-seated movement, a "vibration, laquelle fait trembler les lignes et complète la loi du mouvement éternel et universel" (a). In the *Salon de 1845* he had tried out a weaker expression, "cette pondération du vert et du rouge" (p. 205). In the final version, *vibration* pervades the entire scene beginning with the molecules themselves, an insight fully in accord with the theories of modern physics. An eternal and universal law carries the principle of vibration to its extreme limit and places it also at the seat of consciousness. The spinning top (e) represents not only the ceaseless agitation of nature but also, enfolded into one rhythm, the operation of thought itself.

Here is the innermost burden of Baudelaire's prose poem. In the vibration of color he sees a supreme *correspondance*, linking external reality and the mind. This alternating rhythm finally be- comes the subject of "Le *Confiteor* de l'artiste," which begins to throb between *immensité* and *petitesse*, between *les choses* and *moi* (p. 149). Baudelaire returns to the universal law of alternation at a few other crucial moments of his writing. In "Conseils aux jeunes littéraires," he speaks of "la loi des contrastes, qui gouverne l'ordre moral et l'ordre physique" (p. 268). Chevreul is audible again in this further attempt to find the unifying principle for all domains. Later, after writing on Poe, Baudelaire seemed to find a personification of the oscillating consciousness in the idealized figure of the dandy. But in 1846 he used vibration to express a dynamic combination of materialism and transcendence, in nature and in man. Therefore the strong hortatory tone of the prose poem finds its justification in the vastness of the principle of correspondence Baudelaire is affirming in it. The whole universe vibrates as one— if you can only see deeply enough into the world. Approximately ten years later in one of the journal entries collected as "Mon Coeur mis à nu," Baudelaire caught the principle of vibration in two lapidary sentences that could stand as the inscription for his entire work. "De la vaporisation et de la concentration du *Moi*. Tout est là" (p. 630). The systole and dyastole of the universe itself is reproduced in the contraction and expansion of the mind, alternately concentrating its attention and opening itself to all impressions. The passage we have been studying implies, even more powerfully than a painting of the same subject, that the fascination of sunrise and sunset lies in the fact that these particular moments make sensible for us the earth's harmonious rotation, the generalized vibration of everyting.

Alfred North Whitehead, too, was deeply committed to what he called "vibratory organism." In the fifth chapter of *Science and the Modern World*, he states firmly, on scientific grounds, that, "in a certain sense, everything is everywhere at all times." Baudelaire hoped to initiate us to this vision: neither he nor Whitehead could go further.

For years I have believed that during the nineteenth and twentieth centuries music and painting were ahead of literature in their explorations of the potentialities of human thought. All poetry could do was to try to recover its rightful place.[11] On the one hand

Hoffmann and Schopenhauer and Wagner made deep inroads on the esthetic consciousness of Europe with their pronouncements on music. On the other hand, beginning with Manet and Monet (if not already with Turner and Delacroix) it looked as if the poets could do little more than jog along behind musicians like Wagner and the painters of genius that formed the School of Paris. But an attentive and sympathetic reading of a text like "De la couleur" obliges one to suspend judgment and see the great artistic race as more evenly matched than one had thought.

And I am speaking of a *prose* text, a *poème en prose* to be precise. Mallarmé only called attention to the *crise de vers* that descended on traditional poetry at the end of the century with the advent of free verse. Correspondingly one might speak of an effort in the novel since Flaubert to "reprendre à la poésie notre bien." In the great redistribution of roles and shift of powers that went on during the latter half of the nineteenth century, I feel sure that we could locate and identify a *crise de prose*. It concerns the emergence of the prose poem in French, the claims to authority of certain *poètes fondés en peinture* like Baudelaire and Apollinaire, and Baudelaire's doctrine, powerfully reaffirmed by Eliot, that "tous les grands poètes deviennent naturellement, fatalement, critiques . . . je considère le poète comme le meilleur de tous les critiques" (p. 517).

In order to grapple with these inchoate realignments of the arts and of artists, Baudelaire, aged twenty-five, opened his initiatory prose poem speaking like an engineer or a mathematician: "Supposons un bel espace de nature . . ."

Notes

1. See I. A. Richards, *Practical Criticism* (New York: Harcourt, Brace, 1929).

2. Charles Baudelaire, *Oeuvres complètes*, Marcel A. Ruff, ed. (Paris: Seuil 1968), pp. 230–31. References to Baudelaire's work will be indicated by numbers in parentheses giving the pages in this edition.

3. A few critics have implied as much in passing, but without pausing to examine the merit of the idea. See André Ferran, *L'Esthétique de Baudelaire* (Paris: Nizet, 1933), p. 140; and Enid Starkie, *Baudelaire* (New York: New Directions, 1958), p. 159. Two other books have contributed substantially to my interpretations: F. W. Leakey, *Baudelaire and Nature* (New York: Barnes and Noble, 1969); and Baudelaire,

Salon de 1846, text established and presented by David Kelley (Oxford: Oxford University Press, 1975).

4. One should also compare the prose poem "Le Fou et la Vénus."

5. It may also be his first rendering of a drug experience. The evolution of Baudelaire's prose style shows us that he was able to insert into "Du vin et du hachish" a number of passages transposed from poems—or out of which he formed poems. These exchanges also probably go back to the years just before the 1848 revolution.

6. My colleague Paul Barolsky, who teaches history of art at the University of Virginia, pointed out to me the painterly quality of Baudelaire's prose here and its striking anticipation of impressionism.

7. Chevreul deserves a note as long as I dare make it. In his effort to systematize the subjective process of color vision and interpretation, Chevreul has to develop a psychology of perception virtually a science of sensibility. He distinguishes carefully between simultaneous, successive, and mixed color contrasts, the last being an after-image combined with a new color. In a long section on color and music, successive contrast comes out as melody, simultaneous contrast as harmony. The dynamics of color contrasts are compared in the final section to mental processes in general. Chevreul lays it down as law that comparison exaggerates differences and needs correction. This law applies particularly in solitary thought, in a two-way conversation, and in teaching. "Absolute" judgment is not possible for us because of "relative" circumstances affecting all observation. Because analysis proceeds by dividing wholes into parts, it necessarily distorts. See M. E. Chevreul, *De la loi du contraste simultané des couleurs* (Paris: Imprimerie nationale, 1889), pp. 545–58.

Chevreul wrote a remarkably modern text, in which one keeps hearing anticipations of Eisenstein on montage and of the surrealists on the nature of an image.

8. I might mention that the Monet painting from which the name impressionism was drawn had a subject closely related to that of Baudelaire's 1846 color text. Painted in 1872, *Impression, soleil levant* was one of the major entries in the first exhibit in 1874 of the Société Anonyme des Artistes Peintres. The painting shimmers as vividly as Baudelaire's prose poem.

9. Hippolyte Taine, *De l'intelligence* (1870).

10. See Ferran, *L'Esthétique de Baudelaire*, pp. 139–50.

11. In "Crise de vers" Mallarmé speaks of the need to "reprendre notre bien"—a phrase Valéry echoes almost verbatim in "Avant-propos à *La Connaissance de la déesse*" as the "commune intention" of symbolism.

PART II Definition and Theory

3. Short Epiphanies:
Two Contextual Approaches
to the French Prose Poem

Michel Beaujour

The so-called prose poem, in one or another of its guises, has been the mainstay of modernist poetry in France, where hostility to the "straight jacket" of verse (including *vers libre*) is explicitly or implicitly built into any avant-garde poetics. Indeed the idea of a "prose poem" has been the locus of French poetic, ontological, political, metapsychological, and ultimately anthropological confrontations for more than a century. But despite an abundance of manifestoes and apologias claiming a degree of poeticalness or its equivalent within a given ideological context for short prose texts— a poeticalness increasing in direct ratio to the text's allergy to "normative," informative, or narrative uses of language—I am not aware of any scholarly study purporting to vindicate the prose poem (in any sense of this semantically unstable term) that is not radically flawed by unexamined tenets, by militant ideological guile, by incompetent methodology or methodological legerdemain, or by ontological and hermeneutical assumptions that require a leap of faith precluded by my ontic gravity.

It is impossible to take in at one glance all the heterogeneous issues involved in this problem of "prose poetry," even should one decide to leave aside—as I intend to do—the intimately related question of "free rhythms" in modern poetry.[1] Finally one is even nagged by the suspicion that despite the ideological heat—and dialectical deviousness—surrounding the prose poem (as well as the automatic text, the dream narrative, the short "text" of avant garde—and rear guard—reviews), there is little substance behind the smoke; little at least to be apprehended and described by formalist, rhetorical, or stylistic strategies. One can of course describe discrete texts, but the genre, type, sort of "speech act," kind of discourse, what have you, is so elusive that the theoretician may well wish to decide that there is after all no such thing as a prose poem, since this notion cannot be construed as the object of a poetic enquiry.

Instead of attempting to resolve what strikes me as an essentially insurmountable difference and perhaps a gross aporia, I have chosen to approach the prose poem gingerly within two interrelated, but somewhat staggered, ideological contexts. Both approaches ultimately have to do with the question of what poetry is, but the first one is principally formal, since it tries to account for the belief that the prose poem should be *short*, while the second is mainly ontological, and deals with beliefs about the prose poem as a revelation of Being. There is no attempt on my part to synthesize the two approaches. This self-defeating strategy is, I believe, permissible when one is faced with a literary canon which includes works by Aloysius Bertrand, Baudelaire, Francis Ponge, Rimbaud, Claudel, Jules Renard, and most surrealists, but apparently excludes—who's to say?—Nerval's *Les Nuits d'octobre*, Robbe-Grillet's *Instantanés*, or Jean-Loup Trassard's *Paroles de laine*.

Brevity

The critics, who have failed to provide a definition of the genre able to account for the features of all canonical "prose poems," seem to agree at least on one point: not only are prose poems observably "short" (and autonomous), but they *must* be so, for beyond a certain length, "the tensions and impact are forfeited and [the prose poem] becomes—more or less—poetic prose."[2] Implicit in such a statement (but explicit in Monique Parent's preliminary definition, "autonomous pieces of lyrical poetry devoid of verse structure"[3]) lies a debatable equation of poetry with "lyricism." Lyricism in turn is associated with manifestations ("tension" and

"impact," or "images" and "music") of an *energy*: "This energy,"
writes Parent, "which becomes manifest through music and images, and which is self-sufficient, soaring to the rank of an absolute
and seeking only to express itself in an appropriate language, is
indeed the lyrical state of mind, it is lyricism itself; this state of
mind creates the poem."[4]

Thanks to M. H. Abrams' scholarship,[5] it is easy to trace the
common ideological context of John Simon's factual assertion that
the length of the prose poem is "that of the average lyrical poem,"[6]
and of Parent's complementary outburst. Meanwhile, we should
keep in mind that the energetic metaphor, so widespread in nineteenth-century writings, found perhaps its most polymorphous development in Freud's theory of a sexualized unconscious.

Abrams traced the fortunes of the lyric, rising from a minor
trifle in the Renaissance and classical periods to the status of a
"poetic norm" with preromanticism. Three ideological elements of
poetics came into play in this evolution: expressivity, mimesis, and
moral usefulness. As the mimetic and persuasive function of art,
and especially of poetry, was downgraded, the "expressive" function gained the upper hand, and became the ideological norm for
poetry (as well as the other arts. This foregrounding of "expression" was related to the growing critical interest in the "sublime"
for which the pseudo-Longinian treatise provided a classical
grounding. The sublime was a manifestation of the poet's powers
of "imagination" and "enthusiasm," an ability to project his own
powerful passions through art. Just as it had been in the early years
of the Pléiade (and for similar reasons), the inspired, enthusiastic
ode in principle became the archetype and model of all true poetry,
understood to be an unruly and discontinuous outburst, rather
than a function of the total mimetic or moral effect of a sustained
work.[7] Such psychological—or metapsychological—criteria, which
are inseparable from an emphasis on imagery as the key differentia
of poetry, have ruled poetics—although not unchallenged—in the
modern period. They underly the critical theories of Croce and
Potebnya and play an important part in symbolism, imagism, and
surrealism. Such a conception tends to dissociate poeticalness from
reliance on rhythmical and metrical devices, from genre, diction,
and topic. It also tends to favor short pieces over longer ones.

Although inspiration (and poetic imagery) may flicker here and there through sustained poems, "real poetry" intrinsically is a discharge of short duration. In some cases (imagism, Reverdy's works, surrealism) poetry becomes largely synonymous with *images* understood to be vehicles of analogical revelation occurring in a flash.

Once this ideological context is blocked in, it becomes easier to understand why critics insist on the need for brevity in the prose poem: if even a large piece possessing other traditional differentiae of poeticalness (meter, verse, topic, diction, etc.) cannot be continuous "real poetry," it follows that a prose piece must be short in order to achieve some verisimilitude for its claims to poeticalness. Shortness presents at least a presumption of lyrical energy at work, a presumption which may be confirmed by the presence of specifically lyrical features such as broken rhythm and imagery. As Monique Parent put it: "The lyrical state is a motion, not always a supple and ample motion, but also jerky, leaping, convulsive motion."[8]

Nevertheless, many "canonical prose poems," although comparable in length to lyrics, have none of the rhythmical, syntactic, rhetorical, or semantic features that might conceivably substantiate Parent's orgasmic metaphor. Unfortunately, this is particularly true of Baudelaire's *Petits Poèmes en prose*, which were the first pieces of the kind to have been dubbed "prose poems" by their author. Some of them are so obviously unpoetical according to lyrical norms (except in terms of length) that John Simon cannot, for once, be considered unduly censorious when writing that Baudelaire's prose poem "does not always escape prosaism, and often becomes merely anecdotal."[9] Yet there are no criteria which allow one to exclude such "prosaic" and "anecdotal" pieces from the canon of the prose poem.

Since much the same could be said of other canonical pieces by Jules Renard, Jammes, Fargue, Jacob, the surrealists, Ponge, etc., it follows that *brevity* is the only component of the lyrical-orgasmic metaphor enjoying general pertinence within the canon: the presumption of a "lyrical energy" warping a piece of prose into poeticalness is predicated exclusively and entirely on this single feature. But it would be anticlimactic to conclude that a prose poem merely is a short, autonomous piece of prose, and leave it at that.

We must take a closer look at this elusive artifact, and to that effect it may be useful to adopt another critic's point of view, especially if it is that of a practitioner of the prose poem, whose entire work attempts to claim the inheritance of the past's poetry for his novels and other innovative "prose" structures. In "Le Roman et la poésie," Michel Butor's approach to the prose poem is obviously oblique and self-serving but justifiably so, since the piece is a kind of manifesto. The context of his discussion is the assertion that poetry is not a localized phenomenon and that it can be achieved and modulated through a large literary structure such as the novel:

> The difference between evidently poetical passages—where the words are powerfully tied together, even when isolated from the whole, such as the poems extracted from an unknown novel which make up *Le Spleen de Paris*—and seemingly prosaic passages, which reveal their peculiar virtues through sustained reading, whether linear or spatialized, continuous or discontinuous; this difference is exactly analogous to the one separating this very work [the poetical novel] from the mob of everyday novels and everyday banality.[10]

Butor, then, seems to believe—or finds it expedient to assert—that some prose *passages* (rather than *pieces*, since the latter might connote autonomy, discreteness) are self-evidently and "immediately" poetical owing to some presumably describable "powerful" concatenation of their words, while other "passages" of the (virtual) macrostructure are less evidently poetical (they can even be perceived as unpoetical). Only a global perception of the larger "work" will be able to reveal the poetical function of the latter passages within the macrocontext. There is no essential discontinuity between the highly charged and the more prosaic passages in a sustained work, all passages being functional in producing the work's total poetic effect.[11]

But we have overlooked something: Butor chose for his demonstrative instance of a "poetic novel" that contained both types of passages contributing in their own way to the total effect not so much what he cunningly termed an "unknown" work as a purely and simply non-existent novel. For *Le Spleen de Paris*, despite one isolated and polemical statement in Baudelaire's dedication of the collection to Arsène Houssaye to the effect that these short prose pieces are *like* fragments of a long narrative which, if it existed, would bore the reader, is nothing but a collection of discrete short pieces, whose only suggested coherence is, so to speak, modal (*spleen*) and referential or topographical (*de Paris*). The connective (prosaic, narrative) passages have not been literally subtracted from a longer version of *Le Spleen de Paris*: they never were written.[12] *Le Spleen de Paris* is no *Wasteland*. Nothing that we know of Baudelaire's desultory efforts to stretch his collection to book length (and we know a great deal about this through his correspondence) will substantiate the notion that he ever conceived his *Petits poèmes en prose* to be a virtual or an actual novel. It would take some ingenuity to read a crypto-novelistic intention into the sentence which presumably triggered Butor's speculation on Baudelaire's "unknown novel": "We may," wrote Baudelaire, "cut where we will, I my dreams, you the manuscript, the reader his reading; for I do not suspend his reticent will to the interminable thread of a superfluous plot." However, Butor might have taken his cue from another section of the dedication, a passage which is more attuned to Butor's own esthetic of the novel and prose poem. This passage is preceded by the famous statement concerning Baudelaire's dreaming "of the miracle of a poetic prose, musical without rhythm nor rhyme, malleable and abrupt enough to adapt itself to the lyrical motion of the soul, to the sinuosity of daydreaming, to the sudden starts of consciousness." Baudelaire then goes on to say, and this is the relevant sentence: "It is mainly from the familiarity with enormous cities, it is from the intersecting of their innumerable connections that this obsessive ideal arises." In the transition from a commonplace of lyrical expressiveness to the suggestion of a structural mimesis, Baudelaire created a powerful and fecund metaphor, which offers not only intimations of a new referential, topical system (enormous cities), but, and perhaps more importantly, a new structural, spatial model (innumerable intersections and connections) which would eventually be found in many modern—symbolist and postsymbolist—works.[13]

However, the "poetry of enormous cities" may become structural, as Butor and most modernist writers would have it, or it may remain atmospheric, pathetic, and anecdotal, as it mostly was in nineteenth-century works. Butor would like to confer upon Baudelaire's *Spleen de Paris* the status of a structural archetype, by turning the autonomous pieces into the vestiges of an "unknown novel," thereby stretching the acknowledged poeticalness of the short pieces to the proportions of a large and variegated work. The poetic novel would thus become a synecdochic extension of the prose poem.

But, given the stock definitions (the only ones, after all, having currency), is it acceptable to suggest that a long "spatial" or "topographical" work is indeed a macro- "prose poem"? Is not the lyrical emphasis on shortness and discreteness incompatible with the structural poetics implicit in Butor's conception of the "poetic novel" and, by extension, "the long poetic work in prose"?

These questions are, I believe, at best irrelevant or trivial in the context of literary theory. But they do carry some meaning and affect from the point of view of a literary history—conceived, for instance, along the lines of Harold Bloom's genealogies. It is not as easy as it seems to dare assert that a prose macrostructure (virtual or actual) is indeed a long prose poem, merely because I say so, even though, beyond the constraints of tradition, all it takes is gumption and some plausibility to have what I say go down. Butor did need a paternal Baudelaire, even if only in order to misread him. There is more to this sort of gesture than the mere reshuffling of generic names, for the poets themselves, although perhaps mistakenly, feel that the status of their utterance is at stake, in a world of equivocal labels. And of course anthologists, readers, and teachers of literature are in need of taxonomies. Beyond this, as we shall see later on, the question, although trivial for structural poetics, can be seen as a meaningful, and important, ontological issue.

To get back to the prose poem in the narrow, traditional sense: Baudelaire had insisted on the essential brevity of his pieces, and their autonomy. Of *Le Spleen de Paris* he wrote to Houssaye: "Everything in it is at once head and tail, alternately and conversely." The snake metaphor (drawing on the old belief that the pieces of a cut up snake have an autonomous life of their own, and can join together in any order) suggests unity in diversity. But the book can indeed be published and read in bits and pieces. In short, *Le Spleen de Paris* is not a long poem, but rather like any collection of poems held together by some sort of topical, modal, or generic similarity. Would the reader of the *Petits Poèmes en prose* discover on his own that *Spleen* and *Paris* are supposed to be the poems' topical–modal umbrella without being told so by the author's title? And the other titles suggested by Baudelaire himself while completing his collection do indicate a good deal of semantic–topical leeway: "Petits Poèmes en prose"; "Petits Poèmes lycanthropes"; "Le Promeneur solitaire"; "Le Rôdeur parisien"; "La Lueur et la fumée." Yet several of these drafts bring to the fore a semantic feature which the final title, *Le Spleen de Paris*, somewhat obscures: *le rôdeur, le promeneur* . . .—these two words (leaving aside for a moment the Rousseauesque borrowing of "promeneur solitaire") suggest that these short texts are like picturesque views, tableaux observed in passing by a typical nineteenth-century Parisian *flâneur*.[14] This allusion, of course, confirms that the "poème en prose" is a child of the city (and to that extent the counterpart of Rousseau's rural "rêveries"), presenting verbal genre pictures, typical scenes, picturesque (or worse) happenings, with an explicit or implicit moral provided by the stroller's point of view. A shorter version of a genre created by Restif and Sébastien Mercier, except that unlike Mercier's and Restif's perambulatory narratives, the prose poem is discontinuous, self-contained, descriptive or anecdotal: a verbal equivalent of genre and satirical prints, the prose poem is, in turn, particularly fit to be illustrated, and therefore to serve as the textual component of an album.[15]

The homology—and interchangeability—between prose poem and picture, which Baudelaire seems to take for granted, is of course implicit in the metaphors which accompany the genre through its history, from *Gaspard de la nuit's* explicit emulation of Dutch genre painting, to Ponge's *Parti pris des choses*, which still combines genre painting ("le restaurant Lemeunier") and still life. Ponge's "esthetically and rhetorically adequate definitions–descriptions" (as he defines his short texts in "My Creative Method") are verbal pictures. Thus the prose poem, at least in France, was to remain closely associated with the art of the print (lithograph, etching, etc.) and follow its thematic and formal evolution, as both found their common locus and medium in the album or art book.

As a result, and despite the lyrical myth purporting to account for its genesis and size, the French prose poem did not follow the main ideological tendency of modern poetry away from mimesis and moral teaching. In a sense the prose poem remained faithful to the old apodictic injunction, *ut pictura poesis*: the prose poem is "like a picture" (see Rimbaud's *Illuminations*, Butor's *Illustrations*), and this interchangeability or "correspondence" is particularly evident in the context of the luxury art book displaying text and print on facing pages. It becomes even more so perhaps when the text is published without its "illustration," which then becomes a virtual *double* of the prose poem, a double which may or may not ever become actualized.[16]

The album, often issued by art galleries rather than regular publishers and intended for a wealthy public of connoisseurs and speculators, provided the French prose poem with the sort of *framing* necessary to support the claims that a prose text can indeed be poetic. It would be cynical to say that the high price of the art reproduced reflects favorably on the prose text accompanying it and that the text thus tends to be *precious* because of its contiguity with an expensive work of art. Paradoxically, these texts seldom get read very attentively in the luxurious context which is, so to speak, their artistic–poetic collateral. In order to become "poems" in their own right, rather than skippable pages of stylish typography, they have to be published separately, in non-illustrated volumes.[17] Nevertheless, the genre of the prose poem allowed the French poet to live in symbiosis with the artist and to become his financial parasite; the poet repays his debt with encomiastic *blasons* and that peculiarly French genre, related to the prose poem, the "Préface d'exposition," or catalogue blurb, which usually attempts to give a glowing verbal impression of the exhibited pictures. The close connection between visual art and the prose poem explains why the latter has tended to remain on the whole descriptive, anecdotal, and mimetic: it must be, in some fashion, topically related to a picture. Nowhere is this more evident than in surrealist works such as Éluard's collaboration with Max Ernst on *Les Malheurs des Immortels* (1922) or Breton's textual accompaniment to Miro's *Constellations*. The surrealist conception of *images*, supposed to be at once visual and verbal, provided a convenient theoretical ground for this sort of mimesis.

The mimetic orientation of the prose poem is brought into sharp focus by Francis Ponge's poetics, entitled "My Creative Method," where he proclaims: "No more sonnets, odes or epigrams: the very shape of the poem is to be so to speak determined by its subject-matter." Although Ponge scorns the too obvious imitation of calligrams, he clearly believes that the prose poem tends simultaneously toward semantic and iconic mimesis, thus combining *poesis* and *pictura*. Ponge is evidently aware of some sort of genetic link between the short lyric and the prose poem. But the substance of this filiation is reduced to the dictum that, in order to achieve shapeliness, the poem must be short. Through Ponge's rejection of regular verse forms, one hears a faint echo of the romantic mythology according to which the poeticalness of a prose poem is conferred upon it in a burst of lyrical energy, and a residual belief in the identity between the short prose poem and the inspired ode can be read through the rejection of the traditional genres which are listed.

Yet to anyone who is not prejudiced in favor of the prose poem for ideological (or financial) reasons, and who therefore finds that neither the "lyrical" nor the *ut pictura poesis* argument establishes conclusively the poeticalness of short prose pieces that are often matched with pictures, some of Baudelaire's comments on his own prose poems suggest another approach.

Two of the possible titles, "Le Promeneur solitaire" and "Le Rôdeur parisien," with which Baudelaire toyed while completing his collection suggest that each piece is a textual analogue of a stroll through Paris, and the book as a whole, therefore, a sort of urban counterpart to Rousseau's rural *Rêveries*. But unlike Rousseau's title, which includes a kind of generic marker, the *rêverie* being a sentimental, nonreligious, and loosely articulated meditation, Baudelaire's titles leave out such indications, except in the two variants containing "petits poèmes." His titles focus on the stroller and his moods, rather than on the modes of his discourse: in a flattering letter to Sainte-Beuve, the then famous author of *Les Poésies de Joseph Delorme*, Baudelaire saw fit to write that his own collection was like "a new Joseph Delorme pegging his rhapsodic thoughts to every incident of his promenade, and drawing from each object an unpleasant moral lesson." These small facts, along with Baudelaire's scattered references to such *moralistes* as Vauvenargues and La Bruyère, do seem to indicate his awareness of an affinity between his prose poems and other genres, some of them traditionally considered to be "poetic" (the fable, the epigram, perhaps Juvenalian satire also), and some "prosaic" (the maxim, the Theophrastan character, *moralia*, and, as we said, the *rêverie*, which is a kind of essay on "sentimental" or memory topics suggested by an evocation of referential *places*[18]). Indeed, prose poems, or at least some prose poems,[19] fit within a configuration of disparate, short, prose genres, generated by topical invention and amplification.[20] The nonnarrative prose poem, then, is like a *chria*, topically prompted by some evocative place or event, and building up toward some sort of maxim or moral. It would be easy to prove that the French prose poem, examined from the rhetorical point of view, differs mainly from the essay (and especially the Anglo-American essay, in the tradition of the *Spectator* and Charles Lamb) in that it is generally limited to one *place* and/or *topic*, dialectically uncomplicated, and *short*.

If such is the case, the specificity of this particular type of *chria* becomes somewhat problematic, and its "poeticalness" a matter of faith: it must be asserted metadiscursively within the text, or else suggested by framing and context. All attempts to define the prose poem in terms of lexical, syntactical, or rhetorical (stylistic) deviance from "ordinary prose" are demonstrably ideological, or logically flawed, or both. Ideological, in so far as they presuppose that "poetry" is somehow separable from verbal artifacts, or inconsequential, when they suggest that the prose of the prose poem is not really prose by virtue of its rhythms, figures, syntax, etc.

Ontology

Yet the very polymorphism, indescribability, and elusiveness of this putative genre do make it interesting and problematic: the riddle would not be solved, but merely set aside, if one were to declare, "There really is no such thing as a prose poem," and leave it at that. It might be more helpful to give in to one's impulse and say that the prose poem is "a mess." For if dirt is "a residual category, rejected from our normal scheme of classification," and "where there is dirt there is system,"[21] being repelled—or perversely attracted—to an ambiguous anomaly such as the prose poem may parallel other discomforting and dangerous experiences through which we glimpse the order of our cultural system, perceive the threats against it, and receive intimations of its renewal. At any rate, this analogy might explain why critics get so excited over prose poetry.

At stake then, is Something Important, whose symptoms or epiphanies take the shape of this oxymoronic monster, the prose poem. Its existence can no more be denied than the somatic symptoms of hysteria, or the stigmata of Christian mystics. Literature, and even poetry (in the ontic sense of "what is not prose"), are secondary considerations, along with form, rhetoric, metrics, generic systems, and all the rest of "poetics." The only interesting issues here are transcendental ones, approaches to Being and its unveiling, the suggestion that theological discourse, hermeneutics, and religious ecstasy were misguided archetypes for the true poetic experience and meaningful poetics, which are at last coming into being. Anomalous and ambiguous as it is, the prose poem is the chosen ground for assertions concerning the supralinguistic, metatextual, and ontological status of poetic language: a fantasy, perhaps of poetry as one might wish it to be. Octavio Paz, the great Mexican surrealist, offers one version of this myth: "Poetry transcends language; it is virgin language, preceding the mutilations of prose and, all at once, something which, although reached through language, is more, and inexplicable."[22] The transposition of (Christian) theology is fairly obvious here. And the morphology of an incarnate poetic logos is clearly secondary to its transcendental, preverbal status, about which little can be said, except in negative terms.

From this point of view, it is clear that all semiotic attempts to describe actual linguistic artifacts yield trivial and irrelevant results, since they in no way help to approach the being of poetry, which is only darkly revealed through the glass of language. Or else, it must be said that the language of poetry is not the one that linguists study, although it does, in some minor respects, resemble it. Such an ontological conception of poeticalness is well represented in Jacques Garelli's statement:

Understanding a poem, then, is accepting the risk of pursuing the adventure of language as far as the obscure place where the pre-reflexive temporality is formed, and where, through an ambiguous exchange of images, the mystery, or, if you will, the wedding of material expression with sense is celebrated. On that level of magical participation, there resides the rush of poetic utterance for which neither a theory of concept nor a philosophy of objectivizing intuition can account.[23]

Note that poetic language is equated here with "imaged language," a notion which is just as polymorphous and elusive as that of the "prose poem" itself: an *image* (as the word was used by the symbolists, surrealists, and the like) is much less a rhetorical trope, combining the features of metaphor, comparison, synechdoche, metonymy, and so forth, than a manifest allusion to the alleged power of poetry to recapture the lost heritage of universal analogy, alchemy, *prisca theologia*, etc. In short, although the category of linguistic phenomena designated by the word *image* is heterogeneous and messy in the eyes of the linguist, it is functional as a signal indicating a belief in *correspondences* beyond the reach of ordinary language used by ordinary mortals in a state of ordinary consciousness. One face of the image is this-worldly and linguistic, while its hidden face is magic, supralogical, prelogical, metasemiotic, and *real*. Which is another way of saying that the image is apparently arbitrary, and secretly motivated. On its hidden side, the image ceases to be a diacritic element in the endless chain of signifiers: it signifies itself, as does the eucharistic symbol within the theological context of "real presence."

If images are indeed the only relevant differentiae of "extreme utterances," the existence of a prose poem ceases to be problematic, while all the other traditional differentiae of poetry become superfluous, ornamental at best, a distracting noise at worst: the "world of language, explanation, and history" is the red dust which keeps poetry bound to its literary karma. Only the prose poem can, in principle, achieve the degree of imaged tension which makes it a door to reality. Verse is an ontic compromise which might jeopardize poetry's imaged straining toward being. We now see more clearly the tradition linking Baudelaire (and the German romantics) to Max Jacob, the surrealists, and the postsurrealist practitioners of the prose poem. The focus on prose poems signals the poet's more or less conscious choice of a poetics derived from the quasi-theological belief that "poetic language" is ontologically—rather than formally—different from ordinary language. This ontological difference (and motivation) gives access, through an experience less esthetic than visionary or epiphanic to a "poetic universe" inhabiting, so to speak, the obverse of language, which can neither denote nor connote it.

A few already somewhat forgotten passages from Sartre's *What Is Literature?* may help us better to understand the issue, which grows particularly obscure outside the framework of mysticism, western or oriental. Sartre, as we recall, drew a sharp distinction between the poet and the prose writer.[24] "Poets," he wrote, "are men who refuse to *utilize* language";[25] and further: "One might think that he [the poet] is composing a sentence, but this is only what it appears to be. He is creating an object. The word-things are grouped by magical associations of fitness and incongruity, like colors and sounds. They attract, repel, and 'burn' one another, and their association composes the veritable poetic unity which is the phrase–object."[26] Either one feels such metaphoric strictures to be "right," or they will sound a bit nonsensical. There really is nothing to argue about. But it is well to remember that much modern French thinking about poetry has consistently resorted to this sort of language, which seems to make some sort of sense to both writers and readers. The romantic paradox of success through failure, and the more modern one of the "self-consuming poet," are related to this ideology and find their favorite locus in the work and life of Antonin Artaud. Although one meets with many versions of this type of discourse outside of France (from Russia to Latin America) Anglo-Americans have, on the whole, remained rather cool to it. This may be due to an Anglo-Saxon allergy to symbolism, surrealism, phenomenology, and Heidegger: Anglo-Saxons like their ironies and paradoxes to be large and ethical, while they find word play less revealing than the French and the

Germans do. One culture's meat is another's frivolity. Anglo-Saxon frivolity may find its comfort in the belief that modernity is mainly a formal phenomenon: all is well with expressive literature and the traditional opposition between verse and prose.

That is why it may be useful to insist briefly on a set of French distinctions which gained currency in the modern, post-Mallarmé period. One of them challenges and reformulates the old opposition between poetry (verse) and prose: poetry is antithetical to "literature"; the poet, therefore, is not a mere writer. Cocteau put it amusingly in the film *Orphée*: "A poet is someone who writes without being a writer." *Literature*: loaded with pejorative connotations, the word refers to utterances or texts that use language for persuasive, informative, or entertaining purposes. *Poetry*, on the other hand, denotes procedures—or mysteries (which may or may not leave written traces)—in the course of which the poet shares with an Otherness the initiative of putting language into play. As a conscious, personal, and historical subject, the poet is displaced by another Agent—impersonal language itself, perhaps, or the "discourse" of some occult denizen of the adult poet's self (such as the unconscious, which does not abide by the logic of identity, or the babbling Child, the etymological Ancestor, the rhythmical Primitive, the imaged Visionary, the figurative Schizo, etc.). Of course, such beliefs are more or less secularized versions of the traditional myths surrounding the poet: divine election, inspiration, possession, prophecy, etc. The difference lies in the identification of the transcendental agent: rather than deities, or the poet's overwhelming passions,[27] *language* itself has become hypostasized, as an entity which manifests itself through "nonlogical" and "ungrammatical" utterances or graphemes as they break through or displace the "prosaic" order of "normative" language. And this other language (which is sometimes presumed to be that of the body, entrails, sex, etc.) is endowed with will, passion, and *sui generis* truthfulness. Far from being *used* by the poet, such a language uses the poet up, revealing in the process its own hidden face, its silent side, where, supposedly, the opposition between meaning and meaninglessness is overcome. It follows that in the process of "consuming the poet" (who then becomes a failure and/or a madman in the eyes of the world and merely serves the function of catalyst) language—in the ordinary sense of linguists and psychologists—"consumes itself," or transmutes itself to be reborn as ungrammatical and unsemiotic body, of which one may catch a glimpse through the "poem" and its "images."[28]

Sartre, and French phenomenologists, were still demonstrably under the influence of Mallarmé's theories—and quite close to surrealism in many ways, especially in their urge to refute surrealism's ontology, while retaining its emphasis on the poetic function of *images*. Mallarmé's own positions are well known, though complex. Take for instance this passage, which I shall comment in brackets as I translate it:

The pure work [the alchemical connotations of work-opus are evident in context] implies the elocutory disappearance of the poet [the poet does not "speak" in his own name when engaged in the work of verbal alchemy], who abandons the initiative to words ["words" are agents endowed with will and purpose of their own], when these are mobilized by the jolt of their unevenness [the poet mobilizes words when he produces some metrical pattern: such patterns act like a crystal in the saturated but previously inert solution of language, which henceforth structures itself according to its purposes]; they [the words] are kindled by mutual reflections as in a virtual train of sparkles across gems, thus replacing the perceptible heaving of the old lyrical breath, or the personal control of the sentence in inspiration.[29]

The poet, then, is a self-effacing catalyst who, in principle, relinquishes any sort of control over the shaping of the linguistic crystal. Verbal alchemy produces verbal constructs which are not semantically or formally determined by conscious choices, generic tradition, etc. Distinctions between verse and prose become irrelevant, since the shape, metrics, rhythm of the "poem" result from the workings of language's alien purposes. Besides, whether the poem displays what according to the readers' expectations might be called shape, regularity, closure, etc. becomes an irrelevant matter within this ideological context. And of course, nothing guarantees—or warrants—that texts produced by language, upon the self-effacing intervention of an impersonal poet, should make any discursive "sense" to the poet or to the readers, for the meaning of such a text is a revelation about the transcendence of language.

Since poems are not messages circulating between human agents, they cannot fit within the models of communication theory, or any other rhetorical framework.

Two incompatible conceptions of poetry coexist within modern French culture, as they coexist within the theoretical writings of Mallarmé: (1) Poetry is radically different from other uses of language; and (2) There is no essential difference between poetry and all other artful uses of language. The same Mallarmé who wrote of poetry as though it were a verbal alchemy could also state:

In language, wherever there is rhythm, there is verse, everywhere, that is except on posters and the fourth page of newspapers. In the genre called prose, there is verse, admirable at times, in all meters. But indeed there is no prose: there is an alphabet, and then more or less dense, more or less diffuse, verse. Whenever there is an effort toward style, there is verse-making.[30]

This declaration, which may have seemed paradoxical at a time when "prose poetry" was still an oxymoron, is no more than an unseasonable (and inverted) restatement of traditional rhetorical tenets, according to which prosody and metrics were particular regularizations of verbal figures and schemes found throughout the expanse of artful elocution. But it elegantly resolves the problems posed by prose poetry: since "prose" is a misnomer for a diffuse kind of verse—and "verse" can (when I so decide) be equated with "poetry"—a prose poem is a text where the verse density approaches that of regular metrical forms, while eschewing the anaphoric servitudes of prosody. This solution gives no satisfaction to those who believe in the specificity of prose poetry, for it grants no defensible boundaries to the beleaguered "genre" within the rich territories which, beyond the excluded badlands of journalism and advertising, slope gently up toward the ridge of regular verse. The sacred homeland of verbal alchemy, the place of revelation and epiphanies, is profaned by secularism and a democratic "effort toward style." Not to mention the fact that an absolute distinction between journalistic cacography and artful writing is purely ideological and does not stand up to linguistic or rhetorical scrutiny: it is all a question of taste, and should ideology so decree, *bad* taste might become axiological king of the castle. We know this upset did indeed take place with futurism, Dadaism, surrealism, and their sequels: posters and newspapers became paradigms of artfulness.

In Mallarmé's theory then, the prose poem becomes a red herring across the track leading to much more fundamental matters concerning the status and functions of literature (or poetry) in general. Such is always the case; the question of prose poetry is symptomatic of deep ideological misgivings, the locus of ideological bluster. We have indeed a growing body of short prose texts, some of them clearly labeled "prose poems," which we, as competent modern readers, approach with poetic expectations: we are ready, and even eager, to find such texts to be "difficult"—semantically elusive, syntactically strange, lexically surprising, etc. We fully expect not to "understand" them, and are quite willing to remain baffled, since we have been warned against reducing poetic suggestion to paraphrase. The uninitiated, however, fret and panic when they are, usually for some pedagogic purpose, made to read such texts: they feel frustrated, inadequate; their response is not properly programmed. They attribute their uneasiness to a failure of their sensibility, a weakness of their intelligence. In the face of "prose poems" of this type, the cultural split between the petty bourgeoisie of traditional expectations and the modernist aristocracy of consciousness is seen to gape painfully. This discrimination may well be, in the last analysis, the true social and cultural function of those modernist artifacts which deliberately disregard or reject constituents traditionally built into an art form: representation in painting, the stage in theatre, melody in music, narrative in novels, motion in films, metrical language in poetry. The rejection of poetry's past associations—were they only virtual—with voice and music, with singsong and hypnotic modulation, is made to suggest a higher mystery, which may well reside essentially (as is the case with mysteries) in the difference between the initiate and the unenlightened. The survival of verse and music (singing) in French popular poetry, which the initiates despise, may clarify this assertion.

As Jean Paulhan so patiently and perspicuously explained, the split between two conceptions of language uses and of literature must be enforced by what he called a Terror, the dictatorship of the initiate.[31] The prose poem, with its mystic overtones and its suggestiveness of another, esoteric, and unintelligible language, has been the weapon of Terror in its efforts to protect a higher agonistic and sacred art against the onslaughts of petty-bourgeois levelers. Less is more. Yet, in a paradox which Paulhan well understood, the prose poem also is the locus where rhetoric reasserts its rights and challenges all claims to sacred separateness. In a sense, then, the question of the prose poem allows one to catch a glimpse of all the contradictions which tear modern esthetics asunder.

Notes

1. For an approach to this question, and a survey of the issues, see Benjamin Hrushovski, "On Free Rhythms in Modern Poetry," in Thomas A. Sebeok, ed., *Style in Language* (Cambridge: MIT Press, 1960), pp. 173–90.

2. J. S. [John Simon], "Prose Poem," in Alex Preminger, Frank J. Warnke, and O. B. Hardison, eds., *Princeton Encyclopedia of Poetry and Poetics* (Princeton: Princeton University Press, 1965), p. 664.

3. Monique Parent, *Saint-John Perse et quelques devanciers: Études sur le poème en prose* (Paris: Klincksieck, 1960), p. 12.

4. *Ibid.*

5. M. H. Abrams, *The Mirror and the Lamp: Romantic Theory and the Critical Tradition* (London, Oxford, New York: Oxford University Press, 1953), ch. 4, "The Lyric as Poetic Norm."

6. J. S., "Prose Poem," p. 664.

7. "There was a conspicuous tendency, for example, to identify as 'pure poetry,' or the most poetical poetry, or 'la vraie poésie,' those particular poems or passages which were thought to be peculiarly the product of passion and rapture." Abrams, *The Mirror and the Lamp*, p. 86.

8. Monique Parent, *Saint-John Perse*, p. 13. Parent adduces a passage from Claudel's *Positions et propositions*, where an orgasmic metaphor also is used to justify the features of the Claudelian *verset*. One is tempted to read Parent's description of "lyrical motion" as a variant of the neoclassical opposition between "style périodique" and "style coupé." See also Aldo Scaglione, *The Classical Theory of Composition* (Chapel Hill: University of North Carolina Press, 1972), p. 189. Any rhythmic and syntactic study of the prose poem ought to refer to theories and practice of prose style and composition in order to avoid naive confusions between traditional features of art prose and alleged poetic *differentiae* of the modern prose poems. Scaglione offers many insights, without reference to an "essence of lyricism, into the meanings attached to various types of word orders within the context of theories of prose composition,"

9. J. S., "Prose Poem," p. 665.

10. Michel Butor, "Le Roman et la poésie," *Répertoire II* (Paris: Éditions de Minuit, 1964), pp. 24–25.

11. Such a view, of course, is a commonplace of formalist and postformalist poetics. What remains obscure in Butor's perspective is the poetic status of "everyday novels" and "everyday banality." Butor's argument is, on this score, reminiscent of Mallarmé's distinction between, on the one hand, all artful writing (equated with "verse") and, on the other, "journalism." Seemingly, something like this argument had already been used to elevate the novel to the status of poetry, most notably by Andrei Bely and the Russian symbolists, who were well aware of Mallarmé's and René Ghil's theories. See Georgette Donchin, *The Influence of French Symbolism on Russian Poetry* (The Hague: Mouton, 1958), p. 112.

12. One might also argue that these passages are scattered through the "prose poems" that are "prosaic" and "anecdotal." But then Butor's imagined macrostructure becomes even less plausible.

13. From Verhaeren, Bely, Joyce, Dos Passos to Butor himself, Robbe-Grillet, and many others. It is noteworthy that the title of Bely's great "poetic novel" is *St. Petersburg*, and that Butor's work always is—in one sense or another—topographical. This circumstance may be seen as an urban variant of what Joseph Frank called the "spatial form in modern literature."

14. Note that a collection of "prose poems" published by Lefèvre-Deumier in 1854 was entitled *Le Livre du promeneur*.

15. In a letter to Houssaye, Baudelaire wrote: "I tend to believe that Hetzel [his publisher, who specialized in illustrated books] will find here material for a romantic album" (Charles Baudelaire, *Petits Poëmes en prose*, Jacques Crépet, ed. [Paris: Louis Conant, 1926], p. 224). This kind of album had a dual progeny: the art book—see below—and the French photographic album, with poetic texts facing photographs of street scenes.

16. The question of the prose poem as a *double* is somewhat complicated—and clarified—by some of Baudelaire's *Poëmes en prose*, which also have a verse *double* or intertext: the prose "Un Hemisphère dans une chevelure" or "L'Invitation au voyage" are poeticized by an implicit reference to their verse double ("I can do verse too . . ."). Such doubling will become unnecessary when the prose poem is better established.

17. Prose, and especially the kind of broken prose which, without being calligrammatic, takes it visual cue from Mallarmé's *Coup de dés*, is more interesting for the art typographer to set than regular or free verse, which tends to sit rather stiffly and formally at the center of a page, and resists being turned into a mere typographical contrast to the facing print.

18. On the metaphorical equivalence between *essay* and *promenade*, see Gerhard Haas, *Essay* (Stuttgart: Metzlersche Verlagsbuchhandlung, 1959). The sort of referential place that can trigger the dialectical exploration of a commonplace is culturally coded. For a study of Venice as a literary commonplace, see my essay "The Venetian Mirror," *The Georgia Review* (1975), 39(3):627–47.

19. Several of Baudelaire's "poèmes en prose," such as "Mademoiselle Bistouri," are narrative, and represent instances of the short *conte romantique*.

20. However there is no intrinsic reason why these inventions ought to be in prose. They might be verse, as in the case of the meditative lyric.

21. Mary Douglas, *Purity and Danger: An Analysis of Concepts of Pollution and Taboo* (Harmondsworth: Penguin Books, 1970), p. 48.

22. Octavio Paz, *El arco y la lira*, quoted by Pierre Caminade, *Image et et métaphore* (Paris: Bordas, 1970), p. 65.

23. Jacques Garelli, *La Gravitation poétique* (Paris: Mercure de France, 1966), p. 200.

24. Sartre hardly was a maverick on this issue: all modern French criticism toys with such an opposition.

25. Jean Paul Sartre, *What Is Literature?* Bernard Frechtman, tr. (New York: Harper Colophon Books, 1965), p. 6.

26. We must amend Frechtman's translation in order to grasp the context of Sartre's statement: "burn" ought to be "consume," a word that Sartre borrowed from Georges Bataille. This borrowing conjures up their controversy about Baudelaire, a controversy about the ontological (and ethical) status of poetry.

27. A classic formulation of this ideology is Coleridge's: "Where there exists that degree of genius and talent which entitles a writer to aim at the honors of the poet, the very *act* of poetic composition *itself* is, and is *allowed* to imply and to produce, an unusual state of excitement, which of course justifies and demands a correspondent difference of language, as truly, though not perhaps in as marked a degree, as the excitement of love, fear, rage, or jealousy (*Biographia Literaria* XVIII).

28. The belief in an "other," unlinguistic side of language crops up repeatedly in postsurrealist and post-existentialist writings. Not surprisingly, it is a cornerstone of Lacan's attempt to turn psychoanalysis into an ontology. Although the "unconscious is structured like a language," one would seek in vain for a grammar of that "language." The Other must retain its Otherness.

29. Stéphane Mallarmé, "Crise de vers," *Oeuvres complètes* (Paris: Bibliothèque de la Pléiade, 1965), p. 366.

30. Mallarmé, "Enquête de Jules Huret," *Oeuvres complètes*, p. 867.

31. Jean Paulhan, *Les Fleurs de Tarbes ou la Terreur dans les lettres* (Paris: Gallimard, 1941).

4. Poetry Without Verse

Tzvetan Todorov

*T*he above title should be read as a question: without verse, what is left of poetry? Everyone since the days of antiquity has known that verse in itself does not make poetry: witness, for example, the existence of versified scientific treatises. But the answer is much less simple if one tries to rephrase it in positive terms: if poetry is not verse, what is it? This question gives rise to ı second one, springing precisely out of the difficulty of answering the first: is there such a thing as a transcultural, transhistorical "poeticity," or can one only come up with local answers, clearly circumscribed in time and in space?

In order to pursue this problem, I would like to turn to a literary genre whose very name seems to designate it as the object *par excellence* which will enable our inquiry to advance: the prose poem. Prose is considered to be the opposite of verse; if verse is eliminated, we can ask what the opposite of "poem" is, and from there, proceed backwards toward a definition of the "poetic." It would thus seem that we possess here the perfect experimental conditions for seeking an answer to our questions.

If the prose poem is indeed an ideal place to look for the answer to the question of the nature of "poetry without verse," it is only fitting that we begin by turning to the existing studies of the genre, and first and foremost to that impressive encyclopedia and history

From *Genres du discours* (Paris: Éditions du Seuil, 1978). Copyright © 1978, Éditions du Seuil. Reprinted by permission.

of the prose poem, Suzanne Bernard's *Le Poème en prose de Baudelaire jusqu'à nos jours*, to see whether the answer is not already to be found there.[1] The chapter entitled "Esthétique du poème en prose" indeed turns out to be devoted entirely to this question.

Bernard sees the essence of the genre perfectly represented in its oxymoronic name. "The entire complex set of laws which governs the organization of this original genre is already potentially contained in its very title: *prose poem*. Indeed, the prose poem, not only in its form but in its essence, is based on the union of opposites: prose and poetry, freedom and rigor, destructive anarchy and constructive art." The prose poem's author "seeks a kind of static perfection, a state of order and balance—or else an anarchic disorganization of the universe, from out of which he can call up another universe, recreate a world" (pp. 434, 444).

For the moment we are still confined to the definition of the prose poem and not that of poetry in the absence of verse; however, a preliminary remark is necessary here since it concerns a characteristic feature of Bernard's discourse. It is one thing to state that this genre is characterized by the union of opposites, but it is quite another thing to say that it can sometimes be governed by one principle and sometimes by its opposite (for instance, either by a tendency to order or by a tendency to disorder). The first statement has a definite cognitive content and can be confirmed or invalidated by studying examples, as we shall see; the second statement, on the other hand, has none: A and not-A divide up the terrain exhaustively, and to say of something that it is characterized either by A or by not-A is to say nothing at all. Bernard moves without transition from one statement to the other, as can be seen from the two groups of sentences quoted above, which open and close the first part of her discussion.

But let us now broach the subject which interests us directly, the definition of poetry. Having explained what "prose" consists of (realism, modernity, humor—we will not stop to examine this identification), Bernard turns to the definition of a poem. Its first and most important feature is unity: it is "a definition of the poem as a *whole*, whose essential characteristics are unity and concentration"; "everything 'works' esthetically, everything contributes to the total impression, everything holds indissolubly together in this poetic universe which is both very unified and very complex"; it is a "set of relations, a highly organized universe" (pp. 439, 441).

These statements concerning unity, totality, and coherence will no doubt sound familiar to the reader of today, but he will be more accustomed to seeing them attributed to any *structure* rather than solely to the poem. One could add that while structures are not necessarily all poetic, neither is every poem necessarily structured, at least not in this sense of the word: the ideal of organic unity is that of romanticism, but can we force every "poem" to conform to it without doing violence either to the text or to the metatext, that is, to the critical vocabulary? I will come back to this shortly.

Bernard is aware of the fact that a definition based on unity is a bit too general (after all, isn't a novel just as much of a "highly organized universe"?). She goes on to add a second trait to the definition, actually a more specific version of the first, but one which enables us to distinguish the poetic genre from other literary genres: it consists of a certain relation to time, or more precisely, of a way of escaping time's grasp. "The poem presents itself as a block, an indivisible synthesis. . . . We encounter here an essential requirement, fundamental to the poem: it can only exist as a poem if it reduces all duration to the 'eternal present' of art, if it congeals the process of becoming into atemporal forms—thus rejoining the requirements of musical form" (p. 442).

For anyone to whom these statements are not perfectly clear, and who wishes to know what sort of linguistic realities they cover, it turns out that this particular atemporality is the common denominator of two series of devices. The first is based on the principle that underlies rhyme and rhythm, which are no longer present: it is repetition, which imposes a "rhythmic structure upon the *actual time* of the work" (p. 451). In the second case, time, rather than being suspended, is in effect abolished, either through the telescoping of different moments, or through the destruction of logical categories (a distinction which, moreover, soon breaks down, since Bernard adds, in italics, *"which amounts to the same thing"* p. 455). This last category (or these last categories) manifests itself in the way in which the poem "leaps abruptly from one idea to another," "lacks transitions" (p. 455), or disperses "logical progressions, links between ideas, all sense of coherence in description or order in narration: modern poets, in the wake of Rimbaud, install themselves in discontinuity, the better to negate the real world" (p. 456).

We will not stop to analyze the fact that incoherence is here being presented as a subdivision or specification of . . . coherence, unity, and totality (via the "eternal present"). And we will put off until later the empirical examination of these affirmations. Confining ourselves for the moment solely to the definition of the poetic, we have arrived at its equivalence with the atemporal. But the various "means" for producing this atemporal state—or rather, the different processes which can have atemporality as a *consequence* (repetitions, incoherences)—can only very tenuously and hypothetically be reduced simply to this one common consequence. The deduction which allows one to subsume repetition and incoherence under the notion of atemporality is as fragile as the syllogisms we encounter in the "theatre of the absurd": all men are mortal, all mice are mortal, therefore all men are mice . . . Setting aside the grand principles of unity and atemporality which teach us nothing, it would be more prudent and more precise to reformulate Bernard's thesis as follows: the poetic is expressed sometimes by repetitions and sometimes by verbal incoherences. This may indeed be the case—it can be verified—but it does not give us *one* definition of poetry.

In order to test the empirical validity of these hypotheses, let us now turn to the practice of the prose poem itself, in which the idea of poetry is at work. Among the best known authors of prose poems, two examples will perhaps be able to help us in this research.

It is natural to begin with Baudelaire.[2] He is not the "inventor" of the form, as we well know (provided the notion of "inventor" means anything), but it was he who gave it its title to nobility, brought it within the horizons of his contemporaries and successors, and made it into a model for writing: a genre, in the historical sense of the word. It was he too who popularized the very expression "prose poem," using it to designate the first series he published. Our hopes of finding an answer to our question increase when, in the dedication to the collection, we read that its author dreamed of "le miracle d'une prose poétique, musicale sans rythme et sans rime": this music of the signified which Baudelaire promises us is but a terminological variant of our "poetry without verse."

The question is thus properly set out. The answer given by the texts in the volume, however, is to some extent, at least at first sight, disappointing. The fact is that Baudelaire is not really writing poetry without verse or simply seeking a kind of music of meaning. He is rather writing prose poems, that is, texts which are in their very conception based on the meeting of opposites. (For this reason, one can feel that the collection, whose title Baudelaire long debated, deserves the name *Petits Poèmes en prose* rather than *Le Spleen de Paris*, even if, in some sense, the two titles are synonymous.) It is as though Baudelaire had derived the themes and structure of nine-tenths of these texts from the name of the genre, poetic-prosaic, or, if one wishes a less nominalist point of view, as though Baudelaire had only been attracted to the genre insofar as it enabled him to find an appropriate form (a "correspondence") for a thematics of duality, contrast, and opposition. His prose poems thus aptly illustrate the definition of the genre given by Suzanne Bernard.

This statement can be backed up by enumerating the different figures drawn by this exploration of duality. There are essentially three. The first can be called *incongruity* [*invraisemblance*] (Baudelaire himself speaks of "bizarrerie"): a single fact is described, but it is so out of keeping with ordinary habits that we cannot help contrasting it with "normal" facts or events. Mademoiselle Bistouri is the strangest girl in the world, while the devil is generous beyond all expectation ("Le Joueur généreux"). The most precious gift is refused ("Les Dons des fées"), and it is a mistress' very perfection which brings about her murder ("Portraits de maîtresses"). Sometimes this contrast serves to oppose the speaker to his peers: while they profess a naïve humanism, he believes that dignity can only be awakened by the infliction of pain ("Assommons les pauvres!").

The second type of figure is *ambivalence*. Here, both opposing terms are present, but they are used to characterize a single object. Sometimes this ambivalence can be explained quite rationally as the contrast between what a thing is and what it appears to be: a seemingly noble gesture is actually mean ("La Fausse Monnaie,"

"La Corde"), or a certain image of woman is the truth behind another image ("La Femme sauvage et la petite maîtresse"). But more often the object itself is double, both in its appearance and in its essence: a woman may be both ugly and attractive ("Un Cheval de race"), or ideal and hysterical ("Laquelle est la vraie?"); a man may both love and want to kill ("Le Galant Tireur"), or may simultaneously embody cruelty and the desire for beauty ("Le Mauvais Vitrier"); a room may be both dream and reality at the same time ("La Chambre double"). Certain times or places are valorized for their capacity to serve as figures of ambiguity: twilight, the intersection of day and night ("Le Crépuscule du soir"), or a port, where action and contemplation are combined ("Le Port").

The third and final figure of duality, by far the most prevalent, is *antithesis*, the juxtaposition of two beings, facts, actions or reactions with opposing characteristics. Thus we find man and beast ("Un Plaisant"), man and nature ("Le Gâteau"), rich and poor ("Les Veuves," "Les Yeux des pauvres"), joy and affliction ("Le Vieux Saltimbanque"), multitude and solitude ("Les Foules," "La Solitude"), life and death ("Le Tir et le cimetière"), time and eternity ("L'Horloge"), the terrestrial and the celestial ("L'Étranger"). Or else, as was the case with incongruities, two opposing reactions to the same thing can be juxtaposed, one often being that of the crowd, the other, that of the poet: joy and disappointment ("Déjà!"), happiness and unhappiness ("Le Désir de peindre"), hate and love ("Les Yeux des pauvres"), refusal and acceptance ("Les Tentations"), admiration and fright ("Le Confiteor de l'artiste"), and so forth.

This type of antithetical juxtaposition can in turn be experienced as either tragic or happy: even those who resemble each other can reject each other ("Le Désespoir de la vieille"); even a second child "si parfaitement semblable au premier qu'on aurait pu le prendre pour son frère jumeau" ("so perfectly like the first that one could have taken him for his twin brother") entangles himself with the other in "une guerre parfaitement fratricide" ("a perfectly fratricidal war") ("Le Gâteau"). But on the other hand, the rich child and the poor child, although separated by "des barreaux symboliques" ("symbolic bars"), are united through their teeth "d'une *égale* blancheur" ("of *equal* whiteness") ("Le Joujou du pauvre"). After a brutal attack, the attacker can say to his victim: "Monsieur, vous êtes mon égal!" (Sir, you are my equal) ("Assomons les pauvres!"). And even though dreams are opposed to reality, they can become just as real ("Les Projets," "Les Fenêtres").

Indeed, it is not only in their general composition or thematic structure that Baudelaire's prose poems manifest this constant duality. The reader may already have noticed how many titles are composed of contrasting juxtapositions: "Le Fou et la Vénus," "Le Chien et le flacon," "La Femme sauvage et la petite maîtresse," "La Soupe et les nuages," "Le Tir et le cimetière." Others refer explicitly to duality (not to mention those which present it in its concrete embodiment—the port or the twilight): "La Chambre double," "Laquelle est la vraie?", "Le Miroir." Baudelaire's very sentences often oscillate between two opposing terms: "délicieuse et exécrable femme," "tant de plaisirs, tant de douleurs" ("Le Galant Tireur"), "paquet d'excrément" and "parfums délicats" ("Le Chien et le flacon"). Or witness this series of sentences in "Le Vieux Saltimbanque":

Partout la joie, le gain, la débauche; partout la certitude du pain pour les lendemains; partout l'explosion frénétique de la vitalité. Ici la misère absolue, la misère affublée, pour comble d'horreur, de haillons comiques . . .

(Everywhere, there was joy, profit, debauchery; everywhere, the certainty of bread for the morrow; everywhere, the frantic bursting of vitality. Here, there was absolute misery, total destitution, decked out, as a crowning horror, in comical rags . . .)

Or these, from "Les Foules":

Multitude, solitude: termes égaux et convertibles pour le poète actif et fécond. Qui ne sait pas peupler sa solitude, ne sait pas non plus être seul dans une foule affairée.

(Multitude, solitude: equal, convertible terms for the active and productive poet. He who knows not how to populate his solitude knows not how to be alone in a busy crowd, either.)

Entire texts are constructed on the basis of perfect symmetry: in "La Chambre double," for instance, there are nineteen paragraphs in all, nine for the dream, nine for reality, and one in between which begins with a "But . . ." Similarly, in "Le Fou et la Vénus," there are three paragraphs for joy, three for affliction, and a seventh in the middle which says: "Cependent, dans cette jouissance universelle, j'ai aperçu un être affligé" ("However, in the midst of this universal delight, I caught sight of a deeply afflicted creature"). Even the volume's dedication illustrates, rather than theorizes, this constant meeting of opposites, in its passage, within a single sentence, from the question of poetic form to the theme of the city, both considered by Baudelaire as the distinctive characteristics of the prose poem.

The regularity of these contrasts is such that one tends to forget that they *are* contrasts—contradictions and conflicts which can indeed be tragic. In Baudelaire's work, antithesis is situated within a system of correspondences, and this is borne out not only in the fact that the oxymoronic prose poem corresponds perfectly to the contradictions it evokes. Whatever the thing or feeling being described, it ends up fitting into a plurality of echoes. Witness the woman, the "allegorical dahlia," for whom the poet of "L'Invitation au voyage" dreams of finding an enframing country which would bear her resemblance: "Ne serais-tu pas encadrée dans ton analogie, et ne pourrais-tu pas te mirer, pour parler comme les mystiques, dans ta propre *correspondance?*" ("Would you not be framed by your analogy, and could you not mirror yourself, to speak like the mystics, in your own *correspondence?*"). The multiplication of resemblances is admirable here: the four-term analogy (the woman is to the country as the portrait is to its frame) is reinforced by a similarity between the contiguous elements: the frame must resemble the portrait, and the country the woman, not to speak of the fact that the portrait is precisely a portrait *of* the woman, that it is therefore her faithful image (the only thing missing is a direct resemblance between the frame and the country). Such a superlative "correspondence" is hardly an exception in Baudelaire's poetic world, whether in verse or in prose, and it no doubt constitutes a good illustration of what Bernard called a "set of relations, a highly organized universe." It nevertheless remains that the *unity* of Baudelaire's volume is composed precisely of the *confrontation* between opposites.

The relation between prose poem on the one hand and thematic contrast on the other is not limited to this merely structural resemblance. Numerous are the poems which deal with the work of the poet, thus adding a relation of participation to one of similarity: "Le Confiteor de l'artiste," "Le Chien et le flacon," "Les Foules," "Le Vieux Saltimbanque," "Les Tentations," "Le Désir de peindre," "Perte d'auréole," and many others. But what is even more striking about these poems is that the contrast evoked is precisely composed of the "prosaic" versus the "poetic"—now understood no longer as literary categories but as dimensions of life and of the world. Can it be anything but a poet who dreams of the clouds while the others try to bring him down to earth, nearer to the prosaic soup ("La Soupe et les nuages," "L'Étranger")? Doesn't living as a poet mean living in illusion ("tant poète que je sois, je ne suis pas aussi dupe que vous voudriez le croire" ["however much of a poet I may be, I am not as big a dupe as you would like to think"]—"La Femme sauvage et la petite maîtresse")? Or living like the heedless vagabonds, free from material bondage, who are so much admired by the young child about whom the speaker—the poet—says: "j'eus un instant l'idée bizarre que je pouvais avoir un frère à moi-même inconnu" ("for a moment I had the odd idea that I might have a brother, unbeknown to me") ("Les Vocations")? Isn't the "horrible fardeau" ("horrible burden") of life opposed precisely to the intoxication "de vin, de poésie ou de vertu" ("Enivrez-vous")? And is it not to the prose of life that one devotes the whole day, hoping to balance it off, in the middle of the night, with some more properly poetic activity: "Seigneur mon Dieu! accordez-moi la grâce de produire quelques beaux vers qui me prouvent à moi-même que je ne suis pas le dernier des hommes" ("Dear lord my God! grant me the grace to produce a few beautiful lines of poetry that will prove to me that I am not the very last of men") ("À une heure du matin")?

There is one prose poem which affirms this continuity between the thematic and the formal planes more strongly than the others: it is "Le Thyrse." A thyrsus is an object, a wand, used in religious ceremonies. The type of duality embodied by the thyrsus, albeit a rather common one, is the starting point of the text: the thyrsus is described first "selon le sens moral et poétique" and then "physiquement." The thyrsus is thus an ambivalent object like the port or the twilight, since it is poetic and spiritual on the one hand, and prosaic and material on the other. Soon a second antithesis is added to the first: the opposition between straight and curved lines. And then, as if the relation with poetry and art were not sufficiently clear, as if the structural analogy were not enough, there follows an explicit equation: the thyrsus represents the work of the artist himself.

Le thyrse est la représentation de votre étonnante dualité, maître puissant et vénéré [the text is dedicated to Liszt]. Ligne droite et ligne arabesque, intention et expression, roideur de la volonté, sinuosité du verbe, unité du but, variété des moyens, amalgame tout-puissant et indivisible du génie, quel analyste aura le détestable courage de vous diviser et de vous séparer?

(The thyrsus is the representation of your astounding duality, most revered and powerful master. Straight line and arabesque, intention and expression, stiffness of will, sinuosity of word, unity of end, variety of means, omnipotent and indivisible amalgam of genius, what analyst would have the detestable courage to divide and separate you?)

Being both material and spiritual, the thyrsus first of all partakes of both prose and poetry; as a fusion of straight lines and curves, it is now the symbol of content and form in art, and these in turn ideally extend into the prosaic and the poetic. Who could imagine a better symbol than the thyrsus to stand for the prose poem itself?

Such is the unity of Baudelaire's *Petits Poèmes en prose*, and such also is the idea they convey to us about poetry. As can readily be seen, there is nothing surprising here: the poetic is envisaged only in its contradictory union with prose; it is nothing more than a synonym for the spiritual, the ideal, the dream—and, one is tempted to say, without tautology, for the poetic. According to Baudelaire himself, the poetic thus seems to be a purely thematic category, whose only additional requirement is that it be brief. The text, which in other respects is as likely to be narrative as descriptive, abstract as concrete, must, in order to be poetic, remain short: Poe's rule was perceived by Baudelaire as a constitutive trait of the genre. As he puts it in the dedication, "Nous pouvons couper où nous voulons, moi ma rêverie, vous le manuscrit, le lecteur sa lecture; car je ne suspends pas la volonté rétive de celui-ci au fil interminable d'une intrigue superflue" ("We can cut wherever we wish, me my reverie, you the manuscript, the reader his reading; for I do not suspend the latter's refractory will upon the interminable thread of a superfluous plot"). The poem is brief; the poetic is light and airy: that seems to be all, except for the aforementioned "work" of correspondences, which is as pervasive in the *Petits Poèmes en prose* as in *Les Fleurs du mal*. Through this last characteristic, Baudelaire would seem to illustrate Bernard's first hypothesis, which equates the poetic with conformity to the principle of resemblance.

But let us take a second example, as close as possible to Baudelaire both historically and esthetically: Rimbaud's *Illuminations*.[3] These texts are definitely written in prose, yet no one would contest their poetic character. Even if Rimbaud himself does not call them "prose poems," his readers do, and that suffices for us to consider them pertinent to our debate.

Let us begin with a negative observation: Rimbaud's writing is not governed by the principle of resemblance, which seemed to be at work in Baudelaire's. Metaphor, Baudelaire's master-trope, is all but absent here. Comparisons, when they occur, do not reveal any likeness: they are properly unmotivated. "La mer de la veillée, telle que les seins d'Amélie" ("The sea of the evening vigil, like the breasts of Amélie") ("Veillées III"): we know absolutely nothing about Amélie, and thus will never know what the sea of the evening vigil is like. "C'est aussi simple qu'une phrase musicale" ("Guerre"): musical phrases are not, as far as we know, the incarnation of simplicity, and in any case the text which precedes this comparison and which it is supposed to illuminate is itself far from simple. "Sagesse aussi dédaignée que le chaos" ("Wisdom as disdained as chaos") ("Vies I"): here, two opposites are united by the disdain they elicit. "Orgueil plus bienveillant que les charités perdues" ("Pride more kindly than the lost charities") ("Génie"): again, two unknowns are related by means of a third . . . Far from contributing to the establishment of a universe based on universal analogy, these comparisons only reveal the incoherence of Rimbaud's world.

If one insists on finding tropes in the *Illuminations*, they would have to be metonymies; metonymies do not create a world of correspondences. But even this device is far from certain. It can be argued that, just as those parts of the body or properties of objects which one is at first tempted to see as synecdoches finally turn out to be nothing but literal parts and properties which do not lead to any totality, so too this dislocated and foreshortened world which is literally evoked by Rimbaud's expressions does not demand any organizing process of substitution. There is, however, a great temptation to sense within these texts a call to the metonymic imagination, even if one cannot always know for sure what the end point of the metonymy might be. When we read "notre patois étouffe le tambour" ("our dialect stifles the drum") ("Démocratie"), our linguistic habits lead us to transpose: language here stands for speech, the drum, for its sound; secondly, each of the actions evokes its agent. When one hears "le sable . . . qu'a lavé le ciel" ("the sand . . . which the sky has washed") ("Métropolitain") or "le terreau de l'arête est piétiné par tous les homicides et toutes les batailles" ("the leaf-mold of the ridge is trodden by all homicides and all battles") ("Mystique"), one again has the impression that the use of metonymies of the agent–action or agent–place-of-action type contributes something to the obscurity of the expressions.

One well-known stylistic characteristic of Rimbaud's text can also be related to the metonymic movement: the poet's tendency to describe optical illusions as if they were realities. Something at the top of a picture is said to rise; something at the bottom, to descend. Is it not possible to see this passage—by means of contiguity and not resemblance—from the image to the represented object as a metonymy? Thus we find that, in the woods, "il y a une cathédrale qui descend et un lac qui monte" ("there is a cathedral sinking down and a lake rising up") ("Enfance III"), that "au-dessus du niveau des plus hautes crêtes une mer troublée" ("above the level of the highest crests a troubled sea") appears ("Villes I"), or that "on joue aux cartes au fond de l'étang" ("they

are playing cards at the bottom of the pond") ("Soir historique");
this type of metamorphosis is explicitly motivated in "Après le
déluge": "la mer étagée là-haut comme sur les gravures" ("the sea
terraced up above as in engravings"). Metonymy also seems to be
responsible for expressions like "les herbages d'acier" ("steel grass-
lands") ("Mystique"), "les yeux . . . tricolores" ("tricolored . . .
eyes") ("Parade"), "l'enfance mendiante" ("the beggarly childhood") ("Vies II"), "regards pleins de pèlerinages ("looks full of
pilgrimages") ("Enfance I"), or for strange sentences like the following: "les gentilshommes sauvages chassent leurs chroniques"
("wild gentlemen are hunting their chronicles") ("Villes II"), "les
Rolands sonnent leur bravoure" ("Rolands are trumpeting their
bravery") ("Villes I"), "des scenes lyriques . . . s'inclinent" ("lyrical scenes . . . bow down") ("Scènes"), "les lampes et les tapis
de la veillée font le bruit des vagues" ("the lamps and the rugs of
the vigil make the noise of the waves") ("Veillées III"), or "j'observe l'histoire des trésors que vous trouvâtes" ("I observe the
history of the treasures you found") ("Vies I").

If the *Illuminations* are poetic, then, it is not because they are
"highly organized" in the sense that expression may have in a
Baudelairian context, nor because they are metaphorical (metonymy is reputed to be prosaic). Moreover, organization and metaphor are not the characteristics one habitually associates with
them in any case. As we have seen, Bernard considered Rimbaud
to be the source of the second fundamental tendency of the prose
poem: incoherence, discontinuity, negation of the real world. We
can now sum up the situation in one word: Rimbaud's text rejects
representation, and therein lies its poeticity. But such a statement
demands some explanation, particularly with respect to the representative character of literary texts in general.

It was Étienne Souriau who, in his *Correspondance des arts*,
raised most explicitly the question of representation in art, seeing
it as a distinguishing typological trait.[4] In addition to the representative arts, there are indeed arts which are not representative,
and which Souriau calls "presentative" arts.

In a sonata or a cathedral, all the morphological or other features contributing to its structure are inherent to the being-sonata or the being-

cathedral, whereas in the representative arts there is a sort of ontological duplication—a plurality of such subjects of inherence. . . . It is this duality in the ontological subjects of inherence—the work on the one hand, and the represented objects on the other—which characterizes the representative arts. In the presentative arts, the work and the object are one. The representative work calls up, so to speak, beside itself and outside itself (at least outside its materiality and beyond its phenomena, even though proceeding from it and supported by it) a world of beings and things which cannot be confused with it. (p. 89)

The result is the grand division of the arts into "two distinct groups," "the group of arts where the universe of the work posits beings ontologically distinct from the work itself, and that of the arts where the thingly interpretation of the givens interprets the work without positing anything outside it" (p. 90).

When Souriau turns to the literary field, however, he is obliged to include a certain asymmetry in his table of the "correspondence of the arts": there is no such thing as purely "presentative" literature, at least not in the first degree. The most primal, elementary form of literature would be "the arabesque of consonants and vowels, their 'melody', . . . their rhythm, and, in broader terms, the general pattern of the sentence, of the period, of the succession of periods, etc." (p. 154). This "primary division (which in principle would consist in the art of assembling syllables in what could be called a musical manner, with no intention of signification, and thus of representative evocation) is practically unoccupied—except by 'pure prosody,' which does not exist as an autonomous art: it is only implied in poetry as the primary form of an art which really exists only to the second degree" (p. 132). This type of pertinence of the signifier does enable us to distinguish between poetry and prose (it is thus that Souriau, p. 158, answers the question I am raising here), but it seems to play only a rather marginal role in the entire field of literature: the *Lautdichtung* of the Dadaists, the neologisms of the futurists, *lettriste* or concrete poetry. This marginality, according to Souriau, is due to the musical poverty of the sounds of language in comparison with music as such; and, one might add, to the visual poverty of letters in comparison with the means available to painting.

All this appears quite true, and yet one begins to regret that the dichotomy presentation/representation as applied to literature should yield such meager results. One begins to wonder whether this interpretation of the dichotomy really fits the literary field, or whether it doesn't rather apply only to the material used by literature, namely language. Souriau himself writes: "Literature . . . borrows the entire set of its signs from a system which is already constituted outside it: language" (p. 154). The "primary form" of literature is not sounds but words and sentences, and these already have a signifier *and* is signified. "Presentative" literature would then be not only literature in which the signifier ceases to be transparent and transitive, but also, and more importantly both quantitatively and qualitatively, literature in which it is the signified which does so. What must be put into question is thus the automatic link I quoted a moment ago ("with no intention of signification, *and thus* of representative evocation"), in order to examine whether there might not be a form of writing in which signification would indeed be present, but not representation. It is indeed precisely this type of presentative literature which is illustrated by Rimbaud's *Illuminations,* and it seems to be their presentative character which constitutes their poetry.

The means utilized by Rimbaud to destroy the representative illusion are legion. They range from explicit metalinguistic commentary, as in the famous phrase from "Barbare"—"le pavillon en viande saignante sur la soie des mers et des fleurs arctiques; (elles n'existent pas)" ("the flag of bloody meat on the silk of the seas and the arctic flowers; [they do not exist]")—to sentences which are clearly ungrammatical, whose meaning we can never know, like the last sentence of "Métropolitain": "Le matin où avec Elle, vous vous débattîtes parmi les éclats de neige, les lèvres vertes, les glaces, les drapeaux noirs et les rayons bleus, et les parfums pourpres du soleil des pôles—ta force" ("the morning when with Her you struggled among the bursts of snow, the green lips, the ice [or the mirrors], the black flags and the blue rays, and the crimson perfumes of the polar sun—your strength"). Between the two, a series of devices renders representation at first uncertain, and then impossible.

The indeterminate sentences which fill most of the *Illuminations* thus do not completely rule out representation, but they make it extremely imprecise. When Rimbaud says, at the end of "Après le deluge," that "la Reine, la Sorcière qui allume sa braise dans le pot de terre, ne voudra jamais nous raconter ce qu'elle sait, et que nous ignorons" ("the Queen, the Witch who lights her fire in the earthen pot, will never be willing to tell us what she knows, and what we don't know"), we can visualize a concrete act being performed by a feminine figure, but we know nothing about the figure herself or her relation to what precedes (the floods), and, of course, we don't know "what we don't know." In the same way, we will never know anything about the "deux enfants fidèles" ("two faithful children"), the "maison musicale" ("musical house"), or the "vieillard seul calme et beau" ("Calm, handsome old man alone") in "Phrases," nor about any of the other characters in the *Illuminations*. These beings appear and disappear like heavenly bodies in the dark of night, lasting only the length of an illumination.

Discontinuity has a similar effect: each word taken separately may evoke a representation, but together they do not form a whole, and we are thus forced to remain on the level of words. "Pour l'enfance d'Hélène frissonnèrent les fourrures et les ombres—et le sein des pauvres, et les légendes du ciel" ("For Helen's childhood the furs and the shadows shivered—and the breast of the poor, and the legends of the heavens") ("Fairy"): in this sentence the very multiplicity of the subjects becomes problematic, each one rendering the preceding ones more unreal. The same is true of the prepositional phrases in the sentence from "Métropolitain" quoted above, or of another sentence from the same text where there are "des routes bordées de grilles et de murs," "les atroces fleurs," "des auberges qui pour toujours n'ouvrent déjà plus—il y a des princesses, et si tu n'es pas trop accablé, l'étude des astres—le ciel" ("roads lined with gates and walls," "atrocious flowers," "inns which forever already no longer open—there are princesses, and if you are not too overburdened, the study of the stars—the sky"). This is perhaps why one is always tempted to permute the words in Rimbaud's texts, in an attempt to discover their coherence.

Other techniques serve to make representation not merely uncertain, but truly impossible. Thus we find numerous oxymorons and contradictions, or a shift in the source of utterance, where "je" and "tu," "nous" and "vous" rarely remain constant from beginning to end (see "Après le déluge," "Parade," "Vies I" "Matinée d'ivresse," "Métropolitain," "Aube"); we cannot know, for example, whether the "Être de beauté" ("beauteous being") is internal or external to the subject who says at the end, "*nos* os sont revêtus d'un nouveau corps amoureux" ("our bones are clothed in a new loving body") ("Being beauteous"). The same is true of Rimbaud's propensity, noted above, for describing properties or parts of objects without ever naming the objects themselves, to the point that one really does not know what he is talking about. This is the case not only of texts like "H," which presents itself as a veritable riddle, but of many others as well, as the hesitations of the critics testify. It is this attention to properties at the expense of the objects they characterize which gives us the impression that Rimbaud always prefers to use the generic rather than the specific, proper term, and bathes his texts in an atmosphere of abstraction. What exactly is the "luxe nocturne" in "Vagabonds," or the "luxe inouï" in "Phrases"? Or the "générosité vulgaire" and the "révolutions de l'amour" in "Conte"? Or the "herbe d'été" and the "vice sérieux" in "Dévotion"? "Mes embarras" and "ce vil désespoir" in "Phrases"? The "éclats précieux" and the "influence froide" in "Fairy"? The "horreurs économiques" and the "magie bourgeoise" in "Soir historique"? Rimbaud is also fond of using universal quantifiers, in the manner of a legislator: "des êtres de tous les caractères parmi toutes les apparences" ("beings of all characters among all appearances") ("Veillées II'); "tous les caractères nuancèrent ma physionomie" ("Guerre"), etc.

This analysis of the failure of representation in the *Illuminations* can be countered by two objections. First of all, it is by no means true that all the texts in the *Illuminations*, or all the sentences in every text, display this same tendency: while there are numerous examples of the failure of representation, there are numerous examples of its success as well. Furthermore, the same verbal characteristics which contribute to this failure can be found outside of literature, and thus, all the more frequently, outside of poetry, notably in texts which are general and abstract.

The answer to both these objections is, fortunately, the same. The opposition between presentation and representation in language is not an opposition between two classes of utterances, but between two categories. Language can be transparent or opaque, transitive or intransitive; but these are nothing but polar extremes, between which most concrete utterances are located somewhere in the middle, only approximating one extreme more closely than the other. At the same time, no category exists in isolation, and it is precisely by combining with other categories that the rejection of representation functions as a source of poetry in the *Illuminations*, whereas, for example, the philosophical text, which is equally non-representative, maintains its coherence on the level of meaning alone. If it is indeed their "presentative" character which makes these texts poetic, one could schematize the typological system internalized by Rimbaud's readers, even if Rimbaud himself was not aware of it, in the following manner:

	verse	*prose*
presentation	poetry	prose poem
representation	epic, versified narrative or description	fiction (novel, short story, folk tale)

Which brings us back to our starting point. Atemporality, which for Suzanne Bernard constituted the essence of poeticity, is only a secondary consequence of the refusal of representation in Rimbaud, and of the order of correspondences in Baudelaire. It is therefore a violent distortion of the facts to reduce these two procedures to atemporality alone. But if even the works of two poets barely separated by a difference of ten years, written in the same language and in the same intellectual climate of presymbolism, can be called "poetic" (whether by the poets themselves or be their contemporaries) for such different, entirely independent reasons, and we not forced to admit that Poetry with a capital *P* does not in fact exist, but that varying conceptions of poetry have existed and will continue to exist, not only from one period or country to another, but even from one *text* to another? The polarity presentation/representation may be universal and "natural" (it is inherent in language), but the identification of poetry with the "presentative" use of language is a historically circumscribed and culturally determined fact: in effect, it leaves Baudelaire outside of "poetry."

The question remains—but it can be seen what preliminary work the answer would imply—whether there is nevertheless some affinity among all the different reasons which have prompted mankind to confer the name "poetic" upon a text. The limited objective of the preceding pages has been to show that that affinity does not reside where we thought it did, and to formulate in a more precise way some of the presuppositions and perspectives at work in the decision to call a text "poetic."

TRANSLATED BY BARBARA JOHNSON

Notes

1. Suzanne Bernard, *Le Poème en prose de Baudelaire jusqu'à nos jours* (Paris: Nizet, 1959).
2. All quotes from Baudelaire are taken from *Oeuvres complètes* (Paris: Bibliothèque de la Pléiade, 1976).
3. Arthur Rimbaud, *Illuminations*, in *Oeuvres* (Paris: Garnier, 1960).
4. Étienne Souriau, *Correspondance des arts* (Paris: Flammarion, 1947; rev. ed., 1969).

5. Disfiguring Poetic Language

BARBARA JOHNSON

*B*audelaire's prose poems can often be read as ironic reflections
on the nature of poetic language as such.[1] Yet their way of repeating and transforming traditional *topoi* is sometimes unaccount-
ably violent. Why are Baudelaire's rewritings of poetic figures so
frequently poems of dis-figurement? Is this a mere symptom of
Baudelaire's disturbed psyche, or is there perhaps some fundamental link between *figure* and *violence*?

While the cutting force of rhetoric as persuasion has long been
recognized, the conception of rhetoric as a system of tropes has
always appeared much more static and benign. What I intend to
analyze here is the way in which two of Baudelaire's prose poems
not only *displace* certain traditional poetic figures but also *dramatize*,
in their very plot and framework, the structure and functioning of
figure as such.

Let Them Eat Cake

The first of the two poems, "Le Gâteau," begins with a self-
consciously stereotypical lyric description of alpine felicity, which
is soon subverted by the intrusion of the "real" world of human
ferocity. The poem is worth quoting in its entirety.

This essay is derived from chapters 3 and 4 of *Défigurations du langage poétique* (Paris:
Flammarion, 1979). Copyright © 1979, Flammarion. Reprinted by permission.

Le Gateau

Je voyageais. Le paysage au milieu duquel j'étais placé était d'une grandeur et d'une noblesse irrésistibles. Il en passa sans doute en ce moment quelque chose dans mon âme. Mes pensées voltigeaient avec une légèreté égale à celle de l'atmosphère; les passions vulgaires, telles que la haine et l'amour profane, m'apparaissaient maintenant aussi éloignées que les nuées qui défilaient au fond des abîmes sous mes pieds; mon âme me semblait aussi vaste et aussi pure que la coupole du ciel dont j'étais enveloppé; le souvenir des choses terrestres n'arrivait à mon cœur qu'affaibli et diminué, comme le son de la clochette des bestiaux imperceptibles qui paissaient loin, bien loin, sur le versant d'une autre montagne. Sur le petit lac immobile, noir de son immense profondeur, passait quelquefois l'ombre d'un nuage, comme le reflet du manteau d'un géant aérien volant à travers le ciel. Et je me souviens que cette sensation solennelle et rare, causée par un grand mouvement parfaitement silencieux, me remplissait d'une joie mêlée de peur. Bref, je me sentais, grâce à l'enthousiasmante beauté dont j'étais environné, en parfaite paix avec moi-même et avec l'univers; je crois même que, dans ma parfaite béatitude et dans mon total oubli de tout le mal terrestre, j'en étais venu à ne plus trouver si ridicules les journaux qui prétendent que l'homme est né bon;—quand, la matière incurable renouvelant ses exigences, je songeai à réparer la fatigue et à soulager l'appétit causés par une si longue ascension. Je tirai de ma poche un gros morceau de pain, une tasse de cuir et un flacon d'un certain élixir que les pharmaciens vendaient dans ce temps-là aux touristes pour le mêler à l'occasion avec de l'eau de neige.

Je découpais tranquillement mon pain, quand un bruit très léger me fit lever les yeux. Devant moi se tenait un petit être déguenillé, noir, ébouriffé, dont les yeux creux, farouches et comme suppliants, dévoraient le morceau de pain. Et je l'entendis soupirer, d'une voix basse et rauque, le mot: *gâteau!* Je ne pus m'empêcher de rire en entendant l'appellation dont il voulait bien honorer mon pain presque blanc, et j'en coupai pour lui une belle tranche que je lui offris. Lentement il se rapprocha, ne quittant pas des yeux l'objet de sa convoitise; puis, happant le morceau avec sa main, se recula vivement, comme s'il eût craint que mon offre ne fût pas sincère ou que je m'en repentisse déjà.

Mais au même instant il fut culbuté par un autre petit sauvage, sorti je ne sais d'où, et si parfaitement semblable au premier qu'on aurait pu le prendre pour son frère jumeau. Ensemble ils roulèrent sur le sol, se disputant la précieuse proie, aucun n'en voulant sans doute sacrifier la moitié pour son frère. Le premier, exaspéré, empoigna le second par les cheveux; celui-ci lui saisit l'oreille avec les dents, et en cracha un petit morceau sanglant avec un superbe juron patois. Le légitime propriétaire du gâteau essaya d'enfoncer ses petites griffes dans les yeux de l'usurpateur; à son tour celui-ci appliqua toutes ses forces à étrangler son adversaire d'une main, pendant que de l'autre, il tâchait de glisser dans sa poche le prix du combat. Mais, ravivé par le désespoir, le vaincu se redressa et fit rouler le vainqueur par terre d'un coup de tête dans l'estomac. A quoi bon décrire une lutte hideuse qui dura en vérité plus longtemps que leurs forces enfantines ne semblaient le promettre? Le gâteau voyageait de main en main et changeait de poche à chaque instant; mais, hélas! il changeait aussi de volume, et lorsque enfin, exténués, haletants, sanglants, ils s'arrêtèrent par impossibilité de continuer, il n'y avait plus, à vrai dire, aucun sujet de bataille; le morceau de pain avait disparu, et ilétait éparpillé en miettes semblables aux grains de sable auxquels il était mêlé.

Ce spectacle m'avait embrumé le paysage, et la joie calme où s'ébaudissait mon âme avant d'avoir vu ces petits hommes avait totalement disparu; j'en restai triste assez longtemps, me répétant sans cesse: "Il y a donc un pays superbe où le pain s'appelle du *gâteau*, friandise si rare qu'elle suffit pour engendrer une guerre parfaitement fratricide!"[2]

The Cake

I was traveling. The landscape in which I stood possessed an irresistible grandeur and nobility, some of which no doubt at that moment passed into my soul. My thoughts flitted about with a lightness equal to that of the atmosphere; vulgar passions like hate and profane love seemed to me now as far away as the clouds that filed across the abysses beneath my feet; my soul seemed to me as vast and pure as the cupola of the sky that enveloped me; the memory of terrestrial matters reached my heart greatly diminished and muffled, like the sound of the bells of the imperceptible flocks grazing far, far away, on the slope of another mountain. On the small still lake, black with its immense depth, there passed now and then the shadow of a cloud, like the reflection of the cloak of an aerial giant flying through the sky. And I remember that the solemn, rare sensation caused by this vast, perfectly silent motion filled me with a joy mixed with fear. In short, thus enthused by the beauty that surrounded me, I felt at perfect peace with myself and the universe; I even think that, in my perfect beatitude and total obliviousness to all earthly evil, I had come to the point where I no longer found so ridiculous those tracts that claim that man is born good—when, incurable matter renewing its demands, I gave thought to repairing the fatigue and appeasing the appetite caused by such a long ascent. I drew out of my pocket a thick slice of bread, a leather cup, and a flask of a certain elixir that pharmacists used to sell to tourists, to be mixed with water from melted snow whenever the need arose.

I was calmly cutting up my bread when a very faint sound made me raise my eyes. Before me stood a small, dark, tattered, disheveled creature whose hollow, wild, and seemingly beseeching eyes were devouring the piece of bread. And I heard him sigh, in a hoarse low voice, the word: *cake*. I couldn't help laughing when I heard the appellation with which he deigned to honor my nearly white bread, and I sliced off a nice piece and offered it to him. Slowly he approached, never taking his eyes off the object he coveted; then, snatching the slice with his hand, he leaped back as though he feared that my offer had not been sincere or that I already regretted it.

But at that very instant he was jumped by another little savage, who had appeared out of nowhere, and who was so exactly like the first that one could have taken them for twins. Together they rolled on the ground, fighting over their precious prey, neither one willing to sacrifice half for his brother. The first, exasperated, grabbed the second by the hair; the latter sank his teeth into the former's ear, and spit out a bloody piece of it with a superb provincial expletive. The legitimate proprietor of the cake tried to dig his little claws into the eyes of the usurper; the latter in turn used all his strength to strangle his opponent with one hand while he tried to slip the prize of the fight into his pocket with the other. But, revived by despair, the loser got up and knocked the winner to the ground by smashing him in the stomach with his head. What good would it do to describe a hideous struggle that lasted in truth much longer than one would have expected from their childish powers? The cake traveled from hand to hand and changed pockets once a minute; but, alas! it also changed size; and when at last, exhausted, panting, and bleeding, they stopped out of an inability to continue, there no longer existed, to tell the truth, any object of battle; the piece of bread had disappeared, and the crumbs strewn about resembled the grains of sand with which they were mixed.

This spectacle had clouded the landscape for me, and the calm joy in which my soul had delighted before I saw these little men had totally disappeared. I remained saddened for quite a while, repeating over and over: "There is thus a superb country where bread is called *cake*, a delicacy so rare that it suffices to start a perfectly fratricidal war!")

In the first part of the poem, a state of sublime exaltation is expressed in terms of the perfect correspondence or equivalence between the narrator's inner nature ("my soul") and the surrounding outer nature ("the landscape"). His thoughts and the atmosphere have an "equal" lightness; his soul is as vast and pure as the sky. The first metaphor, then, is an equation between the soul and the scene:

$$\text{soul} = \text{landscape}$$

This equivalence between soul and landscape has as its desired meaning the hyperbolic state of sublime peace felt by the narrator:

$$(\text{soul} = \text{landscape}) = \text{perfect peace}$$

In the second part of the poem, an equation is set up between the two little savages who are "exactly alike":

$$\text{savage}_1 = \text{savage}_2$$

But in this case, instead of a sublime peace, the metaphor engenders a fratricidal war between the two terms, the "legitimate proprietor" or *proper* meaning and the "usurper" or *figurative* meaning. Here, it is the *cake*, a hyperbole for "bread," that functions as the metaphor's meaning—the "object of battle," the "prize of the fight":

$$(\text{savage}_1 = \text{savage}_2) = \text{perfectly fratricidal war}$$

The equations established in the two parts of the poem appear in themselves to be flawless, yet the state of perfect equivalence contains in both cases the very principle of its own destruction. In the case of lyric beatitude, the sublime equivalence between soul and scenery through which terrestrial considerations are forgotten is attained by an act of ascension which brings about the fatigue and appetite that will dissipate the ecstasy. The act of eating is then the literalisation of the ingestion of the sublime ("The landscape . . . possessed an irresistible grandeur and nobility, some of which . . . passed into my soul"), indicating that the state of sublime beatitude rests on the possibility of living on air, of becoming *truly* equal to the inanimate:

$$(\text{soul} = \text{landscape}) = \text{perfect peace} \rightarrow \text{sublimation of the subject}$$

In the second part, the two equivalent terms, distinguished only by the moment of their appearance, can go on fighting over their hyperbolic object only until it becomes equal to the grains of sand among which it is scattered:

$$(savage_1 = savage_2) = \text{perfect war} \rightarrow \text{disappearance of the object}$$

It can easily be seen that the "I" in the first part of the poem plays exactly the same role as the "cake" in the second part—the role of the meaning or value-object around which the metaphor is built. The similarity is reinforced by the repetition of the verb "to travel": the poem begins, "I was traveling," and later, "the cake traveled from hand to hand." Through this isomorphic relation between the "I" and the "cake," between the structure of jubilant resemblance (soul = landscape) and the structure of fratricidal resemblance (proprietor = usurper), the two antithetical parts of the poem have thus become metaphors of each other:

$$\{(\text{soul} = \text{landscape}) = \text{peace} \rightarrow \text{sublimation}\} = \{(savage_1 = savage_2) = \text{war} \rightarrow \text{disappearance}\}$$

Lyric beatitude, in other words, is the very image of realist ferocity. Both are engendered by the same metaphorical structure, which thus posesses the capacity both to exalt and to annihilate. Fraternal peace is structured like fratricidal war, and the sublime subjective internalization of inanimate nature becomes the mirror image of the erasing of all differences between bread and sand.

This is not to say that death is the final meaning of all metaphorical structures. For it is precisely out of the *flaw* or *excess* in an equation that meaning springs. Without hyperbole, the metaphorical energy in the poem would collapse. The meaning of the equivalence between the two savages depends on the maintaining of their *inequality* (the difference between the one that has the cake and the one that doesn't). The moment the cake disappears, the metaphor has no meaning. And yet it is precisely through the way in which the cake vanishes as the meaning of the struggle that the struggle emerges as the mirror image of the lyrical peace that prevailed in the beginning of the poem.

The equivalence between the "I" and the "cake," between fraternal exhilaration and fratricidal obliteration, between the sublime and the inanimate, between the first and the second parts of the poem, thus constitutes a deconstruction of the lyric illusions evoked in the first part. But since this deconstruction takes place precisely through the creation of *equivalences*, it can only demystify metaphor by participating in it. What Baudelaire's prose poem thus engenders as a problem for the understanding of metaphor is precisely the impossibility of finding a critical metalanguage that would not be enmeshed in the very metaphorical structures it attempts to comprehend. And if meaningful metaphor requires that its equations be flawed, then the metaphorical act of understanding metaphor can never even truly be in possession of the meaningfulness of its own hyperbolic aberrations.

A second poem, "Le Galant Tireur," goes even further in its unmasking of the mechanisms of figurative language. By italicizing the sentence *"je me figure que c'est vous,"* this poem explicitly underlines its status as a metafigural allegory.

Le Galant Tireur
Comme la voiture traversait le bois, il la fit arrêter dans le voisinage d'un tir, disant qu'il lui serait agréable de tirer quelques balles pour *tuer* le Temps. Tuer ce monstre-là, n'est-ce pas l'occupation la plus ordinaire et la plus légitime de chacun?—Et il offrit galamment la main à sa chère, délicieuse et exécrable femme, à cette mystérieuse femme à laquelle il doit tant de plaisirs, tant de douleurs, et peut-être aussi une grande partie de son génie.

Plusieurs balles frappèrent loin du but proposé; l'une d'elles s'enfonça même dans le plafond; et comme la charmante créature riait follement, se moquant de la maladresse de son époux, celui-ci se tourna brusquement vers elle, et lui dit: "Observez cette poupée, là-bas, à droite, qui porte le nez en l'air et qui a la mine si hautaine. Eh bien! cher ange, *je me figure que c'est vous.*" Et il ferma les yeux et il lâcha la détente. La poupée fut nettement décapitée.

Alors s'inclinant vers sa chère, sa délicieuse, son exécrable femme, son inévitable et impitoyable Muse, et lui baisant respectueusement la main, il ajouta: "Ah ! mon cher ange, combien je vous remercie de mon adresse!"[3]

The Gallant Marksman
As the carriage was driving through the woods, he stopped it in the neighborhood of a shooting gallery, saying that he would enjoy firing off

a couple of rounds in order to *kill* Time. Isn't the killing of that monster indeed the most ordinary and legitimate occupation of every man? And he gallantly offered his arm to his dear, delightful, execrable wife, to that mysterious woman to whom he owes so many pleasures, so many pains, and perhaps also a large part of his genius.

Several bullets landed far from the proposed target; one of them even lodged in the ceiling; and as the charming creature was laughing wildly, mocking her husband's bad aim [*maladresse*], the latter turned abruptly toward her and said, "Take a good look at that doll down there on the right with her nose in the air, looking so stuck up. Well, angel face, *I figure that that's you.*" And he closed his eyes and pulled the trigger. The doll was neatly decapitated.

Then, bowing toward his dear, delightful, execrable wife, his inevitable and pitiless Muse, he respectfully kissed her hand and added, "Ah! dear angel, how can I thank you for my aim [*adresse*]!")

Killing Time

As of the very first sentence, the question of figure—or the figure of the question—is raised *typographically*. In writing "to *kill* Time" instead of "to kill time," Baudelaire restores to a dead figure the original impact that has been lost through linguistic habit. The italics give back to the verb *to kill* all its literality, especially in this shooting-gallery context. Thus, paradoxically, it is through the verb *to kill* that the "dead" figure is ressuscitated. But the figurality of the figure is also restored by the capital *T* of "Time," which increases the word's personification. On the one hand, then, there is an increase in literality; on the other, an increase in figurality. Some would call this a widening of the gap between figure and letter. But *where*, in fact, is the figure in this phrase? Is the figural space located between the literal and the figurative, or between a dead figure and a ressuscitated one?

In the first case, the figure's effectiveness would result from what Jean Cohen has called "predicative impertinence":[4] the verb *to kill*, which can only apply to an animate being, is here associated with an abstraction, Time, whose meaning is, by association, modified. This, however, brings us to a paradox: the figure endows Time with life only in order to take it away again; Time is personified only to be killed. This paradox is even more subtle than it appears. For in making Time alternate between life and death, the figure "forgets" that there is no other name for such an alternation than, precisely, Time. The text's figural logic can thus be read as follows:

the figurative meaning of *Time*	1.	The figure tries to kill time.
	2.	In order to kill time, the figure grants it life by personifying it; but time is given life only so as to be killed.
the inscription of the figure	3.	The figure thus turns on an alternation between life and death.
the literal meaning of *Time*	4.	The name of such an alternation between life and death is *time*.
the figural paradox	5.	Therefore, if the figure succeeded in eliminating time, it would eliminate the very alternation that alone makes it capable of eliminating time: the figure would eliminate the law that makes it function.
the figure's self-erasure	6.	The figure must therefore "forget" the literal meaning of the word *time* in its attempt to kill time figuratively. And by the same token, it is the very *gap* between the literal and the figurative that is thus eliminated through this foreclosure of the literal meaning. In order to function, the figure *erases* the literal meaning with respect to which it is supposed to constitute itself as a *deviation*.

The gap between the literal and the figurative meanings of the word *time* is then but a mask for the figural work of forgetting, of erasing the gap, an operation that is carried out through the foreclosure of the existence of the literal meaning. Figural space is not located *between* one meaning and another but *within* the very possibility of meaning.

Let us now turn to the second reading, according to which the figure is located not between the literal and the figurative but between a dead figure and a ressuscitated figure, between "to kill time" and "to *kill* Time." If the figure of "killing time" is indeed dead, what can have killed it? The answer, of course, is *time*. The ressuscitated figure, in which the effects of time *on* the figure are erased, thus effectively *kills* the time through which the figure had lost its freshness and "died": this figural resurrection is the very acting out of the sense of the resurrected figure, "to kill time." But the canceling out of the action of time *upon* the figure can only be achieved through the increased personification of the word *Time* *within* the figure. In other words, the time that acts *on* the figure can only be killed if the time to be killed *in* the figure is still alive.

But is this ressuscitated figure the *same* as the one that died? Isn't it rather a *parody* of it? A parody created not only by the hyperbolic setting in which a man literally shoots in order to kill time, but also by the fact that the figure can only ressuscitate itself by *playing with* its own death?

Whether one locates the figural operation in the relation between the literal and the figurative senses of the word *time* or between the dead figure and its reanimation, the figural *functioning* revealed is essentially the same. In the first case, we have shown that the gap between the literal and the figurative could be founded only upon its own erasure. In the second case, we have seen that the ressuscitated figure could live only upon its own corpse. In both cases, fundamental presuppositions are dismantled in the process of arriving at the same paradoxical conclusion: the figure lives only through its own death. In each case the figure's effectiveness depends on the forgetting, erasing, or killing of its component parts. The figure carries its own death within it, not because it contains the seeds of its destruction, but because it is through the destruction of what founds it that it constitutes itself.

Decapitation

While Baudelaire's marksman begins by aiming his gun at Time, it is nevertheless not Time that he ends up shooting, but a doll. A doll whose figurative status is *literally* underlined by the text. "Take a good look at that doll down there on the right with her nose in the air, looking so stuck up. Well, angel face, *I figure that that's you.*" The doll *becomes* the woman by means of a trope, a substitutive *turn* which is also dramatized in the text ("the latter *turned* abruptly toward her"). The text would thus seem to illustrate the traditional conception of metaphor as the substitution of one term for another by means of *resemblance* (we assume that the doll with her nose in the air is being seen by the marksman as similar to his wife).

But this resemblance between the doll and the woman, however vivid, is in fact but a visual screen over the more fundamental *change of places* that constitutes the figure. The doll becomes the woman not because she looks like the latter but because she *takes her place*—the place of her *decapitation*. The meaning of the figure, its signified, is not "woman" but "woman's decapitation." Yet this is precisely the signified the figure will never reach, since in order to *be* a figure it can decapitate but an effigy.[5] While the figure is *aimed* at the woman, it can only *mean* by missing its target. It is thus the figure itself that is decapitated, can never come to a head; it can only continue to aim toward a beheading that will never take place, since the beheading it points to is its own.

Let us now examine the relation between the two figures we have just analyzed: the figure "to *kill* Time" and the figure of the doll/woman's decapitation. There are, clearly, certain analogies between them. Like Time in the first figure, the doll, an inanimate object, takes on the status of an animate being in the act of standing for the woman. But the doll, like Time, is only given life in order to be shot, decapitated. In both cases, the figure goes from the axis animate/inanimate to the axis living/dead. And in both cases, the figure functions only through its own contradiction: Time, in order to be killed, must remain alive; the absence of the woman from the locus of her decapitation cuts the figure off from the meaning it is heading toward.

The two figures, then, like the two parts of the poem "The Cake," turn out to be metaphors of each other. But they are linked by something more than analogy: they are also spatially *contiguous* to each other, since they intersect on the spot where the bullet hits the doll. This spatial relation makes them stand as metonymies, not just as metaphors, of each other. For while the marksman is aiming first at Time and then at his wife, he nevertheless points his gun only at a doll: "to shoot the doll" thus metonymically means both "to kill time" and "to blow the woman's head off."

This apparent symmetry is nevertheless grounded in a fundamental asymmetry: although the doll does stand as the place where the two figures substitute for each other, the second figure arises only because the goal of the first has been missed. "Several bullets landed far from the proposed target; one of them even lodged in the ceiling." In trying to kill time, the marksman was clearly aiming too high. But it is precisely because his wife makes fun of his *bad* aim that she becomes the aim, the goal of the second figure. That is, the woman becomes the target of the second figure only because she stands as the *figure of the failure of the first figure.* The success of the figure of decapitation is inscribed upon the failure of the figure of killing time.

But if the doll signifies at once "Time" and "woman," isn't her decapitation a sign that the first figure, too, reaches its goal? The answer to this question remains suspended, since the correction of the marksman's aim requires the assistance of the figure of his impotence. The success of the figure "to kill Time" can only be achieved by means of the figure of its own failure.

In a sense, it could perhaps be said that *all* figures are figures of the failure of the figure "to kill Time." For what is time but a figure for our own death, that unfigurable source of all figure? As Michel Deguy has put it, "Death, whose reality is entirely metaphorical, sets life at a distance from itself; death is the very epitome of metaphor."[6]

Contradiction in Abeyance

Can it be said, then, that it is the essence of figure to be founded on its own contradiction? In his "Théorie de la figure," Jean Cohen indeed states that since "the principle of contradiction" is "the fundamental principle of logic and the norm that governs both language and metalanguage . . . the semantic rhetorical figures constitute so many violations of that fundamental principle."[7] Cohen's theory, however, goes on to assert that a figure, while it does violate the norm of noncontradiction, can only become *readable* through a process of decoding whose object is to *correct* that violation:

Every figure entails a two-step process of decoding: the first is the perception of the anomaly, and the second is its *correction*, through an exploration of the paradigmatic field in which relations of resemblance, contiguity, etc., are created, in which one can find a signified capable of providing the expression with an *acceptable* semantic interpretation. . . . The figure is thus . . . articulated according to two perpendicular axes, the syntagmatic axis where the gap or deviation is established, and the paradigmatic axis where it is eliminated through a change in meaning.[8]

The figure Cohen chooses to illustrate this process of decoding is precisely a variant of our figure of "killing Time." It is a verse from *Athalie*: "pour réparer des ans l'irréparable outrage" ("to repair the irreparable insult of the years"). Cohen describes the "two-step mechanism" of his decoding as follows: (1) contradiction between "repair" and "irreparable"; (2) substitution of "seemingly repair" for "repair," which removes the contradiction.[9] It could be objected that the substitution of "seemingly repair" for "repair" is not the only *logical* possibility. Why not "seemingly irreparable" instead of "irreparable"? But that is beside the point. For can it not be said that in this play of substitutions it is contradiction itself that has been "seemingly repaired"? How can one maintain that the correct, or rather corrected, reading of this figure is: "to seemingly repair the irreparable insult of the years"? And if the criterion for this substitution is its greater "acceptability," why should "seemingly repair" be more "acceptable" than "repair," when the figure is telling us that it is precisely the *irreparable* that is unacceptable? What is judged "false" by the laws of logic may indeed lie at the very heart of the laws of desire, according to which it is perhaps precisely the law of noncontradiction *itself* that is unacceptable.

If the figure *does* violate the logic of contradiction, it is not in order to call for a "corrective" reading that would bring it back to that logic, but rather to lead us into the domain of a *different* logic. The logic of figure is such that it makes the logic of contradiction *dysfunction*. It suspends the system of binary oppositions on which contradiction is based (presence vs. absence, animate vs. inanimate, life vs. death, reparable vs. irreparable), but without reducing these oppositions to the same. The gap described by such polarities remains as irreducible as it is undecidable, for while each pole can cross over to the other, it is not thereby totally erased. Time remains at once animate and inanimate, reparable and irreparable; the head remains at once severed and attached; the woman is both here and there, present and absent. The figure cannot be fixed on any one of its movements.

Just as the child in Freud's *Beyond the Pleasure Principle* enters into what Lacan calls the "symbolic order" by playing a game that consists of tossing a spool away and pulling it back again while pronouncing the syllables "fort—da" ("away—here"), so, too, the figure, through the detour of its doll, can only "play at jumping" over the contradiction by which it is constituted. As Lacan puts it:

For the game of the cotton reel is the subject's answer to what the mother's absence has created on the frontier of his domain—the edge of his cradle— namely, a *ditch*, around which one can only play at jumping.

This reel is not the mother reduced to a little ball by some magical game worthy of the Jivaros—it is a small part of the subject that detaches itself from him while still remaining his, still retained. This is the place to say, in imitation of Aristotle, that man thinks with his object. It is with his object that the child leaps the frontiers of his domain.[10]

It is by leaping back and forth over contradiction, and not by substituting one thing for another, that the figure deploys the nets of the subject's desire.

But, to return to the figure "to *kill* Time," *where*, exactly, are the "frontiers of its domain"? Doesn't the binary dysfunction that constitutes the figure amount to a shattering of the very boundaries of the figure, a disturbance of the opposition between *inside* and *outside* that would alone enable us to *isolate* the figural phenomenon? Is the word *time*, whose literal meaning is equivalent to the law that makes the figure function, inside or outside the figure it governs? Is the typographical resurrection of the figure ("to *Kill* Time") being carried out *on* the figure or *in* the figure? What logic is the figure obeying if it thus constitutes itself through the principle of the uncertainty of its very frontiers?

The problem is clearly one of isolating the set of elements constitutive of the figure, which, forming a closed system, might be analyzed with nothing left over. Yet modern set theory would suggest that in this case no such set can exist. Just as "the set of all possible sets in a universe is not a set," the set of all signifiers in a signifying system can never be closed.

> One cannot put all the signifiers belonging to the same "family" in the same bag, and, . . . when one tries to group them together, there is a split, an exclusion, through which *one* of the signifiers, which has become other, is carried outside, in such a way that the others can function as such. . . .
>
> The effect of what is thus excluded and detached is to "hold together" the set it is excluded from . . . and, in so doing, to give it a name; or at least to occupy the place from which the law of the name can function.[11]

In the set of elements that constitute the figure "to *kill* Time," it is, as we have seen, the word *time* itself that finds itself excluded, crossed out, "forgotten," in order for the figure to function. The word *time* is thus at once inside and outside: inside, it stands as the figure's target; outside, it is the name of the alternation (life/death) that makes the figure function as such. In the second figure in the text, it is the woman who is both inside and out: inside as the target of decapitation, and outside as the Muse that guides the shot aright. In both cases, one of the elements in the figural set is at once outside, governing the figural operation, and inside, serving as the target of that operation. And hence, it is the very difference between inside and outside that the figural violence undoes.

To split so that what holds it together can leap out, such is the very law of figure. But if the frontiers of each particular figure are thus blown up by the very law that installs them, what about the entire set of figures as such? Can "figurative language" ever constitute a closed object of analysis? If, as Fontanier would have it, the term *figure* first signified "the contours, traits, or external form of a man, animal, or palpable object";[12] if it is *figuratively* that the term comes to designate a rhetorical space—"a surface," as Genette defines it, "marked out by two lines: that of the present signifier and that of the absent signifier";[13] if the term *figure* is thus itself a figure, is it inside or outside the phenomenon it names? And if the set of all figures can be literally named only by a figure, where is the boundary line between figurative language and its other? This detachment of the figure "figure" from what is sup-

posed to be the set of all figures, a detachment which allows it to
fill the role of the name of the set so that the other elements can
function as such, is precisely what prevents that set from consti-
tuting itself as a finite, definite, circumscribed object. By moving
to the outside of the set, the word *figure* destroys the frontiers of
the figural domain. Hence, if the law of figure dictates that the
polarities constitutive of contradiction dysfunction, we can now
see that such a law would end up dismantling and erasing *itself*,
since it would in fact suspend the very difference between literal
and figurative on which it is based.

The Other's Address

Figure, therefore, has always already begun: whenever we
seek to isolate it, it has already invaded the ground we stand on.
But if figure has always already begun, how can one be the originator of one's own figures, the master of one's own rhetoric, the
possessor of one's own figurative *adresse*? This is the question dramatized in the text's final paragraph.

In suspending itself between the failure of one figure and the
success of the figure of that failure, The Gallant Marksman ultimately opens up *between* its two figures (*between* its first two paragraphs) the paradoxical space of a third figure, a figure to the
second power, a figure of the figural operation itself. This figure
of the functioning of figure is given an allegorical name in the third
paragraph's "inevitable and pitiless Muse."

What, indeed, is a muse? According to the poem, she is that
to which the marksman owes both his "*adresse*" and "a large part
of his genius." And what is genius other than a gift for manipu-
lating figure? As the founder of Western poetics puts it: "The greatest thing by far is to have a command of metaphor. This alone
cannot be imparted by another; it is the mark of genius" (Aristotle,
Poetics, 1459a). Yet here, it is precisely such genius that *does* seem
to be imparted by another. It is not the marksman himself but the
"inevitable and pitiless Muse," both target and governing spirit,
both sender and receiver of the bullet, that serves as the source of
the marksman's *adresse*. And she does so precisely because, by

laughing, she had stood as the figure of his *maladresse*. While the marksman is thus aiming at his own bad aim, his success is a proof of his figural dispossession. The straighter he shoots, the more he gets his address *from* the very Muse his bullet is addressed to. It is thus from the Other that his genius must come, an Other that designates not a person but a place: the place of decapitation. For the woman becomes a Muse, the figure of the poet's *addresse*, only when she stands as the *address*—the destination—of the poet's bullet. She is a figure of figurative power only insofar as she is disfigured; she acquires her capital letter through her own decapitation. The Muse's capital letter, which allegorically severs her from herself, is also a sign that the severing has yet to occur, that her head remains potently on her shoulders. And yet that head, always already cut off by a cut that has not yet taken place, springs up out of the figure, never to return to a state prior to the cut, even if the cut, in the end, will never really reach it. An effective Muse is a Muse that is killed, not once, but over and over again; her power is to be both powerful and dead, present and absent, a severed and yet-unsevered head. At the same time the woman becomes a Muse only by remaining *absent* from the place of her disfigurement, so that, in the final analysis, the marksman's address consists of *missing* the address he aims at.

The very notion of transitive action, of cause and effect, of acts and agents, is skewed by the two-way lines of figural force in which the Other, at once sender and receiver, is potent as sender only insofar as s/he is missed as receiver. Indeed, the decapitation which the marksman both succeeds and fails at turns out, unsettlingly enough, to be *his own*. For what has he done to correct his aim? "He closed his eyes and pulled the trigger. The doll was neatly decapitated." The lack of connection between the two sentences, the passive description of decapitation as an effect without an agent or cause, inscribes the marksman's *adresse* in a textual blank. At the moment of decapitation, it is the marksman's own head that is out of the game, and his blindness that somehow insures his good aim. Far from being the origin of his address, his head is rather the address the bullet is sent to. At the heart of the text and of the figure, the decapitated doll is thus literally a *blind spot*, not only because it constitutes the empty space in which the figures of time and woman exchange places, but because it designates the place of rhetorical substitution as a place of darkness, a focus of blindness: the mark is hit only because one remains blind to the law of one's own address. It is thus at the very moment the marksman appears to master figure that he is mastered *by* it. It is always the Other—Time or the Muse—that possesses the Capital.

In reading Baudelaire's two prose poems as allegories of figure, it has not been our intention to reduce all marital ambivalence or fratricidal rivalry to a matter of metaphor and metonymy, but rather to point out the coimplication of human violence and human figuration. If violence is structured like figure, and figure like violence, then the study of rhetoric can hardly remain a subsidiary, trivial matter. But, like violence, it will always be a matter that involves its analyst in greater and greater tangles of its own proliferation. In our search for a language capable of understanding figure, we have indeed not been immune to the law of the Other that robs the marksman of any possession of his marks. For when we speak of dead and ressuscitated figures, of decapitated meanings and battle prizes, is it not always *from the figures themselves* that we derive our language? Whenever we try to comprehend figure, we find that we are already comprehended *by* it. We thus find ourselves in a position similar to that of the prospective hashish smoker who is told by Baudelaire:

Through a singular equivocation, . . . you will feel as though you are evaporating, and you will endow your pipe (in which you can feel yourself squatting, tamped down like tobacco) with a strange faculty for *smoking you*.[14]

Is it not, indeed, precisely the law of figure to erase even the difference between subject and object, Same and Other, and to confer upon each text that strange faculty for *figuring us*?

Notes

1. For a broader development of this perspective, see my *Défigurations du langage poétique* (Paris: Flammarion, 1979), from which, with considerable modification, the present essay is derived. All translations, both of my own original French and of that of others, are mine unless otherwise indicated.

2. Charles Baudelaire, "le Gâteau," in *Oeuvres complètes* (Paris: Bibliothèque de la Pléiade, 1976), 1:297–99.

3. Baudelaire, "Le Galant Tireur," in *Oeuvres complètes*, 1:349–50

4. Jean Cohen, "Théorie de la figure," *Communications* 16:8.

5. The "voodoo" quality of this figural operation casts an unexpected light on the famous Baudelairean conception of "language and writing taken as magic operations, evocative sorcery" ("Fusées," in *Oeuvres complètes*, 1:658). In describing magical operations in *Totem and Taboo*, Freud indeed refers to this same scene: "One of the most widespread magical procedures for injuring an enemy is by making an effigy of him from any convenient material. . . . Whatever is then done to the effigy, the same thing happens to the detested original" (*Standard Edition*, 13:79). It is precisely in *rhetorical* terms—substitution, resemblance, contiguity—that Freud describes such magical operations. The much-vaunted "magic of art" may then perhaps be something more unsettling than the rhetorical prestidigitation that would create out of nothing some "absente de tous bouquets." One begins to suspect that beneath every bouquet of flowers of rhetoric, the "evocative sorcery" of poetry may be producing, somewhere, a severed head.

6. Michel Deguy, *Figurations* (Paris: Gallimard, 1969), p. 121.

7. Cohen, "Théorie," pp. 4–5.

8. Cohen, "Théorie," p. 22; italics mine.

9. Cohen, "Théorie," p. 21.

10. Jacques Lacan, *The Four Fundamental Concepts of Psychoanalysis*, Alan Sheridan, tr. (New York: Norton, 1977), p. 62.

11. Daniel Sibony, "L'infini et la castration," *Scilicet* (1973) 4:81, 120.

12. Pierre Fontanier, *Les figures du discours* (Paris: Flammarion, 1968), p. 63.

13. Gérard Genette, *Figures I* (Paris: Seuil, 1966), p. 120.

14. *Le Poème du haschisch, Oeuvres complètes*, 1:420.

6. Reading Constants: The Practice of the Prose Poem

HERMINE RIFFATERRE

*T*he prose poem has since its beginnings escaped definition. Its oxymoronic name indicates the obvious reason: the self-contradictory, paradoxical nature of the genre. It was a "nom de guerre" (with a little play on words). Something revolutionary had to be done; there had to be a breaking away from traditional poetry; a challenge had to be offered to the esthetics that made versification essential to poetic art. It is with this aspiration that Baudelaire writes in his preface to Arsène Houssaye: "Quel est celui de nous qui n'a pas, dans ses jours d'ambition, rêvé le miracle d'une prose poétique, musicale sans rythme et sans rime? . . ." ("Who among us in his days of ambition has not dreamt the miracle of a poetic prose that is musical without rhythm and without rhyme? . . .")

There have always been two opposing tendencies in poetry: one towards increasing restraints, the other towards freedom from restraints. The prose poem is in the latter tradition. At different periods we observe the push towards elimination of formal rules: rhyme, or punctuation, is dropped, or regular meter is replaced by free verse. The prose poem involves a more radical change, extending through the entire text. It is a whole genre born of this elimination principle.

And two critical currents have sprung out of it. One school obstinately goes on looking for the characteristics of verse in the prose poem. The truth is that these critics have never really accepted the idea that there can be such a thing as poetry without versification, that real poetry outside of verse can exist. Prejudiced critics of this kind are likely to recognize the poetic in prose only where they can detect some disguised or metric framework, or where they think they can prove that the prose poem has the musicality of verse and differs from verse only in its lack of same-length lines or prosodic unity. So holds Monique Parent in her book *Saint-John Perse et quelques devanciers*.[1] Here she used phonetics and acoustics to prove that Péguy's rhythms are so marked that his prose has all the characteristics of verse. Or else she studies prose-poem themes, that is to say facts of content, which cannot be linked exclusively to the prose form and which do just as well in verse poetry (see Saint-John Perse, for instance).

The other critical current acknowledges an authentic rupture between versified poetry and the prose poem, but minimizes its importance and wants to examine it achronically. Even while the prose poetic genre was evolving (by now there is an important corpus), this distinction must have seemed much too narrow and too dependent upon the traditional forms destroyed by the earliest prose poets striving to make their originality felt. And now that the liberation has been achieved it would seem that none of them—not the genre, not its texts, not the authors—need any longer seek their definition in this rupture with tradition; it is no longer this rupture that justifies their creation of poetic experience or their winning of a readership. The attitude is obsolete. If the prose poem is a valid genre for us, it should be able to dispense with such purely historical traits of perhaps only temporary significance.

It is toward this conclusion, indeed, that we see the more innovative, penetrating, and sensitive critics moving, rather than along Monique Parent's lines. Of these critics, the one who has done the most substantial work and made the most impressive efforts to build an esthetic of the prose poem is Suzanne Bernard. We find in her immense volume:

Un Poème en prose a pour nécessité vitale la brièveté, condition sine qua non de l'unité d'effet, que le Poème en prose se caractérise par la concentration, la gratuité, l'intensité. . . . le poème est un monde clos, fermé sur soi, se suffisant à soi-même et en même temps une source de block irradiant, chargé sous un faible volume d'une infinité de suggestions et capable d'ébranler notre être en profondeur.[2]

> (It is vitally necessary for the prose poem to be short, condition *sine qua non* of unity of effect, of its characteristic concentration, gratui-tousness, intensity . . . the poem is a closed world, shut in upon itself, sufficient unto itself, and at the same time it is a kind of ra-diating mass, a small volume charged with an infinity of suggestions, capable of shaking us to the depth of our being.)

I should rather not comment on Suzanne Bernard's final phrases; these sound to me more like mysticism than criticism. But I do want to hold on to the notion of closure: a text can be poetic without being closed, but it will become a poem—something quite different—only if it has a well-marked beginning and end that turn it into an organized whole. Bernard also speaks of rhythm, of the expressive value of sound, and she emphasizes that the prose poem is always poetically liberated compared with versified po-etry. All these characterizations are too vague or subjective or im-pressionistic. Furthermore, many poems lack the concentration and intensity she refers to. Some Baudelaire texts, for example, like "Le Joujou du pauvre" (an anecdote) or "Le Mauvais Vitrier," "La Fausse Monnaie," etc., are relatively long and diffuse.

A merit of Bernard's critical approach is that she tries to define the poem as a closed text; the earlier group of critics does not do this. Yet the traits attributed to the prose are still such as would tend to destroy its prosaic nature. I agree that we cannot do without the fundamental oxymoron: a poem, yes, but a prose poem. The original break with verse is still the genre's active principle, es-sential to its definition, but essential also to its perception by the reader. What strikes him at once is the prose. He reads this and does not feel it is threatened. As he moves forward he discovers specific characteristics that demand a poetic interpretation. What I propose, therefore, is that we seek within the reading experience of the prose poem the clues to this interpretation.

There are in fact two reading stages: reading that is just de-ciphering is incomplete. A true reading is something like the per-formance of a musical score by an instrumentalist. When a pianist plays he deciphers the score and at the same time interprets it.

Reading is thus a simultaneous deciphering and identification of characteristics already known and familiar, of symbols long established, of figures the reader instinctively compares with the fresh examples the text is offering him. It is at this stage of interpretation that the reader notices certain elements of the text are repeating themselves. The repetition may be total or it may be partial—a straight reiteration of a word or phrase—or in anaphoric form, with the text saying the same thing over in various modes, as is the case with rhyme in verse, for instance.

The perception of constants is, I propose, the element that makes the reader sense in the prose before him an organization different from that of mere prose. This element makes him aware of an organization that does not destroy the prose—its rhythm, the variety of its sentences, its absence of preestablished constraints—yet at the same time embraces meaning and form. It is an organization that links up the entire text from start to finish into a single chain, producing the closure that gives the poem its minimum definition. It is an organization that binds the text so tightly there is no possible way of making the poem start earlier or later. Hence this perception of constants must have the same effect upon the reader as the form of ode or sonnet.

The constant varies widely and may take all sorts of forms. It may be a direct reference to another text, hence an intertextual phenomenon, as in the first example we shall consider. Or it may be a rhetorical figure, or a parallelism, or a convergence of picture sequences, as in the Rimbaud poem we shall be looking at. It is this diversity of constants, in fact, that has guided me in choosing the poems I shall try to analyze.

Let me start with something that is not great poetry; I use it for its historical value. It forms part of the first book of what were later called "prose poems": nineteenth-century critics recognized in them the earliest example of the new literary genre.

The poem is titled "Sur les rochers de Chèvremorte" and it comes from Aloysius Bertrand's *Gaspard de la nuit*.[3] This poet was obscurely aware that he was writing "new stuff" without really being able to define it for his contemporaries. Only much later would Baudelaire recognize *Gaspard* as a book of prose poems; it is Baudelaire who invented the phrase, although he said his own

Petits Poèmes en prose were different. Baudelaire thought he was doing the same thing Bertrand did, even though the dissimilarities go far beyond mere content. This gives us one more reason for seeking the nature of the prose poem elsewhere than in established theoretical typology or taxonomy.

I have chosen "Sur les rochers de Chèvremorte" for another reason too: it is one of the poems commented upon by Sainte-Beuve in his 1842 preface to *Gaspard de la nuit*. Sainte-Beuve chose "Sur les rochers" because "il nous rend avec une grâce exquise le très proche reflet d'une réalité douloureuse"[4] ("it renders with exquisite grace the very near reflection of a painful reality").

There is no doubt that for Sainte-Beuve the poem's poetic value lies in this reflection of a poetic reality, of an emotional experience. It is a symbol nestling securely within the corpus of lyrical clichés: solitary contemplation in a landscape that is natural, wild, inhospitable. For Sainte-Beuve, clearly, however the text is written, it will be poetry if the things and acts depicted in it are poetic.

In a footnote to the title Bertrand indicates that Chèvremorte is half a mile from Dijon. He underlines this detail, apparently to certify the authenticity of the sentiments expressed in the poem: we know that these rocks exist, that Bertrand used to wander among them, that he was sad there. The title is regarded as proof of sincerity: the text is accepted as a poem to the extent that it recounts a lived experience with which the reader can sympathize.

Sur les rochers de Chèvremorte

> Et moi aussi j'ai été déchiré par les épines de ce désert,
> et j'y laisse chaque jour quelque partie de ma dépouille.
> —LES MARTYRS

Ce n'est point ici qu'on respire la mousse des chênes, et les bourgeons du peuplier, ce n'est point ici que les brises et les eaux murmurent d'amour ensemble.

Aucun baume, le matin, après la pluie, le soir, aux heures de la rosée: et rien pour charmer l'oreille que le cri du petit oiseau qui quête un brin d'herbe.

Désert qui n'entend plus la voix de Jean-Baptiste, désert que n'habitent plus ni les hermites ni les colombes!

Ainsi mon âme est une solitude où, sur le bord de l'abîme, une main à la vie et l'autre à la mort, je pousse un sanglot désolé.

Le poète est comme la giroflée qui s'attache frêle et odorante au granit, et demande moins de terre que de soleil.

Mais hélas! je n'ai plus de soleil depuis que se sont fermés les yeux si charmants qui réchauffaient mon génie!

(22 juin 1832)

(On the Rocks of Chèvremorte

> And I too have been ripped apart by the thorns of this desert,
> and I leave there every day some part of my corpse.
> —THE MARTYRS

Not from here do you breathe the moss of the oaks, and the poplar buds, not here do the breezes and the waters murmur together with love.

No balm, in the morning after the rain, in the evening at the hours of dew: and nothing to charm the ear other than the cry of the little bird who is seeking a blade of grass.

A desert which no longer hears the voice of John the Baptist, a desert which the hermits and the doves no longer inhabit!

Thus my soul is a solitude where, on the the the edge of the abyss, one hand for life and the other for death, I utter a desolate sob.

The poet is like the gillyflower which attaches itself frail and odiferous to the granite, and demands less earth than sun.

But alas! I have no more sun since the eyes, so charming, which gave new warmth to my genius have closed!

June 22, 1832)

What Sainte-Beuve does not see is that the Chèvremorte of the poem has more in common with the word *rochers* preceding it than with the geographic spot referred to. However they may operate to suggest a verifiable, objective reality, these two signifiers *rochers* and *chèvremorte* function poetically to repeat twice over, by a sort of periphrasis, the notion of desert, that is, a dry and barren region. It is not a question of reality effect, of truthfulness guaranteed, but rather a variation on the word *desert*.

As translator, initiator and adapter, Bertrand does not hide his allusions. The opening epigraph forces us back to Chateaubriand's text.[5] It is Velleda speaking: the Gallic priestess laments her unrequited love for Eudore, the noble Christian Roman. Her passion is doubly forbidden: as that of a pagan priestess for a Christian, and as that of a Gaul for a Roman occupier. The epigraph thus presupposes a lover mourning an impossible love. Let me quote the monologue preceding the epigraph:

"Si tu m'avais aimée," disait Velleda, "avec quelles délices nous aurions parcouru ces champs! quel bonheur d'errer avec toi dans ces routes solitaires, comme la brebis dont les flocons de laine sont restés suspendus à ces ronces."

("If you had loved me," said Velleda, "with what delights would we have traversed these fields! What happiness to wander with you in these solitary roads, like the ewe whose tufts of wool have remained caught on these thorns.")

The world is a hostile wasteland for one who loves and is not loved in return. Lovers seek solitude, which becomes a *desert* when you are alone. In Bertrand's text this notion of solitude = desert is applied through negation to the contrary of a desert. Just the opposite happens at the beginning of Hugo's "Tristesse d'Olympio":

Les champs n'étaient point noirs, les cieux n'étaient pas mornes
Non, le jour rayonnait dans un azur sans bornes.

(The fields were not black, the skies were not somber, no, the day was radiant in an azure without limits.)

Here everything is presented in terms of negative sadness, and the sadness persists. In "Sur les rochers de Chèvremorte" a non-desert, if I may phrase it so, is transformed into a desert by a double negation. The description is made up of pleasant elements negated by the text—"ce n'est point ici qu'on respire la mousse, que les brises et les eaux murmurent d'amour ensemble"—which permits the lingering of something like a memory of life before it turned into a desert. But what does the Chateaubriand text say? The same thing, actually, and I should like to insist upon the fact that Bertrand's intertext is Chateaubriand's text word for word:

"Dis-moi, as-tu entendu la dernière nuit le gémissement d'une fontaine dans les bois et la plainte de la brise dans l'herbe qui croit sur ta fenêtre? Eh bien! c'était moi qui soupirais dans cette fontaine et dans cette brise! Je me suis aperçue que tu aimais le murmure des eaux et des vents."[6]

("Tell me, did you hear the moaning of a fountain in the woods last night, and the lament of the breeze in the grass growing on your window? Well, it was I sighing in this fountain and this breeze! I perceived that you loved the murmur of the waters and the winds.")

In Bertrand's poem this absolute desert, in fact an unrelievable inner solitude, is also developed through another intertextual allusion, this one biblical. Bertrand's desert is compared not to Chateaubriand's but the archetypical desert of the New Testament, where the prophet's voice is lost in the void, and where the seed, as in the parable, falls upon rock and cannot sprout. The profound bereavement, the total emptiness of a life without the beloved where the lover has no one to talk to, this silence, this vacuum, is brought out further through the detour of the Baptist intertext. Even more impressively, the crying voice (*vox clamans*) that cries in vain (*vox clamans in deserto*), that voice itself is silent: still *in deserto* but no longer *clamans*. It is the knife without the blade with the handle missing, an invention of the German humorist Lichtenberg.

The next paragraph describes the lifeless soul, the solitariness that has no limits: "sur le bord de l'abîme, une main à la vie et l'autre à la mort, je pousse un sanglot désolé." In Chateaubriand it is still Velleda speaking: "'Quand je ne serai plus . . . tu m'écriras des lettres et nous causerons ainsi des deux (côtés du tombeau'"[7] ("'When I am no longer . . . you will write me letters and we shall thus chat, from either side of the grave'"). It would seem that Bertrand has made Velleda's desert even more of a desert. His text is a kind of hyperbole of Chateaubriand's. Reading Bertrand today, we do not react to a simple description, or to the symbolism of direct representation of desert reality. The reader reacts to the desert in another text: this he compares with the one in front of him, and he cannot help comparing the two because the epigraph forces upon him a simultaneous reading. What this double reading underscores is that both deserts are only apparently geographical, that the Sinai and the Dijon environs are just a trick. The double reading makes it clear that the desert is an inner one, already defined by Lamartine: "Un seul être vous manque et tout est dépeuplé" ("you miss a single being, and everything is depopulated"). Now we see the importance of the epigraph: once we know Chateaubriand's text, Bertrand's looks like a superlative version of *Les Martyrs*. This interpretation is far from that of Sainte-Beuve, who sees the epigraph as a mere ornament, a pompon as he calls it. On the contrary, the epigraph is essential: our entire reading of the poem depends upon it. It is this epigraph that gives the text its constants and turns it into a poem.

The constant may also be an intersecting of two synonymous series, as in the case of Rimbaud's "Ornières," which I shall now examine.

Ornières

A droite l'aube d'été éveille les feuilles et les vapeurs et les bruits de ce coin du parc, et les talus de gauche tiennent dans leur ombre violette les mille rapides ornières de la route humide. Défilé de féeries. En effet: des chars chargés d'animaux de bois doré, de mâts et de toiles bariolées, au grand galop de vingt chevaux de cirque tachetés, et les enfants et les hommes sur leurs bêtes les plus étonnantes; vingt véhicules, bossés, pavoisés et fleuris comme des carrosses anciens ou de contes, pleins d'enfants attifés pour une pastorale suburbaine. Même des cercueils sous leur dais de nuit dressant les panaches d'ébène, filant au trot des grandes juments bleues et noires.[8]

(Ruts

To the left the summer dawn wakens the leaves and the mists and the sounds of this part of the park, and the slopes on the left keep within their lavender shadow the thousand quick furrows in the damp road. A procession of wonders. All this: chariots filled with gilt wood animals, bright-colored masts and sails, a full gallop of twenty spotted circus horses, and children and men on the most astonishing beasts; twenty vehicles, embossed, decked out, and flowered like carriages of old or of legend, full of children dressed for a suburban pastoral. Even coffins under their night canopy rearing ebony plumes, dashing to the trot of great blue-black mares.)

I offer this second example because it seems to me a case of superficially diverse images finally perceived as a continuum. This perceived but not necessarily interpreted formal continuity represents the equivalent to the challenged meter of the absent prosody. It consists in the joining of two synonymic series at the end of the poem, giving these concluding images a complexity of meaning that links the strands out of which the text is woven. And this final junction, this transformation of an ending that seems just a typographical closure, is the textual component that accounts for the title's plural s. I do not believe anyone has ever commented on this point, but it will make my demonstration complete.

The first synonymous series is the *rapidity* sequence: it starts with "rapides ornières" and goes on with "au grand galop," I should even say with "au grand galop de vingt chevaux." Indeed, the system of literary representation of reality so functions here that the galloping of twenty horses feels faster than the galloping of one, or than galloping in general. The *speed* sequence ends with coffins "filant au trot"—ends, or better, culminates. True, trotting is slower than galloping; but "au trot" has been added on to a verb expressing the height of velocity and agility, *filant*. Most important, this motion feels like top speed because it is so abnormal, so bizarre in connection with coffins. The same anomaly was exploited humorously by La Fontaine in his "Le Curé et le mort": "Un curé s'en allait gaiement / Enterrer ce mort au plus vite" ("A curate was gaily on his way to bury this dead man in a hurry"). Rimbaud uses this incongruity to create not the comic but the fantastic. And the device brings me to the second synonymous series, the *fantastic* or *dream* sequence. It starts out with "défilé de féeries" and pushes on with "des animaux de bois doré" and "des véhicules" that resemble "carrosses," two details that reinforce the circus-and-illusionist-games description, but upon a second reading will enhance our impression of the fantastic. This impression, which at the beginning develops out of the notion of "féeries," is produced by the vision of "bêtes les plus étonnantes" followed by the vision of "carrosses anciens ou de contes" so that "de contes" is analogous to "féeries." The sequence reaches its peak with the appearance of vehicles not only diametrically opposed to the circus vehicles contextually, but actually antonymous: "Les cercueils sous leur dais de nuit." Certainly this dais is appropriate—horse-drawn hearses covered with a black canopy—but it is also metaphorized by the translation of *black* into *night*. The metaphor suffices to give the description the coloration of the fantastic. It confirms and emphasizes how eerie coffins must seem in a parade intended to give delight to the very young and the very old.

Finally, the fantastic is hyperbolically corroborated by the race the coffins run. Funeral processions are by nature slow and solemn, as in Baudelaire's "Spleen IV":

> Et de long corbillards, sans tambour ni musique
> Défilent lentement dans mon âme . . .

(And long funeral convoys, without drums or music, slowly parade by in my soul . . .)

In Rimbaud's poem the speed, as I mentioned before, is an anomaly that may be likened to La Fontaine's and, like his, may be oriented toward humor and interpreted as comic. But if the context does not permit such comic orientation, if humor is blocked, then the uncanny invades the scene. I remember a scene from Dracula where a lost traveler sees a galloping hearse in a moonlit clearing, and the horses are as black as Rimbaud's.

Now we understand how the closure has been effected. The sequence *rapidité* and the sequence *féerie* tie up into a significant knot that turns the race into a fantastic cavalcade. In using the phrase "fantastic cavalcade" I am conjuring up a familiar theme from folklore often exploited in literature for supernatural effects. But if we begin with the second series, we can also say that the race is a brief vision flashing by, or a fleeting dream.

The poetic feature of the text, or what makes this prose a poem, is that within a very realistic, or at least very real, description we are forced to recognize an illusion, a waking dream or vision. The poetic quality is the tension created by an unreality that for an instant becomes real. I must stress that this generative tension of the poetic resides wholly in the combination of the two sequences, the two formal constraints of the text, and in the closure that formally realizes this combination. A formal characteristic is to be observed also in the textual components triggering the sequences: the oxymoron noted by all critics but never explained, which is to say that its function has not been recognized. Also unexplained is the image "défilé de féeries," audaciously concretized through the metonym *féeries*, which is stripped of its abstractness and brought back to its theatrical signification, that is, brought back to the signification it must have within a text of vision or hallucination.

Everything I have been discussing is illuminated by the plural of *ornières*. In the singular the word would have a moral and metaphoric meaning: bad habits, moral stagnation. In the plural it is the reality of a rutted highway. This visible, tangible reality is a reality of absence: it is the traces left by a hurried passage, the glimpse of a race caught by a spectator who is left behind. Thus the title, in an embryonic way, is already suggesting the poetic tension of the text: the empty furrows in the road are a way of reporting the invisible presence of carriages that have literally passed. It is an inverted way of describing, through the medium of abandoned wheel ruts, the imaginary nature of this parade, the fantastic nature of this vision. The text's poetic character is thus inseparable from a unique combination of formal and constant traits. They are constants as verse or prosody might be, but constants peculiar to this text because they depend entirely upon its meaning.

My last example is from Claudel's *Connaissance de l'Est*.

—D'une dent, sans doute égarée, d'entre celles dont Cadmus ensemença le labour Thébain, naquit le formidable aloès. Le soleil tira d'un sol féroce ce hoplite. C'est un coeur de glaives, un épanouissement de courroies glauques. Sentinelle de la solitude, couleur de mer et d'armure, il croise de toutes parts l'artichaut de ses scies énormes. Et longtemps ainsi il montera rang sur rang sa herse, jusqu'à ce qu'ayant fleuri il meure, jusqu'à ce que de son coeur jaillisse le membre floral comme un poteau, et comme un candélabre, et comme l'étendard enraciné aux entrailles du dernier carré![9]

(—From a tooth, probably misplaced somewhere, among those with which Cadmus inseminated the Theban tilling, the formidable aloe was born. The sun drew forth this foot soldier from a ferocious soil. It has a heart of swords, an expanse of milky straps. Sentinel of solitude, the color of the sea and armor, it reaches out everywhere the artichoke of its enormous saws. And for a long time, it will raise its harrow like that, row by row, until having flowered, it dies, until from its heart the floral member leaps forth like a post, and like a candelabrum, and like the banner rooted in the entrails of the last square!)

The subject is an "aloe." Let me say at once that a botanist would be shocked by the *aloès*. Claudel uses the wrong words: he must mean *agave*, but his is a very common mistake. Saint-John Perse makes the reverse error, calling a true aloe an agave. Be that as it may, what Claudel and most of his readers think of as an aloe is a huge plant, much more aggressive than the cactus that botany books characterize as gladiate (from the Latin *gladius*, sword). We can see how easy it is to move from the botanical concept to the hero armed from head to foot. Simone de Beauvoir knows that an aloe is not an agave, but she arrives at the same ferocious image as Claudel: in *Mandarins* she speaks of agaves (alias aloes) "qui poignardent la terre" ("that stab the earth").

It is not surprising, therefore, that the aloe–agave brings the Cadmus legend to Claudel's mind. In Greek mythology Cadmus is the founding father of Thebes: after killing the dragon he sows its teeth in the fields. This myth is recalled in Nerval's poem "Delfica": "Et la grotte, fatale aux hôtes imprudents, / Où du dragon vaincu dort l'antique semence!" ("And the cave, fatal to the incautious guests, where sleeps the ancient seed of the vanquished dragon!"). From these teeth sown by Cadmus as wheat might be sown in furrows, armed warriors spring up. That is all Claudel needs to develop the image of a creature literally born of a seed, the "aloe," which nature has endowed with swords. Here is an extraordinary mixture of exact description, the mythological fantastic, and botanical metaphor.

The aggressiveness of the "aloe" is reinforced by the French anteposition in "formidable aloès." It lends the adjective the strong signification of "that is to be feared," further strengthened by the metaphor "ce hoplite," meaning a heavily armed Greek foot soldier. Since in French the *h* is silent, the pronounciation should dictate *cet hoplite*; but the ungrammatical form is purposely used by Claudel: he is playing with the Greek language. In Greek an initial aspiration is indicated by an accent called *rough breathing*, as opposed to the unaspirated *smooth breathing*. Greek rough breathing is transliterated into French by an initial *h*. But this *h* is not always aspirate, and in the case of hoplite it is not. By making it aspirate, Claudel creates a phonetic effect that evokes something painful. Calling an accent a "breathing" is odd; carry the humanization of breathing further with the adjectives "smooth" and "rough," and a play on words becomes appropriate. Thank to the Greek intertextuality, "ce hoplite" appears to symbolize the soldier's savage cruelty. This brutality is heightened by the hypallage "sol féroce," which makes the soil giving birth to the hoplite exceedingly cruel.

Coeur in "coeur de glaives" is triply determined by a cluster of verbal associations; this alone would suffice to prove that the language of the text is poetic. But poetic prose can exist outside of the genre that concerns us. What still has to be proved is that the piece's "poeticism" is linked to the closure of the text. Meanwhile let us decide what this overdetermination consists of. The word coeur has meaning in three different contexts: the human, the vegetable, and that of the artichoke in particular. We have seen that at the human level the aloe is like a hoplite. At the vegetal level it is the core, the heart of the tree; the floral mimesis is tied up with anthropomorphic associations ("meure," "coeur," "membre") reflecting the tree's vitality. Finally, coeur functions at an intermediate level both vegetable and human, resulting from the wordplay in coeur d'artichaut that must be introduced because "artichaut" is in the text. The artichoke's heart is not only the core of that delectable vegetable, it is also a familiar and pleasing metaphor for the fickle human heart. I do not suggest that Claudel is trying to make us believe in some new aloe form of cruelty in the sense of faithless hearts cruel to their beloveds. That would be ridiculous. But the double literal and metaphoric association between coeur and d'artichaut does make it possible for "artichaut" to reinforce and motivate "coeur," to give "coeur" a reality and a life that in turn bolster the personification of "hoplite."

The set purpose of the text is to develop the warrior image on any pretext, even without the least verisimilitude. This set purpose is flagrant in the case of "couleur de mer et d'armure." "Couleur de mer" is indeed semantically motivated by "glauque," the dark green of the agave–aloe leaves: the dictionary defines glauque as couleur de mer. But "couleur d'armure" does not exist and has only formal reality: within the framework of an alliteration, even of an assonance, with "de mer," "d'armure" writes itself, with no other reason than the desire for symmetry. It is interesting to note that this void within the sentence, opened up by the temptation of assonance and repetition, is filled automatically with a soldier metonym: his suit of armour repeats at the stylistic level what the text has been repeating from the very start. The aloe is like a fierce warrior.

The same effect flows from "artichaut de ses scies énormes," which translates into peaceable garden vocabulary and into artisan-tool vocabulary what has already been expressed in military language. The saw is to the artisan what the sword is to the man of war. The transcode is based upon a semic analogy: the cutting property.

The whole of the last sentence works to develop its most remarkable word, *herse*. It is remarkable first because its aspirate *h* takes on the aspirate *h* of *hoplite*. "Ce hoplite," "sa herse"—the double hiatus stresses their connection: "ce hoplite" is the warrior metaphor; "herse" is the metonymy of this metaphor. As a metonymy "herse" is much more than the agricultural tool it denotes (harrow): "herse" takes up again the aggressiveness of the aloe. This it does on three levels simultaneously, for the word *herse* is a kind of node, a knot where three semantic sequences intersect, three associations of ideas all going back to the aloe. This is the same sort of knot that ties together the *féerie* and *rapidité* sequences in the Rimbaud poem. The threefold association with aloe rests upon the three dictionary meanings of the word *herse*:

1. "Agricultural implement set with several rows of teeths, etc." Claudel's text says: "il montera rang sur rang sa herse."
2. "A gate with spikes, used to close the entrance to a fortified place." The harrow thus serves as a metonym of fortification. The aloe, lacking all vegetable delicacy, is well fortified. The words *poteau étendard*, and *entrailles du dernier carré* are connected to the second *herse* meaning. "Le dernier carré" is a technical military term from ancient army tactics: infantrymen were drawn up in a square formation as a human fortress, with their bodies serving as a rampart (the Waterloo *dernier carré* is a familiar cliché of last-ditch resistance).

3. Finally, the third meaning of *herse* generates the only aloe image that seems to escape war metaphor and is in fact foreign to it: "candélabre." This is an accurate representation of vegetality, for the aloe's trunk and spreading foliage do indeed rise like an enormous lamp of many branches. True to reality as it is, distant from war and the warlike, it still repeats the formal constant initiated with "herse," whose third meaning is "a triangular Church candelabrum with teeth for holding the wax candles."

The nodal words are *Cadmus*, the fighting hero who also sows grain, and *herse*, whose polysemy we have just demonstrated: these words give us the key to the text as prose poem. It is through these nodal words that the two sequences warrior/vegetable intersect: "l'étendard enraciné" is the exemplary form, since it partakes simultaneously in the two sequences.

Now we see, in this game of one for one, that all the signifiers correspond at the same time to the many signifieds. The text starts out with a war image and finishes the same way.

But this proposition is obvious only from the point of view of meaning. Let us examine it from the point of view of form. The text begins with the word *dent* (tooth), the only pertinent tooth in a vegetal context because it is the only tooth that also means *grain*. *Dent* is carried along further in the text by means of *herse*: tooth-sharp in its three meanings. A continuity equivalent to verse runs through the varied images and sounds of these double sequences. The sequences make the text a variation on one motif, a motif whose appropriateness is also overdetermined by a proverbial expression: the aloe is a warrior "armed to the teeth."

This self-sufficient stanza is a reverie upon plant belligerence and forms part of a longer poem called "Heures dans le jardin." The stanza following is a philosophical musing. It is as complex in its construction as the aloe one, and is similarly coextensive with the text. The garden is both a theater of meditation and the grounds for a stroll. Ever since the Peripatetics, taking a walk has meant meditating. On the other hand, going into a question deeply, thoroughly exploring a problem, is traditionally represented by a descent. A famous allegory hides Truth at the bottom of a well. Victor Hugo speaks of *La Pente de la rêverie*, including the slope, the declivity, the inner stairway, these favorite topoi of the imagination ever since the romantics. The spiral staircase is used by Claudel in another of his works, his book on Dutch painting. He describes Rembrandt's *Philosopher* and notes, in a corner of the picture, the symbolic stairwell:

Ce chemin qui a servi autrefois à entraîner l'Enfant Prodigue et à le dissiper du côté de l'horizon, le Philosophe de Rembrandt l'a replié en lui-même, il en a fait cet escalier *cochléaire*, cette vis qui lui sert à descendre pas à pas jusqu'au fond de la méditation.[10]

(This path which used to lead away the Prodigal Son and dissipate him into the horizon, Rembrant's Philosopher has folded it up, has made it into this *cochlear* stair, this spiral which he uses to descend step by step to the depths of meditation.)

The word *cochléaire* is the adjective from cochlea, a medical term for the spiral division of the inner ear. When he describes the painting, Claudel describes at one and the same time the symbolic spiral staircase and the pricked-up-ear—the attentive philosopher. Let us return to the garden where the aloe grows, the Philosopher's Walk. This garden has a very strange shape: not the zigzag of the English garden, or the geometry of the French. Its pathway forms a spiral, and this spiral winds up at a well. You will have guessed the words Claudel uses to describe it: "le repli *cochléaire* de l'allée toujours me ramène vers je ne sais quel point focal qu'indique, tel qu'au jeu de l'Oie, retiré au plus secret, le Puits" ("the cochlear folding in of the path always brings me back to some focal point which is indicated, as in the game of Goose, withdrawn into the most secret part, by the Well") (italics mine).

This is a whole strophe. Its unity depends upon the fact that it is an image of Meditation, a metaphysical listening to the cosmos. A metonymic variation upon the word *philosophe* conveys this image: he is peripatetic (the garden walk); he is attentive (the cochlea); he is a metaphysician (the spiral staircase, the well).

To conclude. I have varied my examples in order to suggest the multiplicity of forms the prose poem can take. I do not pretend, however, that I have indicated all the possibilities, nor have I given any idea of all their categories. But within the limits necessarily imposed, these texts have each displayed constants that differ from one another, yet all share the feature of linking form and content indissolubly, of subordinating the development of meaning to the repetition of a form or variations upon this form. This subordination by itself would be enough to prove that these prose pieces are constructed like poems.

But I should like to go further. The prose poem is instantly recognizable: the text is unversified and yet the reader senses its formal unity as if it had prosodic shape. Hence I propose the following: the difference between the prose poem and the verse poem is that in the latter the formal framework has permanent characteristics peculiar to all its meanings, to all the texts the author wishes to insert. In the prose poem, on the contrary, the formal framework is ad hoc, built out of the content put into it and coextensive with it, just as the content is coextensive with the verse in the verse poem. It is the ad hoc constant that replaces versification. The constant is not prefabricated the way verse is. It does not antedate the text the way prosody does. It makes its appearance in the text the moment there is perception of equivalent elements—equivalent to each other thanks to meaning despite differences of surface; equivalent to each other thanks to form despite differences of meaning. This constant is not set by tradition, like the alexandrine or decasyllabic line; it is created by the text's own internal organization. The constant remains the same from start to finish of the text, just as verse remains the same, always recognizable, no matter what words may give it its concrete reality.

Notes

1. Monique Parent, *Saint-John Perse et quelques devanciers* (Paris: Klincksieck, 1960).

2. Suzanne Bernard, *Le Poème en prose de Baudelaire jusqu'à nos jours* (Paris: Nizet, 1959), p. 439.

3. Aloysius Bertrand, *Gaspard de la nuit* (Paris: Payot, 1925), pp. 176–77.

4. Charles Augustin de Sainte-Beuve, preface to Bertrand, *Gaspard de la nuit*, p. xxxiii.

5. François René de Chateaubriand, *Les Martyrs I* (Paris: Flammarion, 1943), p. 344.

6. Chateaubriand, *Martyrs I*, p. 336.

7. Chateaubriand, *Martyrs I*, pp. 348–49.

8. Arthur Rimbaud, ''Ornières,'' in *Poésies, Une Saison en enfer, Illuminations* (Paris: *Poésie*/Gallimard, 1973), p. 172.

9. Paul Claudel, ''Heures dans le jardin,'' in *Connaissance de l'Est, suivi de L'Oiseau noir dans le soleil levant* (Paris: *Poésie*/Gallimard, 1974), pp. 119–20.

10. Claudel, *Introduction à la peinture hollandaise*, in *L'Oeil écoute* (Paris: Gallimard, 1946).

7. On the Prose Poem's Formal Features

MICHAEL RIFFATERRE

*T*he prose poem has the distinction of being the literary genre with an oxymoron for a name. The two components of the name seem to contradict each other. Some may object that the contradiction is only a leftover from a time when poetry and verse did not seem to be separable. Nowadays poetic expression in most Western literatures no longer depends upon prosodic convention, so we might think the name irrelevant to a definition of the thing. It is not so. The opposition is still quite useful, for you cannot define prose except in opposition to verse. In a versified poem, however, many formal characteristics are linked to prosody. What is it then that makes up for lack of meter in a prose poem? What are the features that substitute for verse? We can assume that these features, if they are to play a constitutive role in the generation of a prose poem, must meet the following conditions.

First, they must be constant, that is, they must be repeated, or at least equivalent to one another—which is to say, they must be recognizable as so many variants of a single invariant. The invariant itself will not be perceived. No structure is perceived directly, but only through its variant actualizations. The reader, however, does get a more or less conscious feel for the invariance: this sensing on his part is an element of the poem's literariness.

Second, constitutive formal features must be coextensive with the text. They have to define it as a formal unit. They must, for

117

instance, confer the same characteristics upon the title, if any, the beginning of the poem, and its close.

Third, formal features must guide the reader to a recognition of the poem as a semiotic unit. That is, its features control the reader's attention and bring him to realize that every component of the text is a transform of one significance. This concept of significance I draw from what seems to me the basic law of poetry: poetry says one thing and signifies something else. Figurative language, tropes, only illustrate this general rule. To account for the general indirectness in signifying, for the systematic, calculated inappropriateness, for what ancient rhetoric called catachresis, we must distinguish between two levels of sense. On the surface lies meaning, based upon a real or assumed mimesis of reality as a reassuring guarantee of truth. Reality, or at least a system of non-verbal shapes. Underneath we have significance, the produce of semiosis. Semiosis, that is, the process whereby mimesis is transformed in such a way that a reader must reinterpret it and end up identifying a new object proposed to him in the guise of representation.[1]

Let us now return to the opposition *verse vs. prose*. In a versified poem the formal unity is assured, if by nothing else, by the meter, that is, by an established conventional system, existing before and outside the poem itself. In a prose poem, on the contrary, the unifying factor will have to be generated by the text itself. The meaning cannot play this role, since meaning will not differentiate the poem's peculiar idiolect from language, from common usage. The unifying factor must be the significance. I propose to find the latter in a constant invariant relationship between text and intertext, in an invariable *intertextuality*. This much-abused and fashionable term designates a function involving three factors: text, intertext, and context. *Text* shall always be understood as the poem under the reader's eye. Let us emphasize that the poem is being read *now*: if it is being remembered it will tend to recede into the intertext. The *intertext* is the indefinite and variable corpus of literary works, written either before or after the text, perceived by the reader as having some relation to his own text. These other works of art are usually connected with his only at some point or points, through a certain detail or episode or image. But once he has caught sight of the detail, episode, or image as the link to his text, he cannot help being influenced by what lies all around that connective in the intertext. Nor can he help comparing or trying to match up the impact of the connective's surroundings in the intertext with the impact of its surroundings in the poem he is reading. Which is why we have to introduce the idea of *context* to designate these surroundings within either the text or the intertext of that text.[2] Intertextuality is activated, actualized, whenever the reader's interpretation is stymied by anomalies he perceives in the text at the mimesis level. The problems they raise are solved as he realizes that while blocking his interpretation here and now in the text, they point to the solutions elsewhere, in the intertext. If the textual dysfunctions that force him from linear to intertextual reading have a common denominator, the reader perceives them as signs of the formal unity and continuous, generalized catachresis that make a text into a poem.

My first example, from Francis Ponge's *Proêmes*, is a prose poem titled "Un Rocher" ("A Rock," or "A Big Stone").[3] Like many poems, it treats of the writer's labors and of the agonies of creation. The central simile evokes a dense, pathless forest to which Ponge compares "le monde secret de (s)a contemplation et de (s)on imagination" ("the secret world of his contemplation and his fancy"). He goes on to say that he has had no end of trouble trying to describe "seulement un petit buisson" ("even a bit of underbrush") in this inner-world forest. He complains that everything he tells about these woods remains obscure to the reader, and even to himself, after he has got it down on paper. As he exteriorizes his inward vision, the aptest phrases turn awkward or bizarre because they are referring to an interior model, to a language the poet alone can speak. The familiar words he uses are not governed by the rules of the sociolect, they rather follow the rules of his own idiolect. To make himself understood, he would have to open up this private grammar to the outside world. The poem ends with an admission of defeat:

Hélas! aujourd'hui encore je recule épouvanté par l'énormité du rocher qu'il me faudrait déplacer pour déboucher ma porte.

(Alas! even today I recoil in fright at the enormous boulder I should have to move to clear my doorway.)

This conclusion refers back to the beginning of the poem; the boulder at the end alludes to the rock of the title. But the two items actually occupy very little space by comparison with the "forêt étouffante" ("stifling forest") imagery, its varied repetitions, and the author's insistence upon the intricate confusions of the undergrowth. This last metaphor seems to evoke much more faithfully the rank proliferation and intermingling of shapes that symbolize ideas, thoughts, poetic visions surging through the poet's mind. Rock and boulder remain marginal as image, an infelicitous choice for the title and for the conclusion of the poem. Even if we admit the rock represents the writer's block, there are plenty of other symbols for that predicament. To be sure, the boulder-in-the-doorway has enough literary precedents: the rock on hinges that blocks entry to Ali Baba's treasure cave—Open Sesame!—the rock Homer's Cyclops uses to keep Ulysses imprisoned inside *his* cave. We might say the *Arabian Nights* and the *Odyssey* are an intertext to the poem's ending, and that they lend it the prestige of literary tradition. Still, that does not make the image any less farfetched, and more important, we still feel it is not really the focus of the poem. We might be tempted to explain this lack of focus as a wilful clumsiness—when a critic is protective of a pet author, he is likely to explain away a blemish by calling it poetic licence or proclaiming the right of genius to play with fire. So it could be said that Ponge is playfully exaggerating his writer's block into the hugest of stumbling blocks.

Here another intertextual reference does indeed seem to suggest that his intention is humorous: Ponge says "je recule épouvanté," and this somewhat comic miming gesture of frustration is made the more comic by its allusion to a familiar tragic passage of Racine's, condemned by the Romantics as classical drama's prime example of the ludicrously unnatural, conventionalized, and overwrought. In Racine's *Phèdre* a sea monster comes ashore to devour the protagonist—an all-too-obvious *deus ex machina*. Writes Racine: "Le flot qui l'apporta recule épouvanté." The sense is: the receding flood leaves it beached—but what the line actually says is: the wave that carried him forward leaps back in alarm. No one who has been a schoolboy in France is going to miss Ponge's allusion or its humor. Somehow, though, we are still left with a poem that does not seem to have definitely chosen between two sets of images, and that has picked the wrong one—the adventitious one—for a weak title and a weak conclusion.

But right in the middle of the poem there is another stone, not a rock but a pebble. And this pebble, I think, brings together forest and boulder, inspiration and what blocks inspiration, as two inseparable facets of the same creativity metaphor. But only by means of the intertext is the pebble (to which the boulder is what hyperbole is to understatement) able to accomplish this:

> Mais si j'essaye de prendre la plume pour en décrire seulement un petit buisson, ou, de vive voix, d'en parler tant soit peu à quelque camarade . . . le papier de mon bloc-notes ou l'esprit de mon ami reçoivent ces révélations comme un météore dans leur jardin, comme un étrange et quasi *impossible* caillou, d'une "qualité" obscure. . . .

> (But whenever I take pen in hand to describe even a bit of underbrush, or just do it in words, if I just tell some friend about it . . . the leaves of my notepad or my friend's mind receive my lucubrations as if they were a meteor falling into their garden, some strange, well-nigh impossible pebble, of an obscure nature. . . .)

Surely this is an unnatural image, if ever one has been, worse than the boulder at the end; yet its extreme discordance with the context is the very thing that tips the reader off, guides his deciphering, and ultimately reveals the image as fully motivated and appropriate. What jolts him into intertextual awareness is the meteorite in the garden. He might have swallowed the pebble, but it has been shoved further down the sentence, it has been demoted to a mere appositive to "météore," because the puny word would not have made enough of a contrast to the proverb "jeter des pierres dans le jardin de quelqu'un" (throw stones into someone else's garden). The *météore* contrast is certainly startling enough. On the one hand, a meteorite from outer space is the foreign body *par excellence*. On the other hand, the garden is surely a good hyperbole of a reality intimately familiar (after all, the proverb equates garden with self: when you cast stones into someone's garden you are attacking his personality, or his way of thinking). Here the pebble makes you stumble on the common paths of thought and of thought expression (my friend and I rereading a first draft that makes no sense).

Now this new language the poet is trying out, this fresh voice that falls out of nowhere, this uncanny message upsetting out linguistic habits—they cannot but remind the reader of another falling star or stone from out of elsewhere: the symbolic meteorite Mallarmé uses to evoke the newness of Edgar Allan Poe's poetic note, the strange voice ("cette voix étrange") he compares with a "calme bloc ici-bas chu d'un désastre obscur" ("a still block of stone fallen down here onto earth from out of an unknown disaster"). In Mallarmé's sonnet the block, the slab, has become the headstone on Poe's grave. It thus represents both the poet's triumph, his stone thrown into the pond of traditional language, and his defeat, the poet silenced by death—not so much his physical death as a metaphor for his failure to get his message across. Everything in Ponge's text derives from Mallarmé's line. That line is a periphrasis skirting a kernel word it substitutes for. Obviously that kernel word should be *météore*. In the following line Mallarmé refers to it as granite; Ponge's "rocher" picks this up (in literary French *granit* is the exemplary heavy stone, hyperbolic stoniness). And Ponge's weird "qualité obscure" echoes Mallarmé's "désastre obscur." Even Ponge's pad of paper, his "bloc-notes," contains Mallarmé's "bloc." The key word in the intertext is repressed, and this repression—through a compensatory mechanism well known to psychoanalysis—produces a sequence of synonyms and paronyms dispersed along the verbal sequence.

Thus Ponge's "rocher," "bloc," "caillou," and "météore" one and all symbolize the same thing. All of them represent the alien uniqueness of the poet's secret language, the near-impossibility of opening it up to ordinary language users. And this makes the rock imagery synonymous with the forest imagery. The title is thus not marginal at all, far from it: it points to the heart of significance. Not only does it bring everything into focus; it also lays down the rule for proper interpretation: every word that belongs to *stone* language, or *stone* code, stands for poetic creativity.

This rule applies, as must be clear, only as a function of the intertext. The special synonymy of "rocher" and "météore," their secret relationship with the first syllable of the word for *writing pad*, all these equivalences are acceptable only because Mallarmé contains them. As long as we are obliged to struggle with Ponge's phrasing alone, the meteor landing smack in the middle of the garden looks odd enough to be hopelessly ungrammatical. Its grammaticality lies within the Mallarmé intertext. Whereas Homer or the *Arabian Nights* or even Racine merely reconfirms an interpretation of the boulder-in-the-doorway that we could have derived quite well enough from Ponge's own ending, the poem as a whole still leaves us ill at ease. But the instant the intertext has been identified, images that at first blush looked aberrant or mutually incompatible harmonize with one another and blend into a coherent whole. The text was first perceived as a loose jumble of sketchy or undeveloped images. The successive segments were mismatched in various ways; now they fit together smoothly. Not directly, along the linearity of sentences, but indirectly, because they all refer to the one intertext, the sonnet. The minute we read Mallarmé's sonnet on Poe into Ponge, Ponge's imagery loses its inconsistency. Out of the needful combining of the two texts is born the prose poem.

We can now distinguish between two types of intertextuality: obligatory and aleatory. The latter type is represented here by Homer and Racine; the obligatory kind, by Mallarmé. Aleatory intertextuality consists in two simultaneous readings. When we assign a meaning to a text or segment of a text, we are attributing a significance to it by recognizing that this text has been seen before, elsewhere. The aleatory intertext is something we quote— quotation being an aleatory process since the ability to recognize depends upon the reader's cultural level. This intertext is perennially threatened by the erosion of culture or memory.

Intertextuality is obligatory where the meaning of certain words in the text has nothing to do with what they should mean in language and can be understood only with the assistance of an intertext. In such a case these words do not carry their normal, everyday linguistic sense, nor is their meaning acceptable to the reader's linguistic competence. Further, the context cannot explain their meaning: the semantic distortion that separates them from linguistic usage does not result from contextual pressure. The reader may not understand them at all, or if he does understand them, the way these words appear to be making sense out of non-sense strikes him as gratuitous and uncalled for. It is this total or relative unacceptability that pushes him to look for, and sooner or later to find, an intertext that happens already to contain the problematic words in the text he is reading. There they are, in the same order, or in something like the same order, and there in that context, within the verbal surroundings of the intertext, they do make sense. For instance, if the intertext uses them metaphorically, the metaphor is readily understood in this other verbal milieu. We do not catch the sense in the present text only because the original verbal surroundings are missing; we have to get back to the intertext if we are to grasp the narrative or descriptive motivations of the metaphor, to compare it with the formal models it follows, and infer the matrix that generated it in the intertext. Which is to say, when the reader has to return to the intertext in order to understand the text, he is not just recognizing the problematic words, the crux, the ungrammaticality, as something seen before. Were he doing no more than this, it would be another sort of reader behavior: spotting a quotation or a literary allusion. Such recognition involves only three possible consequences. One concerns the reader alone and what can be called the pleasure of reading; he recognizes a quotation and feels self-complacent: he shares the culture of an elite. The other two consequences relate strictly to the text, or rather the way it is perceived. Within the sphere of what German theorists today call the esthetics of reception, consequence number two is that the section of the text with the quotation now has a pedigree, its wording is so to speak guaranteed, it stands hallowed, vouched for as true or exemplary, by the authority of the work of art where it first appeared. This instructs the reader to reevaluate the text. As the third result of the identification of a quote, the role of the passage in its new context will be a bit changed by its role in its former context. Its origin may load it with an affect or with connotations it could not draw from its present context alone.

All these behavioral by-products of the quotation or allusion are to be seen in obligatory intertextuality. But what intertextuality does, and mere quotation does not, is provide the reader with an interpretation that lies within the intertext, or halfway between the text and intertext, produced by the comparing or second-guessing that goes on in the reader's mind. And what triggers both this second-guessing and the search in the reader's own memory for an intertext with a solution is the troublesome statement in the text, in other words, the ungrammaticality. This term I use broadly, not as just a sin against grammar, but as any verbal feature of the text that the reader finds linguistically unacceptable or incompatible with the context, or jarring in form and/or content, or, more especially, gratuitous or farfetched or esthetically unpleasing—anything he is tempted to rationalize so he can get safely past it. Any ungrammaticality entails a presumption of grammaticality. Any transgression presupposes a rule. The intertext will therefore be the locus of the corresponding grammaticality, of the rule the text is appealing to when it breaks that rule. The obligatory intertext is thus the object of a presupposition. It must follow that even if historical accident or cultural deficiency cuts the reader off from the intertext, he is nonetheless forced to hypothesize that a solution to the problem the text has raised lies hidden somewhere else.

This hypothesis suffices to draw the contours of the intertext; the text has now gained a potential significance. It may be that the text's unity will be well enough preserved by the reader's conviction that the form of the poem is drawing the outline of the missing significance; the mere postulation of such significance may be enough to make the reading an esthetic experience. In such cases the poem works like a religious or initiatory ritual: it keeps its hold on the believer only so long as its meaning remains partly veiled.

Yet there is one piece of verbal machinery whose presence insures contact between text and intertext. It is some word that functions as a sign not just because it is referential, not just because it points to a thing, for instance, but because it tells us a double reading is possible, or indeed necessary. This piece of machinery is what ancient rhetoric called a syllepsis—a word that is used once, within one context, yet carries two competing meanings. This traditional definition I now rephrase as follows: a syllepsis is a word understood simultaneously in its contextual and intertextual sense, a word understood at one and the same time as meaning and significance. Normally the intertextual sense is wholly incompatible with the contextual, but in such cases the text's ungrammaticali-

ties—all derived from the intertextual sense—are instantly inter-
pretable in the light of that sense. For the syllepsis provides a model
for an interpretation, since the syllepsis is an example, guaranteed
by linguistic usage, of context and intertext with a point in common, the one phonetic or graphemic shape shared by two acceptations. If the verbal sequence is so loose-knit that the reader is
momentarily at a loss to decide which of the two acceptations fits
the context here and now—that is, if we are faced with undecidability—this undecidability is resolved by a derivation from the
syllepsis that presents a sequence of formal features confirming the
impossibility of interpreting by any means save recognition that
the two texts here are interdependent.

My example is the sixth stanza of Ponge's "Prose de Profundis
à la gloire de Claudel."[4] The title does not fail to raise questions,
and these I shall revert to later, but at least it does refer to a traditional literary genre of praise. Stanza six is uncomfortably close
to something nonpoetic, comparative literary criticism. Its style is
that of satire. Certainly Claudel was the greatest living French poet
when Ponge grudgingly joined in the chorus of his admirers to
salute a form of art for which he had little natural sympathy. The
higher to extol Claudel, he compares him with two other practitioners of the prose poem, Péguy and Saint-John Perse, whom he
crushes in the process. There is nothing here that looks like *rational*
literary criticism. Argument is replaced by a pun on Claudel's
name; out of this Ponge extracts a judgment on his poetic manner,
then proceeds to demolish the other two writers. One is put down
because he writes differently from Claudel; this critique might
make some sense if the premise made any. The other victim is laid
low by a pun on *his* name, which yields the antithesis of the pun
on Claudel's.

Ponge starts out with the statement that Claudel's manner is
broad and heavy. This evaluation is impressionistic, but no more
so than many other critics' obiter dicta. It is also accurate (which
does no harm) as applied to Claudel's characteristic rhythms. But
Ponge's remark is not just a piece of criticism, it is also poetic in
being, overdetermined as form and sense by a single matrix: "une
largeur lourde fait claudiquer" ("being broad and heavy tends to
make you limp"). The verb *claudiquer* is at the crossroads of two

associative chains: a metaphorical one derived from rhythm (you can say a verse limps); and a paronomastic chain generating claudication out of Claudel. Then Ponge disposes of Péguy, a poet famed for his repetitive style: "claudiquer, ai-je dit, non piétiner" ("the idea is to hobble along, not to mark time"). Next he turns upon Saint-John Perse, another towering figure, people say, but in Ponge's opinion something lesser:

> Qu'il nous suffise de l'opposer [Claudel] à l'une de ces grandeurs seulement: celle qui lui doit tout.
> Et qui entra dans la carrière avant que son aîné n'y soit plus.
> Elle s'y nourrit de poussière, sans trace de ses vertus.
> Oui, à cette autruche des sables:
> "Le plus gros des oiseaux connus," dit Littré, "et à cause de sa grandeur incapable de voler."
> Oui!
> Et qui s'enfuit dès lors à grandes enjambées dans l'Orient désert, celui de l'Anabase, ne nous laissant plus voir qu'un cul de poule.
> Oui, Oui! Léger, léger plutôt deux fois qu'une.
> Nous en ramasserons quelques plumes.

> (Suffice it to compare Claudel with only one of these eminences [literally, greatnesses]: the one who owes him everything.
> The one who entered the profession [literally, career] before his elder had left it.
> The one who feeds on dust there, showing no trace of his elder's virtues.
> Yes indeed! Let us compare Claudel and this ostrich of the sands.
> Littré [the French Webster, of course] says: "The ostrich is the largest of all known birds. Its size prevents it from flying."
> Yes indeed.
> And a bird that thereupon dashes off in long strides across the Oriental desert, the desert of Anabasis, and all we see of it is a chicken's behind.
> Yes indeed, indeed. A lightweight light in more senses than one.
> We'll be picking up some of the feathers lost on the way.)

The reader is prompt to understand that "carrière" alludes to what for the French is *the* career, the Foreign Service. Saint-John Perse was in fact an ambassador, as Claudel had been before him. Just as easily the reader grasps that a poet of not very high-soaring inspiration may be aptly called an ostrich. This most unkindest cut neatly slices a writer who wrote, among others, a long poem, *Exil*, crammed with deserts, camels, etc. There is nothing startling in the removal of the ostrich from its native Africa to the Near East, the setting of the original *Anabasis*: the Middle East is Saint-John Perse's favorite landscape, and it is also an allusion to the Xenophon story from which he lifted the name of his best-known collection of poems. As for the repeated "light," "light-footed," "light-headed," they transform into a satiric arrow Saint-John Perse's real family name, *Saintléger–Léger*, in an exact counterpart of the wordplay *Claudel–claudication*.

All these images remain nonetheless ill matched. There is a jarring discontinuity between metaphor and metaphor, an apparent gratuitousness suggesting that the sole creative principle at work here is the critic's animus: the end justifies pretty nearly any stylistic means. Literary satire has, to be sure, a tradition of truculent, gleefully shameless bad faith. But what about contradictions like lampooning the victim as a lightweight while comparing him to a bird too heavy to fly? Above all, what about the parody of the French national anthem—a blatant device, utterly uncalled for? As the reader must have noticed, verses 2 and 3 invert the sense of a stanza from the *Marseillaise* word for word:

> Nous entrerons dans la carrière
> Quand nos aînés n'y seront plus!
> Nous y trouverons leur poussière
> Et la trace de leurs vertus.

(We will enter the career when our elders are there no longer. There we shall find their dust [or: ashes—they are dead—dust unto dust] and the footprints of their virtues.)

But lo and behold! it is at this very point of maximum blatancy that a veritable verbal scandal comes into play as our signpost to the right interpretation and to a recognition of a coherence among the images that has thus far escaped us. The signpost is the parody (one of the most visible variants of obligatory intertextuality); or rather, the fact that the parody brings to light that "carrière" is a syllepsis. At first sight the parody is mere caricature: the "carrière" of the anthem is reduced to overseas tours of duty; "poussière" is bureaucratic dry rot, not a fallen hero's ashes; and so forth. But at the same time the parody forces us to ressuscitate the conventional poetic meaning the word *carrière* has in the *Marseillaise* intertext: career as the metaphorical competing ground, the athletic field, the race track for symbolic chariots. The reader is thus shown what the straggling images have in common, the matrix of the metaphors' true relatedness. The elevated sporting style goes well with the image of the swiftest bird, with the hasty retreat of the Greek mercenaries (as described in Xenophon's *Anabasis*), with the otherwise disconcerting final detail of the lost feathers. Most important, *carrière* as race track fits "légéreté," fits the lightness of the "lightfoot lad," of the fleet-footed hero, as well as it does the not-weighty-enough man of letters. Thus we have a fanciful sketch of Saint-John Perse that does not so much give the real artist's likeness as actualize, in three descriptive periphrases, the reversed image, the mirror image of Claudel's claudification. Saint-John Perse is stigmatized through complementary antonymy: he is light and quick. In almost any other context, these epithets would naturally be taken as laudatory—which demonstrates again how mechanical and arbitrary, yet how efficacious this device really is.

The proper functioning of the device and our perception of the unity hidden up till now depend entirely upon our seeing the images as opposites to the name *Claudel*, as the reverse of a textual obverse. This textual obverse is still only a potentiality, but it will be actualized in the ensuing stanzas through the agency of an image of Claudel as a lumbering tortoise. The Saint-John Perse code is significant only in its reversing of the Claudel code.

The parody of the French anthem has two functions. At the mimetic level it makes for humor, it is a means of satire. At the semiotic level it restores to *carrière* its archaic meaning (a race course), and this second meaning enables the word to work as a syllepsis. Only the *Marseillaise* intertext can remind the reader of a usage that disappeared along with the forgotten conventions of classical literary language. Without the quotation the key to significance would be lost together with the archaic meaning.

Of course Ponge's poem runs no risk of obsolescence so long as French children continue to memorize the national anthem. If the impossible ever came to pass, if the anthem ceased to be a patriotic ritual, the text would still be legible, but it would lose its literariness.

We may well ask what it is that makes the whole of "Prose de Profundis" a poem, since I have perhaps arbitrarily limited myself to one of its sections or prose stanzas. One will recall that I laid down a preliminary condition: if formal features are to be pertinent to a definition of the poem, they must all be connected to one significance, and despite their individual differences, they must all appear as variants of the same invariant. My answer is that everything in this text about Claudel is derived from his name; that the text might be prose if it merely were about him, but that it is poetry because form and content together are like one continuous variation on the name of the subject—a variation in the musical sense of the word. The entire text together, indeed, moves from the naming of the subject. Each of the fourteen stanzas is nothing more than a mimetic rationalization of words, or single sentences, that are phonetically relatable to the syllables of Claudel's name.

The process starts, appropriately, with the title—"Prose de Profundis à la gloire de Claudel." If we put the poem's topic in our own flat, matter-of-fact terms, it would run "prose sur Claudel" (prose piece on Claudel). Attach to this minimal statement its first literary handle and you get "a prose celebration of Claudel" (were we not limited to prose, we might have "A Claudel Hymn," or "Ode to Claudel"). Now the syllepsis pistol is cocked, for *prose* in French may mean prose as opposed to verse, but it also designates a special kind of Roman Catholic hymn—not an unlikely association within a context of solemn celebration, and celebration of Claudel, who fanatically identified with fundamentalist popery. Ask a native French speaker for an instant illustration of *prose* in its sacred music sense, and his answer will be, "la prose des morts" (a hymn sung for the dead). *Prose* in its contextual acceptation refers to the prose poem, to the prose form of an ode; but in its intertextual meaning *prose* leads straight to the familiar Psalm 180 in the Office of the Dead, *De profundis ad te clamavi*. This intertext now warrants and redeems the ungrammaticality of the title, where the word *prose* can generate the phrase *de profundis* no longer merely because of a farfetched paronomasia, but because of the availability, in the

syllepsis, of appropriateness at two levels. The supplicant's posture in the psalm ("Out of the depths have I cried unto Thee")
informs that of Ponge singing the ironic praises of Claudel, his
lofty object of (parodic) veneration. Even better, Claudel's own
name, the source of the whole poem, sounds like an echo of the
verb in the psalm's first sentence, "I cried unto Thee." That it is
indeed the starting point, the generator of the whole text, is further
demonstrated by a change of tense in the verb. *Clamavi* in the psalm
is a past tense, but for Ponge's purposes the intertext has a text in
its future; hence the first stanza of the prose poem puts the Latin
quotation in the future, *clamabo*. The very act of speaking, of saying,
of reciting—the gist of the poetic praise—is as it were contained
in embryo within the name of the object praised. Everything anomalous in the text, at least as compared with ordinary usage, refers
to this perfect tautology: where the literary genre, the poem ac-
tualizing it, and the subject of both, all three are encapsulated
within the name.

Whether intertextuality is involved directly, or indirectly
through syllepsis, the matrix of the double derivation, textual and
intertextual, lies within the text. Obviously, Mallarmé, Claudel,
Saint-John Perse, and *La Marseillaise* predate the poems Ponge
builds on them. Likewise, the prosodic structures must exist before
they are actualized in the meter of a verse poem. The similarity,
however, ends here, for in versified poems, the prosodic model is
a convention. It is arbitrary and/or a legacy of tradition. In the prose
poem, on the contrary, the selection of an intertext as a formal
model in lieu of meter is never arbitrary. It is motivated twice, first
by a plausible semic or formal similarity between poem and model,
second, by the fact that the intertext is already an established verbal
monument, a poem or a fragment of it. Years ago Cleanth Brooks
stated as an "article of faith" that "in a successful work, form and
content cannot be separated."[5] The prose poem, where only content dictates the form, comes closest to realizing this ideal.

Notes

1. See my *Semiotics of Poetry*, (Bloomington: Indiana University Press, 1978),
especially pp. 1–22 and 116–38; and "Syllepsis," *Critical Inquiry* (1980), 6:625–38.

This paper is the revised version of an article on Francis Ponge that appeared originally in French in *Études françaises* (1981), 17:73–85.

2. This definition excludes *context* in its looser sense of nonverbal environment—the societal or historical circumstances out of which a work of art emerges, or these same circumstances as referred to by the work of art itself.

3. Francis Ponge, *Proêmes*, in *Tome Premier* (Paris: Gallimard, 1965), pp. 167–68.

4. Francis Ponge, *Le Grand Recueil*, vol. 1: *Lyres* (Paris: Gallimard, 1961), pp. 27–33.

5. Cleanth Brooks, *Kenyon Review*, (1951) 13:72.

PART III Practice

8. A Poetry–Prose Cross

ROBERT GREER COHN

Contemporary literary theory is apt to be too clever:[1] having discovered, for example, the really not very surprising truism that all origins (or cores) are constructs, it becomes thereby intoxicated and "hung up," and rather humorless about the matter. Actually, origins are no more constructs than anything else, or hardly so, and we need them, topologically or typologically, to say anything in an orderly, however hypothetical, fashion. This is the way Rousseau proceeded with his brilliantly intuitive *Origines de l'inégalité*, and even Derrida (in *De la grammatologie*) could sympathize with the procedure, finding it fundamentally wavering and dialectical, like his own trace-presence. Long before him, Mallarmé had carried on in this unduped and undaunted way. Let's try it on the prose poem.

In *Modes of Art* I describe varying basic phenomena as they emerge from an epistemological matrix which I call "polypolar." The binary paradox which is characteristic of other matrixes (such as Plato's *chora*, Mallarmé's *fiction*, Derrida's already mentioned dialectic), when examined critically, doubles on itself into a cross form which can be called "paradox of paradox," "paradox squared," and, as I prefer, "tetrapolarity" (or "quadripolarity"; more complex forms give "polypolarity"). I'll not go over the historical development of this old idea and its modern avatars in Kierkegaard's "absolute paradox" (in *Philosophic Fragments*) and Mallarmé's "symphonic equation proper to the seasons," etc. Rather, let us move on to see how the prose poem arises from it.

First,[2] a "wholeness"—the "poetic" itself in a rich, vibrant sense of the word (recalling the etymological meanings of "making" and "vision" in it)—splits or dissociates (T. S. Eliot's term) into poetic and prosaic branches, giving the main genres of lyric poetry and novel, with epic poetry and drama and, eventually, any ambitious poem or prose masterpiece hovering in between. This process is better seen as a tetrapolar Becoming: a "founding" poetry–prose unity passes through a poetry *and* prose polarity to a poetry–prose (poetic prose or prose poem) "final" unity. This Becoming operates at short range as a constant systole-diastole, in a dialectic internal to each work and indeed each fragment of a work. It also functions over vast cycles of entire cultures: a clear example of the final unity I have in mind is found in the apocalyptic masterpieces of Mallarmé, Proust, and Joyce. Mallarmé was very conscious of the phenomenon, for example in the preface to the *Coup de dés* or related essays in *Divagations*; the prose poem is largely a nineteenth and twentieth century development in this historical view.

Now in a *static* view of tetrapolarity, as opposed to the evolutionary one described above, the basic binary paradox is mutated into a quadripolar one in which all the poles are interchangeable; hence vertical and horizontal axes are paradoxically (interchangeably) related too.

As reality itself does, we can put different entities in the positions of the various poles (including the zero–infinite core, as a third, fifth, etc., entity) and the various axes (or "dimensions"— here we limit ourselves to two). For example, *up* can be superiority, joy, or *Verstiegenheit*, vertigo "wanting down"; *down* may be defeat or basis, "sweet and low"; *front* is advanced or exposed (*future* is promise or "who knows?"; *right* is correct or smug); *back* is outworn or solid (*past* is dead or glorious; *left* is sinister or creative, *felix*); *vertical* can be holistic, visionary, metaphoric, adventurous as well as pretentious, prideful, dangerous, immature, mad; *horizontal* can be serene, mature, rivery-flowing, or tendentious, fragmented, incoherent, metonymic, boring, etc; *center* can be It or a void.

Fortunately for our sanity there are prevailing patterns in existence. For example, it is common (as in graphs) to see space as vertical, time as horizontal. Revolt (or high consciousness, in Camus' use), virility (Icarian), steep vision, poetry, the daemonic and romantic are usually seen as vertical; sleep (recumbency), horizon, maternal or feminine calm, the classic, the normative, etc., are horizontal. But, once again, recalling the underlying paradox of the axes, we shouldn't be too surprised to see classic as dynamite, vision as occult dreariness, maternal calm as suffocation, and so on. Somehow we keep our bearings: in ordinary endeavor by following the herd, in other circumstances by trusting to the more mysterious orientation which guides the creator . . .

This epistemological approach I am proposing can take us through the organic complexities of the modern prose poem in an illuminating way. Assuming that things were slightly neater than they ever are, we can talk about a tradition of poetry and one of prose stretching into the later eighteenth century in France. In the poetic tradition we have approximately Villon-the Pléiade-the baroque poets-La Fontaine-Parny-Chaulieu, etc. Belonging to the prose tradition we have Montaigne-Pascal-La Bruyère-Montesquieu-Voltaire. Although I am well aware that syntheses occurred all along the lines, as I noted earlier—for example, there is plenty of journalistic prose in Villon, dark poetry in Pascal, gay in La Bruyère—as well as all sorts of dealings with other arts and streams of existence, nevertheless, for my purposes, I can say that Jean-Jacques Rousseau represents a notable *cross*, or fusion, of the genres which was to characterize a long and fertile era, roughly the "modern" age, which with fair plausibility (e.g., by Babbitt) has been said to start with him. I am thinking, of course, of famous passages of the *Confessions*, such as the "Nuit à la belle étoile" or the "Idylle des cerises," or of the *Rêveries*, the Île St. Pierre rhapsody . . . These things are well known, as is the fact that Bernardin de St. Pierre, Fénelon, Ballanche, Guérin and many another must not be left out of the picture. But my aim here is theoretical, not historical, and so I'll simply take the potential proliferation of figures and texts for granted and move on to the person who is felt to be an originator of the prose poem form rather more specifically than Rousseau: Aloysius Bertrand, with his *Gaspard de la nuit* (1842). If we look at Bertrand's masterwork through the cross-hair optic of a vertical (poetic) axis fusing with a horizontal (prose) axis, and then try to see what he puts into these polar or axial positions, how they interrelate, and what his successors do in this respect, we'll have a fair chance of detecting an orderly procession of modes.

In his preface, Bertrand refers to the two dimensions as follows:

L'art a toujours deux faces antithétiques, médaille dont, par exemple, un côté accuserait la ressemblance de Paul Rembrandt et le revers celle de Jacques Callot.—Rembrandt est le philosophe à barbe blanche qui s'encolimaçonne en son réduit, qui absorbe sa pensée dans la méditation et dans la prière, qui ferme ses yeux pour se recueillir, qui s'entretient avec des esprits de beauté, de science, de sagesse et d'amour et qui se consume à pénétrer les mystérieux symboles de la nature.—Callot, au contraire, est le lansquenet fanfaron et grivois qui se pavane sur la place, qui fait du bruit dans la taverne, qui caresse les filles de bohémiens, qui ne jure que par sa rapière et par son escopette, et qui n'a d'autre inquiétude que de cirer sa moustache.—Or, l'auteur de ce livre a toujours envisagé l'art sous cette double personnification . . .

(Art has always two antithetical faces, a medal where one side, for example, would resemble Paul Rembrandt and the other side, Jacques Callot.—Rembrandt is the philosopher with a white beard who holes himself up, absorbing himself in meditation and prayer, closing his eyes to better withdraw into himself, holding conversations with spirits of beauty, science, wisdom, and love, and burning himself out in order to penetrate the mysterious symbols of nature.—Callot, on the contrary, is the braggart and salty footsoldier, strutting about the square, rowdy in the tavern and caressing the daughters of the bohemians, swearing only by his rapier and his blunderbuss, whose greatest concern is to wax his moustache.—Now the author of this book has always considered art under this double personification . . .)

Rembrandt is obviously the poetic, vertical axis here, concentrated, transcendent; Callot goes "sur la place" (the flat *a*'s have some bearing), and whatever (limited) action occurs in the prose poem generally moves in this direction: out into the city street, amidst the bustle in the square, the everyday, the commonplace, vulgar, mean, pushy, and sexy, the active and kinetic (in an ordinary way, not a transcendent one: fragmentary or metonymic-*désirant*), the prosaic and narrative, didactic, etc. But remember that the horizontal can become infinite or fluid and transcend in that way; this kind of "vibrancy" between the dimensions, i.e. the tendency to change places or at least waver in direction, will occur in Bertrand.

At times in this wavering atmosphere the dimensions seem to fuse, at times combine in juxtaposition. Impressionist art will evolve in this same pattern, incorporating a new realism as well as a new, vibrant relation between (vertical, subjective) figure and (horizontal, objective) ground; good metaphors and examples of this process are Pissarro's gentle, slope-shouldered peasants, who seem continuous with the landscape, with nature, "porous to the universe" (all is harmonized by texture and light).

Wiser than some of us, at the end of his preface Bertrand refuses to put "some lovely theory about literature," noting that "Polichinelle hides from the curious crowd the conducting thread of his arm." Mallarmé would say later that he had learned from Poe not to show his armature. I favor the image of wires under the carpet, or plumbing in the basement (which I consider *Modes of Art* to be—or else an attic). But our era is nothing if not *impudique*.

Bertrand illustrates an archetypal form of the prose poem, which tends to relate its vertical and horizontal axes in a static, square or rounded, frame, like a picture, a stained-glass window, or just a window (all featuring an epiphanous moment). It is not, I think, fortuitous that his references in the preface are visual; or that the first poem in the collection, "Harlem," opens with a post-card view of a city evoked in the specific terms of its rich tradition of painters; and that the piece should end with the words "à la fenêtre un faisan mort." The window, whether in Baudelaire's great "Les Fenêtres"[3] or Mallarmé's "Frisson d'hiver," will maintain a privileged position in the lineage.[4]

The prose poem seems fated to a *croisée* (casement window) effect, partly by its shape on the page, which reflects the poetic brevity and density (vertically) combined with the horizontal lines of the narrative—despite their being broken up, they suggest the single line which could keep on going through a lengthy narration—and is kept limited this way. To a certain extent the symmetry dictates the shape, and we may say that a prose poem tends toward a balance between its horizontal and vertical elements. When, for example, Baudelaire's more garrulous pieces in the *Spleen de Paris* run on for a couple of pages, one is obscurely aware of a violation of the rules of the game (but there is such a thing as an elongated, or French, window . . .).

"Harlem" is a pretty picture from the past, like all of Bertrand's vignettes; it evokes a scene of bourgeois *aisance* in the lowlands tradition of Breughel, Teniers, de Hooch, and Vermeer. One thinks of those middle-class worthies, their sideboards heaped with game and peeled lemons, with a familiar nostalgia for a bygone equilibrium, akin to Rousseau's dreams of village life. (There may be a certain appropriateness in the fact that the tradition of de Hooch and Vermeer favored square-balanced shapes such as checkerboard tiles or, more approximately, brick facades.) And indeed Bertrand's tone is colored by this backward-looking romantic gaze, as in the Germanic sentimental tradition of Biedermeyer poetic realism, *Hermann and Dorothea*, Gottfried Keller.

We may think ahead to Baudelaire's prose poem "Invitation au voyage," which clearly harks back to this comfortably furnished tradition, perhaps in part through Bertrand. Nothing much disturbs this *arrivé* phase of history, at least not in *Harlem*, which sets the tone for Bertrand's whole collection. Here the horizontal represents the effectiveness of the patient, hard-working, pragmatic bourgeois, religious but not too religious, and rather commercial and phlegmatic in the Dutch manner. Whatever transcendence they display is reasonable, not overly ambitious, cleaving always to the middle line, decorous and decorative like the pictures or carvings which are created for their well-being.

In all such works which seek to recapture a vanished harmony, the aspect of memory—which moves along a serpentine time line—becomes clear if we think of Baudelaire's mood as he evokes the lost paradise of childhood's sheltered calm, perhaps on a balcony (what is more *middle* class, *between* earth and sky, both indoors and out? there is one in *Harlem*) or in a home he once shared with his mother. Glories of mid-nineteenth-century art (prolonged in Proust, happily)! The added horizontal of the prose poem is only a part of this luxurious development, but an organic one, I submit.[5]

A subtler point, essential to understand, is that in the most interesting cases the horizontal does not (only) tame the vertical, as in Spitzer's "klassiche Dämpfung"—though it partially does so, in some of the imagery and other effects it generates—but, rather, dialectically *raises* it through a higher tension to a fuller fused (or combined) presence. To repeat a formula based on Yeats, "we make poetry of our quarrels with ourselves, rhetoric of our quarrels with others," and we make our finest art of the quarrels, and reconciliations, of these two cardinal directions of the human spirit.

The city is, or was, a mother—Dublin his mother ("doublin his mumper"), as Joyce sighed in exile—and it is seen in an almost evening light in the serenity (which can be very intense underneath) of maternal calm. In Bertrand, of course, as in Baudelaire and his successors, this mood comprises the essence of the extensive city.

No doubt there is anguish lurking somewhere; the pain of work leads to the moment of repose, the relaxed sitting of the "insouciant bourgemestre" as if in the cool of the evening which is the bourgeois' reward after a hard day. People generally are seated around casually, but there are ample touches of a working society, a commercial culture. At any rate this is a healthy civilization moving in time with a town clock, earning its keep, and there is little evidence of irony, of "deconstruction" on the part of the artist who works along with and for the burghers. Even Baudelaire maintained a bit of this spirit, in his *Salon de 1846*, where he hailed the bourgeois of his time at least temporarily.[6] Behind this phenomenon is the mood to which Robert Frost ascribed all of his poetry which wasn't dictated by lovesickness or homesickness (they overlap).

Et le canal où l'eau bleue tremble, et l'église où le vitrage d'or flamboie, et le stoël [balcon de pierre] où sèche le linge au soleil, et les toits, verts de houblon;
   Et les cigognes qui battent des ailes autour de l'horloge de la ville, tendant le col du haut des airs et recevant dans leur bec les gouttes de pluie;
   Et l'insouciant bourgemestre qui caresse de la main son menton double, et l'amoureux qui maigrit, l'oeil attaché à une tulipe;
   Et la bohémienne . . .
   Et les buveurs qui fument . . .[7]

(And the canal where the blue water trembles, and the church where
the golden panes leap flame, and the stone balcony where the laundry is
drying in the sun, and the roofs, green with hops;
     And the storks flapping their wings about the village clock, stretching
their neck from airy heights and receiving raindrops in their beak;
     And the nonchalant burgermeister caressing his double chin with his
hand, and the lover growing thinner, his eye attached to one tulip;
     And the bohemian girl . . .
     And the drinkers smoking . . .)

     That "Et" is a heaping up of good things, like the game and
fruit on the sideboards in the paintings. The conjunction obviates
verbs, hence increases the effect of a static view, a "window."
There is a hint also of a biblical transcendence. Each "Et" sums up
the two dimensions in a small way, especially since it is lined up
graphically with the others.
     The second piece in the collection, "Le Maçon," is another
panorama of the city, this time from on high: "Il voit . . . Il voit"
("He sees . . . He sees") is the anaphoric vertical linkage here,
equally static in effect. The poem ends with a cross: "Et le soir,
quand la nef harmonieuse de la cathédrale s'endormit couchée les
bras en croix . . ." ("And in the evenings, when the harmonious
nave of the cathedral fell asleep, its arms crossed . . ."). We note
again an evening calm over the city, the calm of perspective in
space and time. But a slight switch in tone occurs in the remainder
of the sentence: "il aperçut de l'échelle, à l'horizon, un village
incendié par des gens de guerre, qui flamboyait comme un comète
dans l'azur" ("he saw from the ladder, on the horizon, a village
set afire by warring people, flaming like a comet"). The bourgeois-
relaxing "soir," the "croix," and the "horizon" give the tranquillity
of an added horizontal element; the "incendié" stirs up the excitement of a vertical, but from a safe distance—*suave mari magno*—
and a certain equanimity is maintained.
     The foregoing samples give a fair idea of the tone of the whole
collection; some pieces add sprightlier touches, of quarreling rabbis, quaint types, magic, the occult, and otherwordly visitations,
but always a certain humorous distance is preserved, as in the very
title *Gaspard de la nuit*, an affectionate term equivalent to Old Nick.

The sense of a vignette, of a framed picture, of control in an attractive, even yearned-for past culture is maintained. It is against
this rather simple equilibrium of the axes that we will be able to
measure future practitioners of the genre, seeing how they handle
their chiasmus, their warps and woofs, their kite-frames . . .

This balance can pass into bigger forms too, for example Fromentin's *Dominique*, which is like a blown-up prose poem. The
sociability and the ambition of the hero are almost exactly equal in
force, and he is remarkable for his solidity (*carrure*) in this sense.
Country and city, man and woman, all else is notably evenly
paired. Fromentin's interest in art (*Maîtres d'autrefois*) is comparable
to Bertrand's or Baudelaire's. *À la recherche* is a much more global
blowup of the same double principle. (It can be called the masterpiece of "symbolist realism." Is it poetry, as Mauriac preferred,
or prose?) And Proust's adoration of Vermeer is not at all inciden-
tal, viewed in relation to what has just been said about the art of
the low countries.

Baudelaire's preface to the *Spleen de Paris* (1861) pays homage
to Bertrand and says he got the idea from him to "apply to the
description of modern life, or rather of *a* modern and more abstract
life, the process he had applied to the painting of former life, so
strangely picturesque." Then comes the famous passage about a
poetic prose, "musicale sans rhythme et sans rime, assez souple et
assez heurtée pour s'adapter aux mouvements lyriques de l'âme,
aux ondulations de la rêverie, aux soubresauts de la conscience
. . ." ("musical without rhyme or rhythm, supple and jerky
enough to adapt to the lyric movements of the soul, to the undulations of reverie, to the somersaults of conscience . . .")

Evidently, the prose base is the horizontal here, and the
"mouvements lyriques" spring up (and down) in the vertical direction, the poetic one. The "ondulations de la rêverie" do too,
but in milder, more "feminine" waves, as does "souple." The
"soubresauts de la conscience" likewise leap up but in a generally
visionary movement which includes ideas as well as poetry. "Heurtée" is the most interesting, because challenging, entity here: it
belongs, no doubt, to the horizontal, fragmented direction, break-

ing up poetic flights as do humor and reason (cf. Bergson's *Rire*). One thinks of the dryness of Corbière, Laforgue, the imagists, T. E. Hulme, Pound, etc., which renews poetry in this "prosaic," dialectical way. Walter Benjamin wrote a brilliant, though rather poorly organized and unnecessarily difficult essay on the machine age's effect on a previously wholesome, poetic aura, preserved in ritual and art, which is broken up by jerky mechanical motions (as in Chaplin's funny *Modern Times*), fleeting human relations (as in "À une passante"), etc.; throughout he lays heavy stress on the term *heurtée*.[8]

Baudelaire goes on to say that "c'est surtout de la fréquentation des villes énormes, c'est du croisement de leurs innombrables rapports que naît cet idéal obsédant" ("it is especially in the familiarity with large towns, from the crossing of their innumerable relations that this obsessive ideal is born"). Here we have the horizontal *place* of the neat little Dutch city extended mightily. In Baudelaire there is a bigger tension between the two dimensions than in Bertrand; he is unquestionably a more concentrated (prose) poet. Note that I am speaking of a *qualitative* tension primarily, an inner matter, not the quantitative blowup of, say, *Dominique* (though the latter has some of both these features, as compared to *Gaspard de la nuit*). The *croisement* indicates the spontaneous existence of at least potential vision—poetic and/or ideational—*within* the prose dimension of the city (recalling that the frame shapes always incorporated an *Aufhebung*, a crystallization into an incipient network, transforming a base, a prose reality, into something else). We have here an advance hint of what is going to happen in the collection: the vertical and the horizontal, in Baudelaire, *interpenetrate powerfully* (though delicately), for the huge tension between them makes for a remarkable attraction over a wide gap. We may say that they tremble on the brink of changing places, as always occurs in lively mating, crossing, or multiplication. This is what T. S. Eliot had in mind when he said that Baudelaire elevated the "sordid metropolis" to "poetry of the *first intensity*" ("Baudelaire," in *Collected Essays*). The *Tableaux parisiens*, such as "Le Cygne," are miraculous in this sense, and are often compared to the prose poems—for example by Philippe Soupault—as high points of Baudelairian art. In "Le Cygne," the city is so obsessively inside the poet, in a tension between past and present, it and him, that it *crystallizes* and becomes like "rocks" in his pregnant-creative belly-womb. In the best of the prose poems, such as "Les Veuves," this epiphany occurs too. On certain days, almost Zen in mood, the ordinary "takes off" in a manner reminiscent of Beckett's "automatic symbolism" (*Proust*), or Kafka's "true miracles are in the street" (as Camus notes in *The Myth of Sisyphus*). This poetic realism also approaches the mood of camp and pop art, [9] but those later manifestations are short on the poetry side and represent a decadence of the development; they are, accordingly, deficient in terms of overall tension, overall art. Yet they do illustrate how daringly far one can go in this new course. Camus's descriptions of Oran and its boring stone lions, its dirty trams and store windows, and similar passages of *La Nausée* are more effective steps in this direction, contemporary to us. And Huysmans' metallic flowers in *À Rebours* belong strangely in this picture (-frame) as plastic flowers might in modern camp. But I cannot follow all these leads, not yet, in any event. I have my hands wonderfully full with Baudelaire, starting with "Les Fenêtres."

Here the axis of *la place* is occupied by something characteristic of both Bertrand and Baudelaire: a plunging view of the city "par delà les vagues de toits." As did his predecessor's, Baudelaire's glance reaches an Other, so that between the two poles of a dimension there is the plenitude of *exchange* going on between the dimensions: "Et je me couche, fier d'avoir vécu et souffert dans d'autres que moi-même." To get out of the self is to have really lived, supreme paradox. This polar vibrancy overlaps, is paradoxically the same as, the dimensional vibrancy: the self is easily, for Baudelaire, seen as a dimension, vertical; the Other is the ground for this erect figure (dandy), this Individual; the Other is a beginning of a crowd, as in "Les Foules," that which you go out to from your individual center, in a sort of "prostitution." But in both texts it is a "sainte prostitution"; and, to repeat, in these liveliest of Baudelairian works such ironies are rife: life here is global, a rounded crystal, complete. (Note that a window can be a *bay* window, cf. Mallarmé's "carreaux bombés par les rêves" and my forthcoming observation on the "thickened" pane.)

In Bertrand the backward look often encountered *extreme* others, eccentric, "outsider" types, such as bearded rabbis quarreling in their synagogue. In Baudelaire, even more, an understandable dialectic, compensating for his "sulking" isolation, flies out to an extreme object of compassion, of "charity."[10] At times it can be wizened old ladies, bent-over *vieillards*, homeless dogs. In "Les Fenêtres" it is an aging, lonely woman who never goes out;[11] he compares her to a "pauvre vieux homme."[12]

This elongated axis across the city, flatter and more obsessively realistic than Bertrand's yet poignant, profoundly touching, rich in the feel and pulse of experience, is the essence of the *Spleen de Paris*, e.g., "Les Désespoirs de la vieille," "Les Veuves," and "Les Bons Chiens," with its "Muse familière, citadine!" At the same time, the vertical axis is also stronger in Baudelaire: "Il n'est pas d'objet plus profond, plus mystérieux, plus fécond, plus ténébreux, plus éblouissant qu'une fenêtre éclairée d'une chandelle" ("There is no object deeper, more mysterious, more fecund, more shadowy, more dazzling than a candle-lit window"). Here is the daemonic depth of your true modern poet with his *frisson nouveau*, the dialectic of *fleurs–mal*, the pain of distance (barrier: window) versus love (light: candle).

I have noted various ways the dimensions interpenetrate; Baudelaire makes a specific tie in "dans ce trou noir ou lumineux vit la vie, rêve la vie, souffre la vie" ("in this black or luminous hole life lives, dreams, suffers"). The flatness is in the lengthy "vie" and its repetition; the transcendence arises from "rêve" (mildly), and particularly the intense "vit" ("la vie")[13]—compare "Ivre, il vit" in Mallarmé's poem "Les Fenêtres," which antedates Baudelaire's—the feverish "souffre," or the concentrated "trou noir ou lumineux." The tension which sets up the vibrancy in this *croisée*, and *chassé-croisé*, grows daringly and masterfully.

"Les Foules" is very much in this line: "être lui-même et autre" is the main cross, "poésie et charité" ("to be himself and another, poetry and charity"). Baudelaire, patently under the spell of Poe's crackling "Man of the Crowd," vaunts his brand of emotion, contrasting it with mediocre compassions or loves: "Ce que les hommes nomment amour est bien petit, bien restreint et bien faible, comparé à cette ineffable orgie, à cette sainte prostitution de l'âme qui se donne toute entière, poésie et charité, à l'inconnu qui passe" ("What men call love is quite small, restricted and weak, compared to that ineffable orgy, that sacred prostitution of the soul which gives itself completely, poetry and charity, to the unknown person passing by"). He prizes the supreme tension of poles and dimensions which almost crucifies him—"les mille amours qui m'ont crucifié," as Rimbaud cries in one of *his* bursts of poetic prose—until, like the character in Kafka's *Penal Colony* under such duress, he *glows*. On good days when he could take It, Baudelaire went farther in both directions of the spirit, up and sideways, until It relented and he gave gladsome birth to these masterpieces.

The old artist of "Le Vieux Saltimbanque" is another such extreme Other, but also linked to Baudelaire more directly: Baudelaire sees his future self in him, and the shock of recognition—a wide gap followed by an identification—is intense. And it is all part of the vast *croisement* of the city: the self–Other line, parallel to the past-self–future-self line and overlapping it; it thus collapses into the vertical figure of self-involvement, and the whole is alive with such cross-purposes, like a *carrefour* in the fateful park. This domain has been explored fecundly in Mauron's study of the prose poems;[14] though his psychological approach lacks the openness of an epistemological view, it roughly illuminates.[15]

In "L' Étranger" the Other is a "stranger" in the same sense, strongly resembling Baudelaire (and Claude Debussy). Baudelaire looks *over* at him as they both look *up*, meeting in the target, "far out" as intersubjectivity. The cross is sufficiently in that; but here we are perhaps closer to Bertrand's shallower estheticism than to the "Muse citadine."

"Un Plaisant," the Other in this figure, incorporates the modern city on a holiday binge, and even reaches out to encompass "la France"; but he is a "magnifique imbécile," in the wake of Flaubert's hated-savored bourgeois, exuding the ambivalence of the *hénaurme* (or the *Garçon*, cf. the absurd, Ubu, and the like). As in Beckett, Nabokov, and even pop art, the very flat, dreary, boring, imbecillic can "take off" into a vertical "magnifique." Baudelaire's mood, leaning a bit toward the vindictive rather than the fully ambivalent, points to something quite modern . . .

"Le Fou et la Vénus" features a character close to the "vieux saltimbanque" in sympathetic pathos. The equivalent of *la place* is a most Parisian "vaste parc" (with flat *a*'s appropriately); the glance plunges across the space to a poor eccentric looking up to a monumental Venus, Oedipally gigantic and as indifferent as Baudelaire's "Géante" or "Beauté." Like the clouds of "L'Étranger," the shared ideal is too remote, perhaps, for warm reciprocities with other poles and directions of reality; so to that extent the poem is less alive.

In "La Chambre double" the city condenses into the poet's room and its threshold. An artist's room, it undergoes the extreme polarization (like polarized lenses) of pleasure–pain, daemonically same–different like his sado-masochism, mania-depression, starkly circular like the swirl of the Tao. This is the steep dimension (and whole). But the city's horizontal comes to Baudelaire as grinding time and an Other, "un huissier qui vient me torturer au nom de la loi" ("a bailiff who comes to torture me in the name of the law"); he sums up the hell of Others generally as "la Vie, l'insupportable, l'implacable Vie!" The old figure we saw elsewhere is now a Father Time, "le Temps . . . hideux vieillard." Although Baudelaire blames the outside world for changing his room into horror, actually it is a mitigating diversion; on better days it enters into fertile reciprocal relations. Here the mood is too manic, one-sided, for that; but even so, along that steep route, what glorious art! As in calculus, one dimension can be reduced to a near-zero point and pour itself (*verser*, as the French technically say) into the other, giving it all its psychic energy. At such moments, balance, genre, theories be damned: if it is great poetry, who cares? We note that *tantôt* the old are the object of Baudelaire's extreme charity, *tantôt* they prefigure his death-in-time and frighten him, as here. At other instants he is ambivalent, shakily fascinated, as in "Les Sept Vieillards." But these cases generally overlap.

The dog of "Le Chien et le flacon" could be a distant Other, an object of sympathy like the dirty, mangy, but free "bons chiens" of another piece, but it, too, illustrates the mutability of poles in our epistemological purview: this dog bothers the poet like the petty *huissier* and other city types who come to bug him and who on another day might elicit his fellow-feeling.

In the same way, Baudelaire turns against the "mauvais vitrier"—"le pauvre homme"—as he moves into his perverse vertical à la Poe ("The Imp of the Perverse"). The axis of the city is suggested—he is "the first person I saw in the street"—but the vertical obliterates it—"I let my war engine fall perpendicular"— and it smashes his "poor walking fortune." The idea of intersection is very specifically present in these terms, especially "perpendiculairement," but again, as in "La Chambre double," an individual concern takes most of the life out of the rest of reality, smashing it (*its* window-pane is only "bad"). There certainly is a meeting of the dimensions, but it is too negative for characteristic prose poetry.

There are a number of pieces in the collection which are marginal to the genre for similar reasons ("Le Confiteor de l'artiste," "À une heure du matin"); even "Un hémisphère dans une chevelure" or "L'Invitation au voyage," though gorgeous, are too private to resonate with the beauty-and-humanity we see as the main line of *Spleen de Paris*. The horizontal axis becomes voyaging or exotic nature, and these do not really resist the poet the way the city does, or people of his own culture. They are too soft and feminine for that and besides consist mostly of fantasy or mere memories of real travels. The Other as person is passive, probably recumbent, just a listener or receiver of caresses.

In the city poems the tension, as I said, is two-dimensional or tetrapolar (and, more complexly, polypolar). This is the structure, as I define it in chapter 3 of *Modes of Art*, which gives off expression at a peak of "excruciating" tension from its core; Baudelaire's *frisson* is parallel to all such wave-movement phenomena of expression as they move into fallen time, e.g., a line of writing on a page, or sound waves. One may imagine a crystal as the static polypolar network (including cross) emitting such sound waves, and one recalls the crystallization of art, as in the organic image of the window ("cristal par le monstre insulté," Mallarmé's phrase in his "Les Fenêtres"). When a poem is tight, dense, tense, and lively enough it gives off a thickened texture you can almost feel and taste, evokes something like a shiver. It rises under the leavening of inspiration, like a brew of malt ale leavened by yeast, or a good peasant soup— both are useful metaphors here, being staid and exciting at the same time. They rise from the page, as MacLeish would say, almost spill off it; and stirring is very much part of the process in all these contexts. In crystal formation one sees the whirling in films made of those kaleidoscopically twisting, spiralling axes; Mallarmé's *tourbillon*, prime symbol of art, reflects distantly the awesome spirals of the galaxies, of worlds in formation ("un compte total en formation"), or the swirls of mitosis. *It* is stirred and crystallizes, then from the crystalline structure of the words on the page a "shivering" expression emerges and *we* are stirred.[16] And our psyches are restructured, crystallizing a new view of the world.

All this happens in (spiraling) stages, as is usual in organic phenomena: since writing is linear as well as approximative of the lost circle in its spiraling references back and forward, up and down (compare Lacan's "insistence" as opposed to Saussure's theories), we move on gradually from provisional *paliers* of crystallization to a hypothetical total and final crystallization, the window of the poem.[17] And each stage has its accompanying levels of release as expressive and moving psychic rhythms, including *frissons nouveaux*.Parallel processes are at work in visual art, not only in series of versions or sketches, which often shift around a core (like Matisse's many variations on the *Girl in the Peasant Blouse*), but more evidently in the archetypal swirls, vortices, and whirlwind forms in Renoir, Monet, Redon, Rodin, Münch, Van Gogh, Wyndham Lewis.

Under the dialectic of vertical (holistic, metaphorical, etc.) and horizontal (fragmented, metonymic, etc.) lies the elemental, eternal circle-and-line, the metaphysical Eve-and-Adam pair. Their mating is often visible as a spiral—as in our stirring, our *tourbillon*—and this is what Baudelaire's metaphysical prose poem, "Le Thyrse," is about. It is the epistemological source and a concrete–abstract poetic–prosaic crown of the collection, at least from a theoretical point of view.

Looking back over the types which emerge from this matrix, one concludes that the poems which center in the artist, although naturally ambivalent, can have a positive or negative accent in relation to the dimension of the real, the Other. For example, "Perte d'auréole" emphasizes the negative aspect of the vertical, "Le Confitéor de l'artiste," complex as it is, comes down finally on the positive side for the poet. The same ambivalence characterizes the horizontal: "Les Foules" gives it a hearty plus, "Un Plaisant" a

disgusted minus. A full typology must start from these four positions of the axial relations, with variations according to the ac-
centing of the different poles (self–Other, past–future, here–there,
indoors–outdoors, up–down, etc.). Then, according to the amount
of "stirring" and "crystallization" present—looking at each work
either microcosmically, in terms of its quintessential zero-infinite
core, or (a paradoxically related aspect) in terms of the macrocosmic
totality of it—one can say whether it is very alive or flaccid, and
whether its "brewed" tone is characterized by fusion or is more
heurté, i.e., involves a degree of juxtaposition (as in tachism or
pointillism), rather than a blending, jagged as it may be (as in the
grotesque and stark contrast, of the baroque).

   This tonality has largely to do with the dosage of the dimensions, or of their underlying qualities, metaphoric and metonymic,
etc. The different dosages give variations of what we can think of
as total rhythm or texture. (Tone, which is traditionally a matter
of brightness or color, can be extended to include this corollary
matter; perhaps Stimmung would be an appropriate term, too). The
precise texture is often a very subtle affair to determine, just as it
is not always easy to say whether a poem finally emerges with an
accent on the light or dark side, or, in the more evidently in-be-
tween cases, to ascertain the degree of its (juxtaposed) chiaroscuro
or (blended) greyness.[18] Nonetheless these final accents do exist,
just as major and minor modes or differing keys exist in music,
and it is quite possible and good fun to pin them down with reasonable conviction. To illustrate: "Enivrez-vous" is bright in tone,
as is "L'Invitation au voyage" (with a Vermeer light); "La Corde"
is dark, "Le Gâteau" darker; "La Chambre double" is patently in
between, chiaroscuro; "Les Veuves" and "Les Bons Chiens" are
characterized more by a blended greyness, yet with an important
reservation which takes us to the heart of our present dimensional
concern in the matter of texture—"Les Veuves" has a strong heurté
quality, with a really lively prose-poem texture like a homespun
weave, burlap, or monk's cloth, whereas in the splendid pieces
such as "L'Invitation au voyage," both light in tone and smooth,
the blend is more legato, fused. For the heurté texture to occur,
there must be gaps, strong resistances, not only between positive
and negative, unidimensionally (fleurs and mal), but also between

poetry and prose, polydimensionally. Over these gaps, like the flickering caressing flame of a *réverbère*, which was Mallarmé's prime symbol for Baudelaire in his "Tombeau" sonnet, up and down, straight and sideways, words and ideas wrestle and become reconciled, sparkle with true life.

As I have shown, the vibrancy of impressionism, which is very much in the light and air of this period, the chiaroscuro of Rembrandt, which was very much on Baudelaire's mind—*vide* "Les Phares"—and that of his predecessor Bertrand, the grotesque and stark contrasts of the baroque, which overlap it (see "À une Madone"), are among the many possibilities for rhythm (texture, *Stimmung*) which Baudelaire exploits. The *Confiteor* comes close to impressionism in its mingling of harmony and taste of acid, *heurté* vibrancy. "La Femme sauvage" is closer to the grotesque, as is "Un Plaisant" and "Une Mort héroïque" "L'Invitation au voyage" is more akin to Vermeer, as I have said, than to Rembrandt (or Van Gogh) in its serene blending of the vertical (the poet's soul and dream) and the horizontal (the voyage; the low country bourgeois "furnished" atmosphere surrounding the Other/lover; realism); the evening light is as settled and gentle as in Bertrand's end-of-day evocation of Dutch cities. The melting of the extreme poles ("aller vivre . . . aller mourir") is equally serene and liquid, made so largely by the *r*'s (cf. the coalescing *"or"* and *"moire"* of "La Chevelure," the fusing of light and water).[19]

The preceding argument assumes that there is a unity of tone, an artistic integrity in the considered works. This too is a varying matter. Baudelaire, of course, believed in it as fervently as his master Poe or his coeval Flaubert. But he wasn't always at his best. Each work can be evaluated in terms both of its unevenness or failed aspect, as well as of its integrated dialectic tensions. Generally, Baudelaire performs at or near a peak and we can more or less forget the problem of integrity, having taken this dutiful theoretical account of its existence. But lingeringly we note that a poem can be very lively—dialectically advanced and ripe in that sense—and imperfect (or blemished, caved in). "Les Veuves" illustrates, *nec plus ultra*, all my points about the genre at its apogee.

The full ambivalence of the horizontal, and of the vertical, and of their relation, is the armature of "Une Mort héroïque." The despotic Prince has the cold, flat quality of objective reason as opposed to the daemonic, steep, ambivalent artistic love-death of the clown Fancioulle. In fact he reminds one of the dimension of lucid reason in Poe's *Philosophy of Composition, detective* reason murderously tracking down a murderous beauty ("it takes one to know one") with the ruthless analytic (root: *lysos,* destruction) penetration of a detective story (a genre Poe practically invented), hounding the beloved, criminal alter ego in self and life.[20] Thus the Prince, like a Nero (*qualis artifex pereo*), is also said to be artistic, at least potentially. The ironies are manifest and manifold. As Mauron rightly observed, the Prince is another dimension of Baudelaire (but then what in a good artist isn't also he?). What he missed is the fantastic reversibility, which is duplicated in similar terms in Baudelaire's "De l'essence du rire": "le personnage de Giglio Favio, le comédien atteint de dualisme chronique . . . il se déclare l'ennemi du prince assyrien . . . et quand il est prince assyrien, il déverse le plus profond et le plus royal mépris sur son rival . . . Favia" ("the character of Giglio Favio, the actor afflicted with chronic dualism . . . he declares himself the enemy of the Assyrian prince . . . and when he is the Assyrian prince, he pours out the deepest and most royal scorn on his rival . . . Favia"). (Fancioulle too conspires against his Prince.) Rimbaud's "Conte" prolongs this intimate *chassé-croisé* in self–other.

But the crystallization of all these elements in "Une Mort héroïque" is rather loose, spun out over a certain narrative extent. A distinct tone, very much in the self-controlled, cool, tight-lipped Poe and Conan Doyle tradition is emerging prominently here, and is a key aspect of modernity. As in the best of the tradition, this vertiginously stirred and stirring brew curdles, and curdles the blood, in a disciplined way.

The *frisson* here is one of Baudelaire's many. In "Chant d'automne" (a poem), the negative–positive tension released as a wave movement stems from winter cold encountering, in the poet's frightened soul, disappearing summer warmth; and a delightful shiver marks the triumph of life over death (warmth over cold, inwardly) and, expressing itself, enters in its fallen, temporally strung-out rhythm the healthy ongoing dimension of élan vital.[21] The *frisson* is a tight and intimate lyric shiver,[22] closely analogous to the one which characterizes the twilight moment of "Crépuscule du soir" (prose poem and poem) or "Crépuscule du matin" (poem), masterpieces all. In the last-mentioned work, "l'air est plein du frisson des choses qui s'enfuient." Mallarmé's equally intimate, special moment in "Don du poème," at cold–warm bright–dark indoor–outdoor dawn, is expressed by the word *frémi* (the window is there too).

I could go on, voluptuously, but this sampling gives the seminal trend, and something of the range, of Baudelaire's prose poems. I am swiftly running out of allotted space, and I want to get on to Mallarmé for a lick and a promise at least (mindful of, and grateful to, Ursula Franklin's fine book[23]).

In Mallarmé the paradoxical tension (and its crystallizations and expressive releases) goes farther than in Baudelaire. Mallarmé is known (though not often by comtemporary critics) for extreme opposites that meet, as in Pascal (the spirits of geometry and finesse). He stands archetypally for the principle of separation of "l'état brut de la parole" (a kind of base popular "coinage") and poetic language, well before Jean Cohen's simplistic *écart* gimmick and Barthes's equivalent gimmicks (but Barthes at least admits that "all we do is repeat Mallarmé");[24] and yet Mallarmé is the one who maintains staunchly that poetry and prose are in one continuum, in the "Enquête de Jules Huret!" Mallarmé is wide open, and he is equally closed, wild and meaningful, universal and specific. His poems, resolving all these facets, are vertiginous and *frémissants* (as if recalling the "vertige" and "frissonne" of "Autre Éventail," caught between a father's love and his *pudeur*, the elite emotion frantically spinning on itself and beating out immortal and ecstatically blood-curdling rhythms on the pure page). The dizziness and the shiver are their temporally strung-out expression; the static aspect of it is the crystallization, as in "Les Fenêtres."[25] Each work is specific, individual, a microcosmic completion, a homunculus which can *speak* to us (as in "Surgi de la croupe et du bond"), and yet all are part of the *Jeu suprême*, the one all-embracing Work, "l'ensemble des relations entre tout," of which the *Coup de dés* was a sketch. These master paradoxes are at the core of our classic moderns such as Proust, who, like his partial mentor, saw each artist as a separate universe (e.g., Vinteuil), yet viewed all great works as part of One Great Work (in "Contre Sainte-Beuve").

With Mallarmé, the tension—tetrapolar or polypolar—leading to (static) crystallization and (dynamic) shiver-rhythm and expression-in-time, such as writing, sound waves, and all the psychic analogies,[26] predominates so utterly that his works, including the prose poems, are notably concise. The narrative aspect of the horizontal dimension tends to be foreshortened accordingly. Still, for example in "La Pipe," the personal autobiographical narrative, combined with a perspective of travel in the background plus the broad city of London, is ample enough to provide excellent resistance to the poetic stance. The prose poem tone, in that respect, is quite ideal. And the shiver that arose from Baudelaire's encounter of "sulking" self and reality, poet and city, is marvellously alive here. The *frisson* is also, overlappingly, a product of the shock of warm and cold, indoors and out, intimacy and the fog-bound expanse of London (represented closely by *la place*, the public *square*). The crystallization is like the one that occurs in Baudelaire's "Le Cygne," arising from a tension of past and present, loss and love (which will become Proust's epiphanous memories).[27] It is the nostalgic resurrection, catalyzed by the puff on the pipe, of an anxious moment in Mallarmé's life when Marie, his fiancée, was teetering in and out of it, waving goodbye from a steamer crossing the Channel, in an atmosphere of savory uncertainty and perhaps peril: the tobacco aroma, "bitter and delicious as life," (Apollinaire) is linked to, and catalyzes the resurrection of, this hovering *reality* that is gradually crystallizing. It all comes back, solidly, like the block of ice which stands for a poet's past in "Le Vierge, le vivace"—polypolar dream space ("le transparent glacier des vols qui n'ont pas fui" ["the transparent glacier of the flights that have not fled"])[28]—or Baudelaire's "rocks," palpably like the Japanese paper flower which was Combray rising, another *Ys*, from the cup of linden tea, with its houses, gardens, all.

In "Frisson d'hiver," the shiver is similar. The Other is Marie who came from far away in Germany, while outdoors there is wintry alienation and cold. The crystal, which is the static mate of the shiver, is once more present in a window, a "croisée"—a term thrice repeated (plus, once, "vitres"). The "toile d'araignée" quivering in the window frame is, as we know from Mallarmé's correspondance, a closely related syntactic essence.[29]

To be sure, the window is a major image throughout Mallarmé's verse poetry, but this overlap is hardly surprising in Mallarmé, for whom the two realms, prose and poetry, were in a continuum, theoretically. "Les Fenêtres" (Mallarmé's verse poem) is very static, centered in a solitary sick man's hospital room. It is, to use the jargon, "narcissistically" self-involved. In "Frisson d'hiver" there is a couple: they look at, or out of, the window together, and a going out, or coming from other lands, is narratively sketched or suggested.

In "Le Démon de l'analogie," the "vitrine," which is the window to the main event, is part of a street scene; the crystallization which is the essence of the "story" (as a shiver was, consciously, that of the preceding one)—telling how a psychic structure, solid as a block, builds up through universal analogy, starting from a haunting germ of wordage—occurs in an ambulatory city setting. There is a notable shiver here too, both taking place during the account and emerging from its final structure, a blood-curdling mystery with Poe-like (a comparison of the title with "The Imp of the Perverse" is suggestive) detective tones in the deliberate account that builds up a dimensional tension with the private *hantise* until we start shivering with (releasing the tension of) anticipation. As in crystal formation, the tense poles and dimensions whirl on each other, "go round and round," as in the American expression for an incipient fight: two poles that don't give in, that start to *tourbillonner*, lead to vertigo, just as piston movement leads to wheel movement (cf. the dizzying jump–don't jump sollicitations from a high place or in front of a train). This stirring forms the crystalline new reality and meanwhile (as well as in the final *frisson*) stirs our blood, which curdles, starts to rise, and thickens into high presence. The crystal, which I have called the static aspect of all this being that is pinned on the page and which is, in its symmetric shape, a *frozen* crystal, a window, can be seen as this thickened solid: the block can be imagined as having to do with a certain thickness of the panes. Since they can mirror, etc., Mallarmé associated them with ice, *glace–glace*, cf. *verre–hiver*.[30]

The minstrel child of "Pauvre Enfant Pâle" is entirely of the streets, as much as Baudelaire's "bons chiens"; yet he is fascinatingly close to Mallarmé, linked with his other sacrificial figures, including the decapitated St. John. The cross here, in a complex

sense, is very alive, very *frissonnant* . . . This child imagines he is
going to lose his head because of a crime. His melodic complaint
goes high, high, too high perhaps for a bourgeois society to tol-
erate. There is a strong hint of social malaise here, as elsewhere
in Mallarmé, especially when he is thinking of his own underpri-
vileged son, Anatole: the smallness of this self-masking alter ego
works up indignation, like the defeated human wisp in the cosmic
water of "À la nue." But the political note is too kinetic, too tendentious to interest the poet for long: no Sartrean *engagement* for
him, despite *Tel Quel*. Out there among the mass of ordinary folk,
including the bourgeois who were an extension of his family,
amidst the "Foule (où inclus le génie)," perhaps at the Sunday
concert "listening to its own grandeur" underneath, is a sea of
sacrificial heads, all to be annihilated some day. The urchin is not
only of the streets, he is of life; and life is rounded, rich in ironies,
reversibilities, and mobile truth to Mallarmé, who believed, as
much as Proust, in real life "la vraie vie." Mallarmé sympathizes
with the child, but he is mainly Other; he, the poet, classes himself
with those for whom the criminal will pay as a scapegoat: "tu
paieras pour moi, pour ceux qui valent moins que moi" ("you will
pay for me, for those who are worth less than me"). There is more
than a touch of ambivalent guilt here. He seems to be thinking: I
am a bourgeois too, and we are exploiting your Billy Budd naivety
as you die for society in need of a safety valve. The *chassé-croisé* is
indeed complex in this vignette. As so often, Mallarmé is inexhaustible.

The window is present here too, suggested in the words *volets*
and *rideaux*; the poet hears the child through an open window,
just as St. John's eerie hymn comes through a window in the fragments of the *Noces d'Hérodiade*. The tension of self–Other, indoors–
out, poet–city occurs on this threshold of art, and in a sense it
weaves the expression's syntactic shape, though here the window
is only a ghostly hint.

"Plainte d'automne" evokes memories of the dead sister,
hence the deepest ambivalence of selfhood as well, all mingled
with the street sound of the "orgue de Barbarie"—heard through
a "fenêtre"—which creates an excruciating combination of banality
and poignancy. The flat *a*'s are particularly effective here: *Barbarie*

. . . suranné banal . . . ballade romantique; the time-horizontal of "sur-anné"—overlapping the theme of decadence—parallels the street platitude, almost pop art or Brecht–Weil campy in tone.

"Réminiscence" is an encounter with the Other, who, like Baudelaire's "vieux saltimbanque," is a version of the self: "le futur et que je serais ainsi" ("the future and that I would be so"). But the scene is definitely excursive, a wandering abroad into the world and the real, with the wonderfully everyday quality of the cheese sandwich which "takes off" into lyric and indeed cosmic streams of analogy.[28] The "out there," the real, is both horizontal, ordinary reality in the form of cheese sandwiches, and yet it is circus magic too, vertical and miraculous like Kafka's streets. The Other he comes upon is in one way flatter than the narrator, less sacrificial; he has parents, and the narrator is the orphan. But the boy Other is an incipient performer, perhaps a high-wire artist . . . Once more we are in a space that allows for reversibilities in all directions.

In "Un Spectacle interrompu," on a banal stage—its frame replacing the window—a bear rises to cosmic proportions in an anxious moment. Again, it and the poet are brothers under the skin. We can situate them at two poles, up and down on an evolutionary scale, or positive and negative in that sense. The play on the two *dimensions* is made very explicit in the important formula "artifice que la réalité, bon à fixer l'intellect moyen entre les mirages d'un fait" ("reality is artifice, good for settling the average intellect between the mirages of, an occurrence"). As much as to say that art and reality are brothers under the skin too: all is *fiction*, "parfait terme compréhensif" as Mallarmé called it. Which is what my polypolar epistemology, echoing his jottings (especially those dramatic crosses and the like in *Le Livre*) is largely about.

Something similar happens in the vulgar carnival tent of "La Déclaration foraine": an ordinary (amateur) woman-performer becomes "infinite," vertical as the stunning statue of "Le Phénomène futur." The cross-play and cross-purposes between the poet and/or his anima and the crowd are featured resonantly in one of his most compelling demonstrations of sheer mastery of language combined with cosmic syntax, "l'ensemble des relations entre tout."

From the quintessential empty egg of a zero-non-event at the core of our cross in "Le Nénuphar blanc," an absent, imaginary ecstatic woman arises, intersecting a real day ("la nature existe") with a rather boring rowing expedition up a drowsy and resistant summer river: an *excursion*. This network-trellis blooms with some of Mallarmé's most enticing flowers of expression, seen as a static, constellar—or crystal—simultaneity; more movingly, they are blown along melodiously, thrilling us, as if caught in a Botticelli storm of petals. One thinks too of Monet.

"La Gloire" opens with the perspective of a cityscape being fled by train, versus tall autumnal trees in the forest of Fontainebleau, symbolizing modest self-glorification beyond the market of ideas, in anonymous nature, as just a man in the world, that being tremendous enough. In a way, the multiplicity of the forest is the dimension of the Other, and Mallarmé implies that being a man among other creations, or a man among men, is true glory (cf. "Conflit" and "Confrontation"). In this poem cross is an understood intersubjectivity between the hero-poet and the genius-including crowd—the distant city—recalling the anonymous ritual in which he and audience would be at one (*Le Livre*). The play, the *Jeu suprême*, is very active here and resonates with Mallarmé's deepest theorizings, which, as Barthes remarked, "all we do is repeat."

In Mallarmé, the prose poem is a microcosm of everything. No wonder then that Huysmans in *À Rebours* saw it, with specific reference to Mallarmé, as the elite form summing up and climaxing a dying civilization—and leading, by a natural extension, to a Work in which all would be "supreme Game," concise constellar arrangement of words, without clutter or waste motion, words which by their multiple permutations and reciprocal relations as foretold in "Crise de Vers," would say it all. The *Coup de dés* is not far off. In his preface to it, Mallarmé sees this piece as participating in a number of convergent tendencies of his time, including music, the prose poem, and "notre recherche" (his ambitious epistemology). So it can be said to be a sort of blown up, complicated, and to say the least ambitious prose poem. He called it a "Poem," but that, in his view and that of our culture generally, can be almost anything (I noted its total matrix impact in my opening remarks). The two dimensions I have featured in my discussion are put to work directly in his revolutionary use of type on the page.

We could easily press on to look at Rimbaud and others, but it is time to stop for this one modest venture. My aim was to provide some sense of direction through the genre, or of "What goes on here?" as Bellow might say. I end with the feeling that these things, rather commonplace after all, were really known by everyone, well, practically everyone, before I started, at least instinctively if not in conscious, articulable fashion. And that is good in a way; it's a cross we all bear . . .

Notes

1. A prime example: in his *Univers imaginaire de Mallarmé* (Paris: Seuil, 1961), Jean-Pierre Richard justifies thematically rearranging Mallarmé's *oeuvre*—pulverizing the poems, etc., and putting them in a new synthetic order—by claiming that Mallarmé does so in a lecture on Villiers, or operates on nature that way. This argument is disingenuous: it is obvious that a more responsible critical approach would respect both the *integrity* of individual works (their specific forms, sequences) and the intertextual connections in a sort of ambitious spiral (each theme, the chronology, evolutionary aspects, etc.). That spiral would minimize the damage and approximate Mallarmé's true universe. Richard's world is largely an artificial construct, *his* world, as Genette notes. However dazzling, it is also partly *faux-brillant*. What I am doing in this essay is quite different: I am not aiming at criticism proper but *precriticism* (in the sense of critical theory).

2. The following paragraph is adapted from my *Modes of Art* (Saratoga, California: Anma Libri, 1975), p. 118.

3. Note that Mallarmé's poem "Les Fenêtres" preceded it by a year or so.

4. The illustrator who put a stained-glass window on the cover of my edition (Montreal: Parizeau, 1945) of *Gaspard de la nuit* was right on target.

5. How the different phases of an archetypal horizontal movement work up in a spiral through humanity, civilization, bourgeois spirit, feminine influence, etc., to this specific nineteenth-century phase I endeavor to show in *The Writer's Way in France* (Philadelphia: University of Pennsylvania Press, 1960). Volume 2 of *A Critical Work*, in preparation, will go this same route. Realism generally raised modern art dialectically, as with impressionism.

6. Later, Baudelaire moved to a truer position, one between, and provisionally above, both bourgeoisie and minor artists of his time ("a plague on both your

houses"). Sartre, who worshiped Vermeer's bricks (in "Tintoretto"), occasionally owned to being bourgeois.

7. All quotes from Baudelaire are taken from *Oeuvres complètes* (Paris: Bibliothèque de la Pléiade, 1976).

8. Benjamin extends this "divide and rule" (my term) device to general mental functions such as memory, citing Freud, Bergson, etc., but not controlling the flow, or articulation, of his argument very well. His confusion is largely ascribable to his extreme nostalgia for a past "aura" his Marxism is killing.

9. See my "From Poetic Realism to Pop Art," *Modes of Art*, ch. 10.

10. This element is constant in Baudelaire, cf. "de la vaporisation et de la condensation du moi. Tout est là" from the *Journaux intimes*, or his favorite quote from Emerson, "the hero is he who is immovably centered" (a powerful half-truth).

11. Cf. Camus's old woman whom nobody wants to stay with in *L'Envers et l'endroit*.

12. Cf. Camus's lonely old man, *ibid*.

13. The *i*'s accentuate the intensity. See *Modes of Art*, ch. 4, for a discussion of phonostylistic effects.

14. Mauron, *Les Derniers Poèmes de Baudelaire* (Paris: Corti, 1966).

15. See Jeffrey Mehlman, "Baudelaire with Freud," in *Diacritics* (Spring 1974), 4(1):7–13. Mehlman detaches himself from his former idol Mauron in this piece, finds a more open model in Lacan, and points out some further ironies in various of the prose poems.

16. For a discussion of this motif, see my *Oeuvre de Mallarmé*, (Paris: 1951), *passim* and especially pp. 241–48; *Modes of Art*, p. 175, *n* 75; and "Mallarmé contre Genette," *Tel Quel* (Spring 1977), no. 69, pp. 51–54.

17. In *Oeuvre de Mallarmé* I show how the static (i.e. constellar) tetrapolarity turns into dynamic wave movement through an archetypal "twist" or shift from circular to linear, as in the shift from crystal to shiver. Thus the final crystallization, echoing the first, can be a window, as often in Mallarmé and other poets, or a constellation (viewed in it and intimately related to it, or seen in the nearby mirror, like a snowflake crystal), as in "Ses purs ongles."

18. See *Modes of Art* ch. 7, "Poetry of Light and Radiant Darkness."

19. Compare Debussy's use of a "drowning" pedal in *Reflets dans l'eau*. Note that dark and light are clearly corollary to positive and negative (and eventually all else) and come out of the same epistemological chain, which emanates from a common matrix, so that critical terms and critical matter are in a paradoxical same–other continuum. See *Modes of Art*, p. 51.

20. A recent study of the detective story observes that the name of Dickens' Inspector Bucket is at just such a crossroads of up and sideways. A bucket is a common object, yet has a certain depth (or well-plumbing depth). As I predicted in 1951, in *L'Oeuvre de Mallarmé*, our era is moving massively into this fuller epistemology. That is the main line of structuralism, as represented by Lacan and Foucault.

21. See *Modes of Art*, ch. 3, "Tone," pp. 65 and 68 in particular.

22. See *Modes of Art*, p. 60.

23. Ursula Franklin, *An Anatomy of Poesis: The Prose Poems of Stéphane Mallarmé* (Chapel Hill: University of North Carolina Press, 1976).

24. In his interview with Stephen Heath, "A Conversation with Roland Barthes," from Stephen Heath et al., eds., *Signs of the Times: Introductory Readings in Textual Semiotics* (Cambridge, England: Instant print, 1970), pp. 41–51.

25. See my article "Mallarmé's Windows," in *Yale French Studies* (1977), 54:23–31.

26. See *Modes of Art*, p. 59.

27. See my "Proust and Mallarmé" in *Yale French Studies*, (1970), 24(3):262–75.

28. See my *Toward the Poems of Mallarmé* (Berkeley: University of California Press 1965), pp. 129–30.

29. *Ibid.*, p. 216 and *passim.*

30. A marvelous example of the solidification of the *frisson* into a three-dimensional block of vibrant, shivery texture is the image of the "bûches qui tombent" ("logs that fall") on the pavement in "Chant d'automne" with a "choc sonore." The whole of that poem is alive with this phenomenon. Note the relatedness in letter-effect (*br*) and substance of the following: *vibre-fibre-timbre-brr*. Mallarmé plays on it considerably, e.g., in "La Musique et les lettres," as does Verlaine: "L'ombre des arbres dans la rivière embrumée" (The shadow of the trees in the mist-covered river").

In "Le Démon de l'analogie," the final "thrilling" shock, as in all such revelations, is the explosive mating of two entities which are carefully kept apart by civilizing bad faith, as in the myth of the *Doppelganger*. Here, as in the sense of déja vu, a past and a present disconcertingly coalesce; compare Proust's staggering experience of past-in-present, or any uncanny prediction. Part of the shock is an unconscious approach to incest, as in the *Doppelganger* myth, a "narcissistic" return to total *self*, real *self* (Nature or Totality); Heideggerian *Geworfenheit*, phenomenology, etc., deal with parallel paradoxical *experiences* of shocking truth. Mallarmé's formula of a terrifying leap of tautological vision to the "total arabesque" of "all Being alike" in "La Musique et les lettres" is a clear expression of this experience. The network of imagery generated by the fertile bad faith of the artistic *career* as revealed in this prose poem is organic, central to Mallarmé's whole poetic universe. (See *Toward the Poems of Mallarmé*, p. 94.)

9. The "Alphabet" of Paul Valéry

JAMES R. LAWLER

*T*hree decades after Valéry's death, *Alphabet* takes a place as a major composition that shows him at a summit of his powers.[1] His great poems in regular verse were behind him when he turned to a genre he had by and large eschewed. The critic of prose, who had contrasted its facile walking to the arabesque of poetry, developed a manner that increased his range, deepened his voice, and permitted an intensity he had not known before. Like Baudelaire and Rimbaud, he came to see the prose poem not as raw material ("poésie brute," "poésie perdue"), nor as a lesser manifestation of the lyric, but as a distinct mode sufficient unto itself and subsequent to formal regularity.

One may guess the reasons for this evolution. The ten years he devoted to *La Jeune Parque* and *Charmes*, to the series of so-called exercises he pursued in personal ways, had left him feeling that a certain creative capital was spent. He needed other resources than those he had handled with singular finesse. But as in 1912 when Gide's urging him to collect his early writings brought about a splendid invigoration, so chance provided the occasion for renewal. A publisher requested twenty-four passages in prose or verse, all beginning with different letters of the alphabet, which they would serve to illustrate: twenty-four, and not twenty-six, since the engraver had excluded *K* and *W*. "Some years ago, I was asked to write twenty-four pieces in prose (or different forms of verse) in which the first word of each was supposed to begin by one of the letters of the alphabet. The engraver had omitted two

163

letters, the most clumsy and moreover the rarest in French, the *K* and the *W*." Such were the conditions of the contract that Valéry accepted and turned to his advantage. For he decided to match his twenty-four pieces to the successive hours of the day so that each would introduce an attitude, treat an activity, expand on a mood, or, as he put it, illuminate "un état et une occupation et une disposition de l'âme différente" ("a state of mind and a pursuit and an individual disposition of the soul").

The point of origin was, then, a bare sequence of letters. This was the formal stipulation that gave the outline of a series without fable. Nevertheless Valéry well knew the Cratylian thesis, in particular from close acquaintance with Mallarmé's *Les Mots anglais*, and we likewise see him using alliteration to generate ideas and imitate actions. Thus, for the letter *C*, "calme," "colorée," "commencement," "crainte," "contemple," "coeur" bring together a palette of dawn, the dominant tones of an aubade evocative of all beginnings. But Valéry's mimetism was customarily less obtrusive, and more often than not he was content to adopt a mere few words from his initial letter (*B* leads to "bouleversant," "bord," and nothing more; *Z* to "zénith" and "zone"), proposing thereby—with no obvious alliteration to carry him—the motif he would expand.

The gamut of themes is not gratuitous, however, but consonant with his notebooks, his poems, his essays. Already the substance is familiar: we are offered the mechanism of self-awareness as it untiringly plies its moments of being and knowing. "Mon amour devant toi est inépuisable. Je me penche sur toi qui es moi . . . Tu m'attends sans me connaître et je te fais défaut pour me désirer." ("My love before you is inexhaustible. I bend over you who are me . . . You wait on me without knowing me and I am absent from you so as to desire myself.") The texts are so many metalepses of previous representations of sleep, waking, waiting, wonderment, loneliness, despair; the extension of the central images of diamond, sun, sea, flame. Once again the poet finds his gods and loses them, declares the marvel of mind, his ability to know yet failure to understand. We are in a Mediterranean setting: the light is strong, the ocean close by; the park abounds in trees and flowers. No events of consequence occur during an indifferent summer day and the twenty-four scenes are without anecdote. What matters is not incidents themselves but their inscape and resonance, for, as Valéry writes elsewhere, "les événements sont l'écume des choses mais c'est la mer qui m'intéresse" ("events are the froth of things but what interests me is the sea"); or, as we read in the grave terms of *Alphabet*, "faut-il interpréter toute chose sensible et réelle comme Joseph et Daniel faisaient les songes des rois?" ("must we interpret each real and sensible thing as Joseph and Daniel interpreted kings' dreams?")

Yet despite the correspondence of themes to those of his better known writings, it becomes evident that self-quotation is part of a wholly new structure that stands at controlled distance from his earlier ones. The author of *Alphabet* is not he who wrote *La Jeune Parque*, since in the meantime he had suffered the fire that the *Cahiers* have shown: he had lived through the drama provoked by his meeting with the poet Catherine Pozzi and the emotion—the spiritual crisis—that informs his work of the twenties. "Un homme avait trouvé un joyau," he writes, "une merveilleuse pierre—et elle fit explosion entre ses mains" ("A man had found a jewel, a marvellous stone—and it exploded in his hands"). Again, "Je croyais que mon univers était l'univers. Mais j'ai vu quelque chose au delà. Et ce devint une cage. ("I thought my universe was the universe. But I saw something beyond. And it became a cage.") Yet again, in words that place his experience alongside the inner revolution of his twenty-second year from which he dated his pursuit of analysis, "J'ai lancé la foudre sur ce que j'étais en '92. Vingt-huit ans après, elle est tombée sur moi—de tes lèvres." ("I threw a bolt at what I was in '92. Twenty-eight years later it fell on me—from your lips.") The history of these years has not been attempted but it must be, for it involves the return of the hypersensitivity he had thought to have banished once and for all. Catherine, whom he named Béatrice, reintroduced values whose obliteration he had resolved so as to ensure impregnable calm: "Ma vie était comme une maison que je connaissais dans ses moindres parties. Et tant je la connaissais que je ne la voyais presque plus . . . et voici qu'une porte secrète s'est ouverte. Je suis entré dans des appartements étranges et infinis"

("My life was like a mansion that I knew in its least parts. And so
well did I know it that I almost saw it no more . . . and now a secret
door has opened. I have entered apartments limitless and strange").

With poignant directness the notebooks of the twenties are totally
at odds with the author who proclaimed himself Caesar of the
sensibility, the word *douleur*—pain, grief, solitude—unlocking the
indeterminate schemes of another poetry.

Valéry did not immediately conclude that the prose poem
suited his ends. He undertook *L'Âme et la danse* and *Eupalinos,*
which treat as never before the erotic foundations of an esthetic
and its harmonies of body and mind; but his Socratic dialogues
had to accommodate constraining disciplines and manners. He also
worked at two long poems in alexandrines—the second and third
sections of "Narcisse" and the conclusion of "Profusion du soir"—
which he had begun in 1898. They reveal, in their late versions, a
frenzied aspiration oblivious of all else, which terminates in the
one case with the nocturnal absorption of the object of desire, in
the other with a gesture of fervent supplication:

> Et toi, de ces hauteurs d'astres ensemencées,
> Accepte, fécondé de mystère et d'ennui,
> Une maternité muette de pensées . . .

(And you, from those heights sown with stars, accept, fertile with
mystery and monotony, a mute motherhood of thoughts . . .)

But he was not content with either piece, deeming the finished
"Narcisse" no more than "fragments" and "Profusion du soir"
an "abandoned" poem. He required both greater depth and concentration, a continuity to espouse the smoothness of thought, an
attendant discontinuity to engage its drama. The prose poem was
seen to be such an answer, conceived as an entity within a network
of compositions of roughly similar length. In contrast to the fatal
voice of *La Jeune Parque* and "Le Cimetière marin" which deduces
the song (*deducere carmen*), unraveling the implications of an initial
rhythm or image or tone, that of the prose poem is by nature undefined, and the alphabet the arbitrary means to a sequence of
moods.

The technical and spiritual heritage now stems not from Mallarmé but from the properly classical tradition: we are far from the wit of *Divagations* as Valéry has recourse to biblical, liturgical, and mythological references and as his language discards measure for visionary appetence. It is this latter element I would wish to emphasize, since never before had he gone so far in isolating a strangeness within thought. The poetry of *Alphabet* gives shape and power to reality of a second order. Although the Parque was aware of darkly mysterious promptings in the coils of her obsessive serpent, she was led back on sure-footed couplets to the enduring presence of the self, "as a sea-anemone is held to its rock." But here the form of the whole, and above all the use of prose, allow a keener sensitivity to disparate perceptions. In several essays posterior to *Alphabet*, Valéry tried to define a "mystique sans Dieu" that postulates no divinity, no consoling response, but an imperious resonance. This was a language that, using ordinary discourse, might pass uninterruptedly from common usage to the extraordinary, from tangible to intangible, from quotidian to essential: "L'ambiguité de cette double fonction [de la parole] a pour conséquence la facilité de passage de l'état normal à l'état privilégié, *le va-et-vient sans effort* entre deux mondes" ("The ambiguousness of that dual function [of discourse] has as a consequence the ease with which transitions are made from a normal state to a privileged one, *the effortless coming and going* between two worlds"). It was the mode of expression that the mystics usurped, their writings combining just such equivocalness of reference with spiritual intensity. Yet one needs to envisage Valéry also—the Valéry of *Alphabet*—as another poet who sought in prose the passionate convergence of normalcy and elevation.

The poems of *Alphabet* are patterned after the Divine Office that consecrates each hour, the first moment that of waking, the last a vigil in the following night. In the shifts of time and sensibility, one sees the potential for multivalence. All is ritualized according to an exact span of time and the secret movements of desire and disarray. Yet the several pieces one by one gauge the force of apprehension which could be realized by this system of poems alone—not sonnet nor elegy nor continuous monologue. One may, in illustration, choose at random *O*, which forms part of the second series of poems, the first group of twelve being devoted to nature, the second to love.

The text may be defined on the twin axes of lyricism and ritual. *O* is stylistically unique, its tone and structure unidentifiable with those of any other piece in *Alphabet*; yet the level of discourse and the character of the theme have a solemnity that only a particular self might formulate. Beginning with an adverb that signals a parenthesis, supposing the linear drama of events after and before, the poem crystallizes an instant of portentous suspense.

OR il y eut pendant quelque temps dans le jardin, et pendant la durée infinie de la vie d'une douleur, il y eut comme un abîme mouvant, allant, errant et s'arrêtant sur la figure ordonnée et odorante de ce jardin. Sur la terre grise et rose, sur les ombres et les lumières, parmi les touffes, entre les arbres et les arbustes des allées, un abîme se déplaçait comme l'ombre d'un nuage. Un esprit l'avait aperçu, les yeux ne le voyant pas. Il y avait comme un abîme entre deux pensées qui étaient presque la même; et des deux côtés de l'abîme une même peine, ou presque la même. Car deux âmes divisées se mouvaient séparément vers leur ressemblance; car chacune se tourmentait à cause de l'éloignement intérieur de son autre même, et se la créait et se la recréait en soi indéfiniment comme supplice, et se la faisait tantôt trop méchante et tantôt trop aimable. Et tantôt trop haïe, et tantôt trop aimée, l'amour inquiet formait et déchirait l'image![1]

(Now there was for some time in the garden, and for the infinite duration of the existence of a grief, there was as it were an abyss moving, proceeding, wandering, and stopping over the ordered sweet-smelling image of this garden. On the pink and grey earth, on the shades and the lights, among the tufts, between the trees and the shrubs along the paths, an abyss was moving like the shadow cast by a cloud. A mind had perceived it, for the eyes saw it not. There was as it were an abyss between two thoughts that were almost the same; and on both sides of the abyss, the same pain, or almost the same. For two divided souls were moving separately toward their likeness; for each was troubled by the inner distance of its other self, and created it for itself and recreated it endlessly within itself like a torture, and made it now too cruel and now too kind. And now too hated; and now too loved, troubled love formed the image, and tore it asunder!)

Valéry had not previously achieved a comparable pathos. His prose is a phonetic complex of homophones, alliteration, and assonance, in particular of one sound—not *o* but nasal *a*—which recurs like the audible image of immobility. However, it is not only this sound but the vocabulary itself that is heard over and over again to the point where it becomes incantation. Such is one typical aspect of Valéry's lyricism in prose: its mode of repetition, its insistency of voice within a continuous paragraph.

Yet this pattern constructs a meaning, precipitates a drama. The poet sees the invisible, discovers a polysemous image where to the eye nothing appears. There is no single sense to define the abyss of expectancy that is sought, feared, detested, and that proposes itself against the mythical background of the Fall—"dans le jardin," "sur la figure ordonnée et odorante de ce jardin." The opening words create the duality of surface and depth, of time and timelessness—"pendant quelque temps," "pendant la durée infinie de la vie d'une douleur"—of locale and legendary locus. The strangeness is an unbodied shade named four times like a numinous apparition, like the vertiginous space separating two lovers. Nevertheless, the second part of the poem takes up once more the same abstract action in changed terms. It seeks to explain ("Car deux âmes divisées . . ."; "car chacune se tourmentait . . ."), but no conclusion emerges other than the tugging to and fro of good and evil, hatred and love alternately victorious, and each at odds with the sensibility. The poem becomes not a balanced structure of nexus and dénouement, but a furious naming coterminous with desirable pain, a shrill development based on phonetic, rhythmic, and semantic doubling.

So, introducing the fantastic yet avoiding narrative, drawing a pathetic vision from its own sensuous substance, *O* maintains with respect to familiar prose its angle of liturgical divergence. If we look now at another page from the same collection we see that it has certain important traits in common with *O* but that, in the way of other pieces in *Alphabet*, it develops an individual style. *H* does not employ the impersonal, but a strongly personal mode, by which the irreparable is declared. A severe design is traced as sound and sense gain the pitch of dramatic monologue.

HÉLAS! au plus haut lieu de sa puissance et de sa gloire, hélas! au point suprême, au séjour le plus élévé, rien n'échappant à la lumière, je heurte à la place de l'astre une tache brûlante ténébreuse; et le haut dieu a pour moi le coeur noir. Absent est le soleil dans toute sa force, invisible est celui que les yeux ne peuvent soutenir. Il se cache dans son éclat, il se retranche dans sa victoire. Au sommet de la nature vivante j'ai trouvé la terreur et la nuit dans le centre de tes feux. Sur mes mains, sur le mur, sur une page pure, une tache vivante s'impose affreusement, une macule sombre et violacée s'attarde, une morsure de pourpre renaît devant moi sur toute chose. Voici que l'essence du visible dévore ce qui se voit. Cette marque m'accuse. Je la fuis; c'est me fuir. Je descends vers les fleurs, aux bosquets, sous les arbres; j'y transporte le mal ardent. Le fantôme du dieu m'affecte en chaque fleur. Je ne laverai plus mes regards du crime d'avoir vécu par eux dans le soleil.

(Alas! at the height of its power and glory, alas! at its topmost point, at its most elevated peak, when nothing can escape light, I strike instead of the sun a dark yet burning spot; and for me the lofty god has a black heart. The sun in all its force is absent, what the eyes cannot bear is invisible. In its brilliance it hides, in its victory it disappears. At the summit of living nature I have found dread and night at the center of your fires. On my hands, on the wall, on a pure page, a living spot puts a terrible mark, a dark violet macula lingers, a purple bite reappears before me on every single thing. Here the essence of the visible devours what it is seen. This mark accuses me. I flee it; which is fleeing myself. I go down toward the flowers, to the woods, beneath the trees; I bring with me the burning pain. The ghost of the god affects me in every flower. I shall never cleanse my eyes of the crime of having lived by them in the sun)

Here affectivity has the first and last word. The initial letter produces the two occurrences of "hélas," "haut lieu" and its variant "haut dieu," "heurte," all in the first sentence; after which, though the same letter does not recur, the tone is established for the poem to amplify. Across phonetic echoes, syntactic inversions, rhythmic regularities, semantic iteration, a close-knit texture achieves the plaintive resonance of a modern Phaedra newly self-aware. Once again the aim is to turn functional prose into the ceremonial, to elaborate a distinctive tone that has the accent of tragedy. A transgression has occurred, a taboo has been violated, and the self chants a solemn lament. This is the fatal insight, the obsessive chimera, of one who presumed to live by light.

In similar fashion to *O*, the text depends on the principle of repetition, the words sustaining each other as a binary structure is composed. The first half urgently affirms the fascination of the sun: "au plus haut point," "au point suprême," "au séjour le plus élevé," "au sommet de la nature vivante"; while the second half, with emphasis no less great, underlines the consciousness of guilt: "tache vivante," "macule sombre et violacée," "morsure de pourpre," "marque," "mal ardent," "crime." The symmetrical parts offer the interplay of identity and contrast, underline the transformation of ordinary discourse, bring to bear the resources by which a timeless actor of myth goes to the extreme point of despair.

We may come now to one of the most unusual poems in *Alphabet*, one that asks for close analysis. Under the letter *F* a text is offered of greater complexity than either of those we have seen. No words could be more direct, yet the vision is unique, as it turns on the wonder of awareness: this is Valéry's high ode to dawn which galvanizes the soul. The joy evoked is that of the union of thought and desire, of spirit and sensibility focused, of consciousness fixed by indeterminacy alone. One thinks of Valéry's own "Les Pas," or perhaps of Mallarmé's "Eventail."

> Vertige! voici que frissonne
> L'espace comme un grand baiser
> Qui, fou de naître pour personne,
> Ne peut jaillir ni s'apaiser.

(Vertigo! space is shivering now, like a vast kiss which, wild to be born for no one, cannot burst forth or grow still.)

No consummation is more fervent than this prelude enunciated on the frontiers of a day still virginal. At its climax the poem discovers an abstract formula, an intuition captured in the full stretch of mind.

FAIS ce que tu voudras, bel Instant: Âme, fais ton office: Est-il espoir plus pur, plus délié de monde, affranchi de moi-même—et toutefois possession plus entière—que je n'en trouve avant le jour, dans un moment premier de proposition et d'unité de mes forces, quand le seul désir de l'esprit, qui en précède toutes les pensées particulières, semble préférer de les surprendre et d'être amour de ce qui aime?

L'âme jouit de sa lumière sans objets. Son silence est le total de sa parole, et la somme de ses pouvoirs compose ce repos. Elle se sent également éloignée de tous les noms et de toutes les formes. Nulle figure encore ne l'altère ni ne la contraint. Le moindre jugement entachera sa perfection.

Par la vertu de mon corps reposé, j'ignore ce qui n'est point *puissance*, et mon attente est un délice qui se suffit: elle suppose, mais elle diffère, tout ce qui peut se concevoir.

Quelle merveille qu'un instant universel s'édifie au moyen d'un homme, et que la vie d'une personne exhale ce peu d'éternel.

N'est-ce point dans un état si détaché que les hommes ont inventé les mots les plus mystérieux et les plus téméraires de leur langage?

Ô moment, diamant du Temps . . . Je ne suis que détails et soins misérables, hors de toi.

Sur le plus haut de l'être; je respire une puissance indéfinissable comme la puissance qui est dans l'air avant l'orage. Je ressens l'imminence . . . Je ne sais ce qui se prépare; mais je sais bien ce qui se fait: *Rendre purement possible ce qui existe; réduire ce qui se voit au purement visible.* Telle est l'oeuvre profonde.

(Do what you will, Fair Moment: Soul, do your duty: Is there hope more pure, more free of the world, more liberated from myself—yet more wholly possessed—than that which I find before daybreak, in a first moment of proposition and union of my strength, when the mind's desire alone, which precedes all individual thoughts, seems to prefer to come unexpectedly upon them and to be the love of that which loves?

The soul enjoys its light without objects. Its silence is the total of its speech, and the sum of its powers composes this repose. It feels itself to be equally removed from each name and form. As yet no figure alters or constrains it. The least judgment will stain its perfection.

By the virtue of my rested body, I am ignorant of that which is not *power*, and my waiting is self-sufficient delight: it supposes, but defers, all that can be conceived.

What a marvel that one universal moment should be constructed by a man, and that one person's life should breathe forth this small eternity.

Is it not in such a detached state that men invented the most mysterious, the most audacious words of their language?

O moment, diamond of Time . . . I am but details and miserable cares, outside you.

On the peak of being, I breathe an indefinable power like the power in the air before the storm. I experience imminence . . . I do not know what is being readied; but I well know what is taking place: *To make existence pure possibility; to reduce the visible to pure visibility.* That is the profound task.)

F elaborates a pattern of supple counterpoint. The first words express the poet's integral yielding to his apprehension: by two imperatives and a long question that merges into an affirmation, the opening paragraph states an encounter with time. The moment is hailed impatiently, the soul will give its all. Here is the fatal conjuncture of world and self, which stand in the mutual vigilance of lover and mistress. An identical tension is taken up and glossed in the second paragraph, where the self is, however, not describing but described. Conscious distance prevails with the use of the third person and, through the sequence of virtual negatives, light reigns without individual objects, speech exists beyond words, rest itself is power; here neither name, nor form, nor change holds sway; no single idea detracts from thought's coherence. Thus the initial élan is overseen and defined by the language of self-qualification.

The second section turns again to personal discourse in order to relate the mind's energy to that of the body. One sentence establishes the balance of exclusion ("j'ignore ce qui n'est point *puissance*") and inclusion ("mon attente est un délice qui se suffit"), of acceptance ("elle suppose") and postponement ("elle diffère"). In general terms the antipoles of calm and alertness, expectancy and resolution, anticipation and deferral designate the responsiveness of the intellect. The next paragraph confirms this by an exclamation, avoiding once more the first person as in paragraph 2, speaking of a man nameless. The pattern again is one of alternation as lyricism stirs universal delight.

The next two paragraphs show the same characteristics, but the movement is reversed. Language becomes aware of itself and of its age-old strangeness that poetry ever renews. Its words are free of selfish ends, as the abstract expression reminds us: they are the way men name their gods. But in the next lines the rule of duality restores the personal vision; before being the discourse of others, the poem is an individual voice which conceives its ideal lucidity: "Ô moment, diamant du Temps . . ." The octosyllabic rhythm, with its apostrophe, elevated tone, alliteration, and assonance, is the genesis and magical seed of the soul's dance, the future poem. The self can only contrast this instant beyond price with the opaqueness of ordinary existence.

The coda brings a resolution that combines the personal and the impersonal. We return to the first person, which intones its joy and twice repeats the word *puissance* from paragraph 3. But if the fruit is not yet visible, the lesson is patent in the manner of an abstraction: the injunction gives a formula for creativity which is the refusal of life restricted to any one life but endless potentiality; the refusal also to define things seen according to convention but with reference to the abundance ever discoverable. Our deep understanding—"l'oeuvre profonde"—is to adhere to the surface, in a constant readiness similar to morning twilight, so that we can be present at the time of creation. The ode thus shows us a flexible art that treats its complex theme with economy. Attention—which Valéry once described as "le refus indéfini d'être quoi que ce soit" ("the indefinite refusal to be anything at all")—is embodied dramatically; image engenders thought, self informs symbol, the particular enriches the universal. The fourfold structure modulates a master pattern that places F amongst the most accomplished shorter works of its author.

Two other short pieces will enlarge our notion of the collection. The first is G, which offers no paragraphing but, like O and H, the unified contour of a mature thought. Nevertheless a ternary progression occurs which denotes a metrics of the mind: first, the declaration, then the confession, then the affirmation both moral and spiritual.

GRACIEUX, gai, noble jour, qui me retires maintenant de mes fatigues, qui me reprends mes regards, qui me consoles mes esprits, tu leur parles, tu changes leurs peines en palmes, car tu les attires vers les jardins, vers des ombres, sur mainte douce terrasse confusément peuplée d'arbres noirs et légers que la lumière immense irrite et fait frémir. Ils palpitent de plaisir. Mes paroles intérieures se taisent, le cèdent aux cris purs des oiseaux. La mer lointaine est une coupe pleine de feu tout auprès de *mon âme*. Je goûte à l'horizon étincelant qui est posé sur ces feuillages, et mes regards sont des lèvres qui ne se peuvent détacher de cette chose pleine éblouissante. Les cieux là-bas, versent *la flamme* sur les flots. La ferveur et la splendeur suspendues entre ciel et mer sont si *intenses* que le bien et le mal, l'horreur de vivre et la joie d'être, brillent et meurent, brillent et meurent, forment le calme et l'éternel.

(Gracious, gay, noble day, you who now take away my tiredness, who relieve my glance, who console my spirits, you speak to them, you change their pain to comfort, for you draw them to the gardens, to shadows, to many a gentle terrace thronged with dark and tenuous trees that the huge light irritates and causes to tremble. They palpitate with pleasure. My inner words grow silent, and yield to the pure call of birds. The distant sea is a fire-filled chalice next to *my soul*. I sip the sparkling horizon which is placed on this leafery, and my eyes are lips that cannot leave this full and dazzling object. Over there the heavens are pouring *flame* on the waves. The fervor and splendor suspended between sky and sea are so *intense* that good and evil, life's horror and joy, shine and die, shine and die, and form calm and eternity.)

Day is transformed into a kind of eternity, voluptuousness into idea. The external scene being without drama, the poet invests it with his own ardor. In the space of six sentences he invokes the godhead of light, surrenders to its consolation, finds fire and water which he would drink endlessly; at last he achieves a peak of acuity. From the initial image an elevation is composed in the classical tradition of the *Élévations sur les mystères*.

It becomes clear from this and earlier readings that the prose poems constantly aspire to the register of prayer. A natural force is treated as if it were divine grace saving, pacifying, comforting: sense interpenetrates intellect as pleasure nourishes awe, which in turn leads to a passion of pleasure. One discarded image from a manuscript of "Le Cimetière marin" is taken up ("C'est une coupe auprès de moi posée, / Toute ma soif y place une rosée . . ." ["It is a chalice set next to me, all my thirst loads it with dew . . ."]), but now the chalice of the sea has the intense unexpectedness that prose allows, the evidence of a vision of the soul—"tout auprès de *mon âme*." One last example in a vastly different mode confirms this properly religious strain of the Valéryan prose poem. *X* is a *contemplatio* in the strict sense of the word, a meditation on the sky. A group of stars forms the cross of the constellation Orion, a jewel, a nexus, an initial unadorned: from time immemorial men have written their imaginings on the stars, but they have also inscribed, in the midst of names that read like an exotic horde, this sign of the fathomless.

X nom du secret, appellation de la chose inconnue, je te vois inscrit dans les cieux. Betelgeuse, Bellatrix, Rigel, Kappa, quatre sommets de l'X écartelé sur cette nuit si pure et populeuse. Au centre de l'immense figure,

Anilam, Alnitak, Mintaka sont les joyaux du noeud qui attache les membres de la lettre imaginaire. Un signe de l'algèbre brille et palpite sur la ceinture de notre monde. Mon front se presse au verre qui me sépare des ténèbres, et le frisson du froid qui règne entre les étoiles me parcourt. X! me suis-je dit, quoi de plus admirable!

Quelle idée plus digne de l'homme que d'avoir dénommé ce qu'il ne sait point? Je puis engager ce que j'ignore dans les constructions de mon esprit, et me faire d'une chose inconnue une pièce de la machine de ma pensée. J'appuie mon front à la vitre glacée; la question du savoir et du non savoir me semble suspendue éternellement devant mon silence, et une sorte d'équilibre stationnaire entre l'homme et l'esprit de l'homme s'établir.

(X name of the secret, designation of the unknown thing, I see you inscribed in the skies. Betelgeuse, Bellatrix, Rigel, Kappa, the four points of the X spread out on this night so pure and populous. At the center of the huge figure, Anilam, Alnitak, Mintaka are the jewels of the knot that ties the members of the imaginary letter. An algebraic sign shines and pulses on the girdle of our world. My brow presses the glass that separates me from the shadows, and the shiver of the cold that reigns among the stars traverses me. X! I have told myself, what is more admirable!

What idea more worthy of man than to have named what he does not know? I can introduce what I am ignorant of into the constructions of my mind, and make an unknown thing into a piece of my thought's machinery. I press my brow to the icy window; the question of knowing and not knowing seems to me eternally held in suspense before my silence, and a kind of stationary balance seems to be established between man and his mind.)

The two paragraphs form a binary development, the first conveying the surprise of the neophyte astronomer, the second the philosopher's speculation. Both parts, however, are infused with an immediacy of awe, sustained by the tension of object and name, man and spirit, knowledge and mystery. Around this division the poem calls in turn to sensation, feeling, intellect, and the temporal and the timeless. Each half qualifies the other, accomplishes the balance. In solemn and varied rhythms X is the lyrical celebration of the figure of consciousness, known yet properly inexhaustible. "Et pendant une éternité"—as Valéry writes in his last published poem—"il ne cessa de connaître et de ne pas comprendre" ("And for an eternity, he did not stop knowing and not comprehending").

It would no doubt be important to look at these texts in detail with a view to gauging their accomplishment in fuller terms; yet from the foregoing remarks we may make some provisional deductions. That Valéry turned to the prose poem when he did is significant. That period of his writing bore the impress of crisis, so that his choice implicitly rejected the poet he had been and gave voice to the need for ritual utterance. He came to discover this language in the apparent transparency of prose. "The essence of prose is to perish," he wrote, "that is, to be 'understood.'" He would snatch it from mortality, work it as densely as a fixed form. He did not, however, opt for the model of Mallarméan wit but for music and liturgy. Having found the measure of "Le Cimetière marin," the clarity of "Narcisse," the closed sphere of "Le Serpent"—the enchanted circle of the creative sensibility—he sought here to construct a visionary drama of awareness.

For the reader the first contact is no doubt relatively casual: each passage offers itself as a continuum not regulated by meter or bound to its matter in the way of a poem; by its nature it is bare. Yet Valéry forged the countervailing techniques that changed the transitive into the intransitive. The primary feature of his art is, as we saw, auditory: phonetic reinforcement is achieved by multiple echoing, symmetries of rhythm, formal compactness. His lexicon is small—"un petit nombre de mots, et aucun d'extraordinaire" ("a small number of words, and not one extraordinary one")—its basis, repetition. Yet the musicality proceeds not only by words and phrases but by complete themes such as the binary structures we saw. Valéry composed in paragraphs whose dense sonority achieves a manner of incantation. Nevertheless, if the richness of poetic voice is clear, we also recognize the literary mode of *Alphabet* with its embodied references to a mythico-religious line—that of Bible and liturgy, of Racine and classical eloquence. Calling on a tradition, Valéry beckons now to one, now to another figure of a rhetorical heritage. Thus he establishes the gamut that makes of his poems unique texts, and of the whole an admirable virtuoso sequence in the high register of French prose.

Yet, while attesting a musical and literary specificity, the poems plainly offer a semantic one also, which may be described by the term Valéry used so often in the latter part of his life: "mystical." He compensates for abstraction by increasing the affective charge and raising emotion to the level of fascination. The moments of day, the diverse phases of love, are not idiosyncratic images but substance and symbol of a scheme that confounds paraphrase. Unlike *Le Spleen de Paris*, which has, in Baudelaire's phrase, "ni queue ni tête, puisque tout au contraire y est à la fois tête et queue"; or *Divagations*—"un livre comme je ne les aime pas," Mallarmé wrote, "ceux épars et privés d'architecture"; ("a book of the kind I dislike, scattered and devoid of architecture") or *Les Illuminations*, whose order is fortuitous; or *Connaissance de l'Est*—"un album de dessins," "un recueil d'explications"—Valéry's work is a single sequence, the complex system of mobile consciousness whose total surpasses the sum of its parts.

Why, then, *Alphabet* being such as it is, did its author withhold it from publication? We have a collection which, however different from *Charmes*, answers to his definition of poetry as that which is distinguished by "the miraculous," by "a quality untranslatable into prose." But he knew that perfecting is an endless task and carried his work *in petto* as long as he could. It is undeniable that some of the pieces do not reach sharp focus, as if the poet had become discouraged as he went. He was, moreover, concerned at what he took to be the obscurity that derived from the special conditions he set himself: could prose, finally, allow itself to be so indirect? Yet one further possible reason for the collection's not having appeared—this perhaps crucial—we should not dismiss. Although *Alphabet* began as a problem of form, it grew to be one of Valéry's most revealing works and subsumes deep poignancy. The prose poem served him to inhabit the turbulence of his fifties— that moment when, "blasé des choses de l'esprit," he lived his disorder: "enfer et paradis," "quelque chose d'illimité et d'incommensurable," "éclats sombres de la destruction d'une substance intelligente." The freedom of prose, and the limits he wrote into it, enabled him to go as far as despair and beyond; but to publish such a work could not be without terror for the author of *Monsieur Teste*. For us his psalmody of the intellect is a discourse more pathetically intimate than *Charmes*, to which an observation from one of his last notebooks can doubtless apply: "J'ai connu fortement le sentiment singulier que publier certaines pensées serait me désarmer—et davantage, me dégoûter de celles-ci, qui m'étaient chères, comme mes maîtresses favorites" ("I had the strange and powerful feeling that, were I to publish certain thoughts, I would disarm myself—more, that I would lose all taste for them, which were dear to me, like my favorite mistresses").

Notes

1. Paul Valéry, *Alphabet* (Paris: Blaizot, 1976).

10. The Self-Defining Prose Poem: On Its Edge

MARY ANN CAWS

> Mais il faut toujours tenir compte du cadre.[1]
> —Pierre Reverdy, *Main d'oeuvre.*

*T*his paper seeks to explore the limits of a few prose poems as they help to frame in the completeness and the coherence of this otherwise undefined genre within its own borders, in its own voluntary and involuntary self-definition. Part of the contemporary fascination with the prose poem has to do, I think, with its supposed potential for multiple perspectives, changeable limits, floating borders, and shifting contours. Just as in narration tales can be embedded one inside the other, the textual elements boxing in or framing each other, the prose poem permits the same sort of complication and adds to it a lyric preoccupation. The reader's sight fixed upon a variable series of lines, levels, and surfaces, upon a convergence of the horizontal and the vertical axes, perhaps, as well as on the juncture of poetry and prose, often finds a peculiar depth for itself, in the passage of one perceptual level to another, so that the depth is balanced by a heightening of poetic consciousness, or, as Pierre Reverdy puts it in an ardent poem entitled "Fire," the visual is placed in ascent: "the field's level rises." The reading of the containing frame may facilitate the reading of a content and vice versa, in alternation, as if the eye needed to renew the object of its gaze.

In the prose poem, the final framing edge is of especial importance, acting retrospectively to construct or destruct what has been built. Here, a single-line stoppage may resume and contain the previous steps in the poem leading to it, or may cast in an entirely different light the picture made until that point. This forms the limit of our knowledge.

The two poets who here exemplify this discussion of limits are deliberately chosen from opposite poles of sensitivity and language; their very contrast figures again the contrast of prose and poetry. The convergence of those two elements within the limits of that form bears witness to the vitality of this intermingling of opposites, and to the kind of knowledge which is contained within these necessarily self-defining limits.

Claudel's Knowledge by Water

> Il n'en est aucune qui à côté de ce qu'elle dit tout haut
> n'ait quelque chose qu'elle *veuille dire* tout bas. C'est à
> nous de l'écouter, de prêter l'oreille au *sous-entendu*.
> —Paul Claudel, *Introduction à la peinture hollandaise*[2]

Besides their obvious application to Dutch art, Claudel's comments in the volume *L'Oeil écoute* may be seen or heard as an illumination both positive and negative of the prose poem as it is conceived of by some eyes and ears. Its defining characteristic is its own self-definition. Having no necessary exterior framework, no meter or essential form, it must organise itself from within and find there its own center of gravity, its own hearth of energy, its own intimate depth of understanding.

If the figures in Dutch painting as rendered by Claudel perform "an act of presence," precisely because of their lack of fixed limits, the same might prove itself true of the figures in the prose poem, human, natural, or artificial. When "reality" is emptied out of the painting in honor of this presence, the strength of the inward pull fits and fills it entirely:

. . . we are within, we inhabit it. We are taken up, contained . . . We are present at this work through which exterior reality transforms itself in our depths into shadow and reflection, the line by line movement of the day rising or sinking upon this wall we present to it.[3]

Now "the mirror as purified water," ubiquitous in this school of painting, the mirror breathing in and incorporating the exterior spectacle through an intense concentration, serves to transmute the outer into the inner. Water itself in its many forms, not yet hardened into mirroring substance, serves as that bridge of inner and outer in Claudel's extraordinary prose poems of *Connaissance de l'Est*, directed, as their title indicates, toward another sort of knowledge than that of the Low Countries and their painting, and yet toward the same interior understanding, dependent neither on representation nor on outer form. The eye chooses its matter, so that the poet's reflection upon it is self-instructive and all-inclusive.[4]

The poem "Peinture" captures, as in a painting, the moon at three-quarters in the blue-grey of a pond, and "Pluie" makes its own capture of a raindrop within a drop of ink, ending as it does with a brilliantly self-conscious flourish toward the act of poetry, celebrating itself in permanence:

> Je fais aux tempêtes la libation de cette goutte d'encre.
>
> (I make to the tempests this libation of an ink drop.)

The line preserved is hardened into a text, retaining a rounded finality, at the source. This is a prose poem in itself, visually and conceptually circumscribed, framed in the smallest possible space to a perfect completion. Its shape is defined by its choosing and not by exterior dictation.

These two poems can be seen as the emblems of the numerous water poems of *Connaissance de l'Est*, all of which are at once paintings and celebrations whose subject, and whose end, is understanding. There is little distance felt within the space of the poems, so that the reader is plunged, like the narrating poet, into the element from which he learns. The fall of rain perceived through a six-part windowpane, and resumed within the drop of ink like yet another rain drop (reminding us of Ponge's poem on rain which culminates in the single and complete expression: "Il a plu" ["It has rained"]) makes of Claudel's "Pluie" a perfected metapoetic statement about itself as well as about the seeing of the element and its transcription, in a text which—if we did not know—we would scarcely date from 1897. Claudel's relationship to the element of water was always intimate; the contemplation of it, as in "Le Contemplateur," brings out the most reflective of reflections, and the deepest.

Here the waterfall contemplated at the heart of a stone, and of a destiny, brings coherence to thought and sight; elsewhere, the sounding of a river as if to penetrate a mystery serves to deepen the sense of the poem and the metapoetic interest also. In line with contemporary self-consciousness in reading, we may well take the image as pointing to the way to read the poem, for the sounding or plunging can be considered indications of the depth, the *probability* of the text as probed or plunged into. The prose poems of water compose a picture of knowledge, no less the knowledge of the perceiving self than of the East: these are at once the texts of the landscape as observed, or of the seascape or the riverscape, and of perception, intense and urging in its turn an intense participation in sight as in text.

"Tristesse de l'eau" teaches a convergence of nature and the human, as water and the human eye share their melancholy in some doubling of the soul as it were, animate and inanimate:

Du ciel choît ou de la paupière déborde une larme identique. . . .
Que ces eaux sont copieuses! et si les larmes comme le sang ont en nous une source perpétuelle. . . . (pp. 86–87)

(From the sky falls, or from the pupil spills, an identical tear. . . .
How abundant are these waters! and if tears like blood have in us a perpetual source. . . .)

After this single tear, a copious sharing of substance and form builds up to a final abundance, against the background of which a single raucous cry resounds, as an ironic response of the animal world to the single tear for which no reason is given or needs to be given.

The two poems I shall single out make a duet, opposed and complementary. The first is a poem of possession through dispossession, and the second, of dissolution through reassembling. Both address the question of how to receive what is seen and felt and desired, and the ways of receiving and of seeing, the ways of understanding or knowing through a poem.

"La Dérivation" initiates its attack by a refusal of all that is not the subject of the poem's own immersion, thematic and linguistic, imaged and phonetic, taking place in the liquidity of a desire strongly charged, freely avowed, plentifully rewarded:

Que d'autres fleuves emportent vers la mer des branches de chêne et la rouge infusion des terres ferrugineuses . . . que la Seine, par l'humide matinée de décembre, alors que la demie de neuf heures sonne au clocher de la ville . . . que la rivière Haha à la crête fumante de ses rapides dresse tout à coup . . . le tronc d'un sapin, à plat ventre, amarré à contre-courant, la largeur de celui-ci ne suffit pas à mes bras et son immensité à mon engloutissement. (p. 68)

(Let other rivers carry seawards oaken branches and the red infusion of iron-laden earth . . . suppose the river Haha with the foaming crest of its rapids erects in an instant . . . some trunk of fir, flat against the bottom, moored in mid-current, the breadth of this is insufficient for my arms and its greatness for my absorption.)

Immersed with such gusto in language, as in the figured water, the narrator is possessed by river and by poem, his absorption indicated by the roundness of the syllable *ou*: first in "engloutisse-ment," then in the direct statement of his erotic enjoyment— "l'examen de la jouissance est de cela que je possède sous moi," where the roundness is once again audible and visible. Entirely prostrate, the poet lies counter to the flow where he is totally immersed; the culminating word of the stanza stresses the reversal of ordinary expectation and reaction: rather than enclosing the object desired, he is the enclosed, the absorbed, the swallowed up.

This initial imploration represents the flow of underwater desire attached to the surface by the visible and audible repetitions, "que . . . que." The long flow of the watery text gives way to a strong statement of negatively stated profusion, doubly rich in its interior rhyme: "Les promesses de l'Occident ne sont pas men-songères! . . . Les richesses de l'Ouest ne me sont pas étrangères"

("The promises of the Occident do not lie! . . . The riches of the West are no strangers to me"). All the stronger for the phrasing by way of the negative, such a positive claim then leads to an oblique refusal of all the other elements, magnifying by contrast the vertiginous reception given to the source and the abundance of its cornucopia of offering: "Puisque d'un pied étonné descendant la berge ardue j'ai découvert la dérivation! . . . Tout entier par moi, versé par la pente de la Terre, il coule" ("Since, descending the arduous bank with an astonished foot, I discovered the diversion! . . . Entirely through me, poured out through the slope of the Earth, it flows").[5] The flow of the poem is, then, what is desired, expended, enjoyed, and yet refulfilled; and that is the flow of the prose itself.

As the extent of the riches, heaped heavy, transcending the power of sight, is enough to overwhelm and to force the rejection of civilized posture, the narration from here on has its own source in the flattened-out possessor, swallowed up, already visible to himself at once as possessing and possessed: "J'ai trouvé qu'il est insuffisant de voir, inexpédient d'être debout; l'examen de la jouissance est de cela que je possède sous moi" ("I have found seeing insufficient, standing inexpedient; the examination of enjoyment is of what I possess under myself"). As all the riches of the West spill forth from the horn of plenty provided by nature and culture, the richness of the poetic prose in the poem of plenty rolls out once more through the orifice *ou*, which we have seen opened in "engloutissement," "sous," "jouissance," and then there is the flowing itself, "coule." The heavy flow and the positive and double possession—the rich text by the possessive narrator, in turn possessed by the sweep of the flow—the very immensity of the absorption as the substance sucks in the describer of the substance, all this prepares the responding negative flow of the catalogue of comparison:

Ni la soie que la main ou le pied nu pétrit, ni la profonde laine d'un tapis de sacre ne sont comparables à la résistance de cette épaisseur liquide où mon poids propre me soutient, ni le nom du lait, ni la couleur de la rose à cette merveille dont je reçois sur moi la descente. Certes je bois, certes je suis plongé dans le vin! (p. 68)

(Neither the silk shaped by hand or foot, nor the wool piled deep for a coronation rug can be compared with the springiness of this liquid thickness where my own weight sustains me, neither the name of milk nor the color of rose to this marvel whose downfall I receive. Indeed I drink, indeed I am plunged in wine!)

The downward force is to be discounted no more than the almost excessive weight of the flow: the "descente" of the liquid picks up, with its thick-piled wool, the image of a bedside rug (a "descente du lit") where even the notion of bed, as in the riverbed, is elided. This underlying image, suppressed on the surface of the text, gives its springiness to the texture of the text, all the more resistant as a notion precisely because it does not appear but only motivates the rest. Taking the inebriating plunge, the narration combines the skeins of luxury (silk, thick wool, coronation) with the skeins of delicacy in a liquid vein (milk and wine, mediated by the rose color), all the while making or pouring out a libation (milk, roses), as in the Ronsard sonnet to Marie in which those two offerings unite in celebration of loveliness, in homage to life and to death:

> Ce vase plein de lait, ce panier plein de fleurs . . . reçois,
> Afin que vif et mort ton corps ne soit que roses.

(This jar of milk, this basket of flowers . . . receive, so that living or dead, your body might be but roses.)

The inebriation only reinforces the considerably erotic weight of the lines, again flowing towards the culmination of the stanza in an evocation of enjoyment in the strongest sense of the word. The whole stanza in its reinforcing repetitions ("Certes . . . certes," "Que . . . que . . . que," "voici . . . voici") helps the stream bear heavily upon all the senses, past that of simple sight:

Que les ports s'ouvrent pour recevoir les cargaisons de bois et de grains qui s'en viennent du pays haut, que les pêcheurs tendent leurs filets pour arrêter les épaves et les poissons, que les chercheurs d'or filtrent l'eau et fouillent le sable: le fleuve ne m'apporte pas une richesse moindre.

(Let the ports open to receive the cargos of wood and grain coming from the high country, let the fishermen stretch out their nets to catch the flotsam and the fish, let the gold-seekers filter the water and forage in the sand: the stream brings me no less a richness.)

The eye alone cannot suffice for this accumulated charge, and it takes a more subtle touch to comprehend the kind of possession so violently stated in the last paragraph by the repetition of the deictic "voici," bringing to the sight and to the hold of reader and poet the knowledge so captured, and rendered finally within the presence of the poem. The rich and royal colors will be distinguished only just prior to their entry into blackness, for the poem will end in immobility and dark, penetrated by all the stars the black water prepares and then mirrors.

This scene, heavily charged and cumulative in its energy, will lead to a culminating point of possession, of inebriation, and of mystery, as of understanding, both of the seen and the unseen:

Entre ces gras replis violets, voici l'eau peinte comme du reflet des cierges, voici l'ambre, voici le vert le plus doux, voici la couleur de l'or. Mais taisons-nous: cela que je sais est à moi, et alors que cette eau deviendra noire, je posséderai la nuit tout entière avec le nombre intégral des étoiles visibles et invisibles. (p. 68)

(Between these thick violet creases, this is the water painted like the reflection of the candles, this is the amber, this the softest green, this, the color of gold. But let us keep silent: what I know is mine, and when this water becomes black, I shall possess the night entire with the integral number of visible and invisible stars.)

The sacred ceremony continues by the light of candles and stars, joined in the mind and in the water, which is counted for its gold, the real possession of the lover of rivers and poems. The subtlety of touch guarantees that the brush strokes on the watery canvas and the silent knowing will take proper account of the number of reflections, poetic or celestial, painted or mirrored, not only as they are seen, but also as they are not.

After the gluttony of self-absorption and the delight of drunkenness, the truest interior understanding ("jouir, c'est comprendre") is that which the touch, like light itself, decomposes, composing thereby the poem, whose every word is quiet finally, whose end is not in sight and cannot, precisely, be counted on.

In a parallel discovery through the prose of a poem, Reverdy's "Chacun sa part" in his *Poèmes en prose* composes a similar refusal of counting, except as part of understanding. Stars fall from the sky into running water where a greedy fisherman fills his pouch with the pieces of apparent gold.

Mais un autre attendait plus loin du bord. Plus modeste il pêchait dans la flaque de boue qu'avait laissé la pluie. Cette eau, venue du ciel, était pleine d'étoiles.[6]

(But another was waiting farther from the edge. More modest, he was fishing in the mud puddle that the rain had left. This water, having come from the sky, was full of stars.)

While the streak of gold disappears in his pouch, like some flash in the pan, these stiller and more modest waters according with the other, less imposing fisherman, capture an undying sparkle, more lasting as it is less expected.

"Dissolution" supplies the finality of the knowledge, this last poem like a witness born and lost, a testimony to a sight now vanished. Dating from 1905, it is eight years later than "La Dérivation," and the lusty "immensité" of its absorption and self-absorption, the delicate nuances of its colors, their loss and their replacement by the invisible which can enter into account.

The outcome is not possession, I have said, but dispossession, of outer world and self. Beginning in the middle of a statement, the poem begins in indifference also, and in pain, repeated, prolonged, echoed, and intensely present even as it is vanquished only by the future:

Et je suis de nouveau reporté sur la mer indifférente et liquide. Quand je serai mort, on ne me fera plus souffrir. Quand je serai enterré entre mon père et ma mère, on ne me fera plus souffrir. On ne se rira plus de ce coeur trop aimant.

(And I am carried back out upon the indifferent liquid sea. When I am dead, I won't be made to suffer any longer. When I am buried between my father and my mother, I won't be made to suffer any longer. This too loving heart won't be laughed at any longer.)

The very liquidity of the sea, banal to the point of tautology, reassures, exactly like the obvious cessation brought about by death, and the repetitions serve to stress the evidence of it all. As the body disintegrates in the earth—dust to dust—the soul, reduced to a single cry, has no need to wait for its own painless future in the bosom of Abraham: its repetition is its own passionate being, its dissolution its present possession, in accord with the horizon-less seascape. No division there, none of the singling out which has caused such prolonged suffering:

Maintenant tout est dissous, et d'un oeil appesanti je cherche en vain autour de moi et le pays habituel à la route ferme sous mon pas et ce visage cruel. Le ciel n'est plus que de la brume et l'espace de l'eau. Tu le vois, tout est dissous et je chercherais en vain autour de moi trait ou forme.

(Now all is dissolved, and heavy-eyed I vainly look around me for the usual countryside with its road firm under my feet and that cruel face. The sky is no longer anything but mist, and space—water. You see, all is dissolved and I'd look in vain around me for a stroke or a form.)

Natural forces aid the *decomposition* of the very seascape from which the poem has sprung, whose shapelessness gives it form and birth. There is nothing to possess other than this dispossession of line, nothing to set off sky from land, color from the grey of mist, water from tears, hope from despair:

Rien, pour horizon, que la cessation de la couleur la plus foncée. La matière de tout est rassemblée en une seule eau, pareille à celle de ces larmes que je sens qui coulent sur ma joue.

(Nothing, as a horizon, but the cessation of the deepest color. The matter of everything is gathered in one water, like that of these tears I feel running down my cheeks.)

The tautology of the opening, these restatements resulting from the grave hurt inflicted, lead the evolution of the text toward this dissolution of the psyche within its setting.

But the build-up of hammering sadness—"Et je suis . . . Quand je serai . . . Quand je serai . . . on ne me fera plus . . . On ne se rira plus"—is itself the creator first of the Other, who rises as the addressee—"tu le vois"—and then of the unity of the seen—"tout est dissous . . . tout est dissous . . . La matière de tout."

Moreover, in the conclusion of this very brief text, in the summation of all the preceding repetitions—those of seeking and of nothingness as response, those of country as it is familiar and of the beloved face as it is identified with that country—two changes of importance have been brought about, both stated in such a low key that they are practically, like the horizon, indistinguishable in and from the text.

First, the confession has been made, finally, in the last word: "J'aurais beau chercher, je ne trouve plus rien hors de moi, ni ce pays qui fut mon séjour, ni ce visage beaucoup aimé" ("Look as I might, I find nothing any longer outside myself, neither this country which was my dwelling, nor that face, greatly loved"). The "cruel face" has been swallowed up within the mist, like any face loved and lost, yielding in memory only the love. Above all, the self that formerly found nothing around itself on which to count, now finds nothing outside itself, which leaves us to suppose that perhaps there may be found within the self another landscape, or seascape. The positioning alone of the third reference to looking and not finding stresses its difference from the first two, as in folk adages (if at first you don't succeed, try, try again) or in legends of three sons, where the third member always stands out: "je cherche en vain autour de moi . . . je chercherais en vain autour de moi . . . j'aurais beau chercher, je ne trouve plus rien hors de moi" ("I look in vain about me . . . I'd look in vain about me . . . look as I might, I find nothing any longer outside myself"). For the first time also, the I initiates the sentence: always before, a conjunction or an adverb, another person or another thing took the lead. In the course of the narration, the text has provided the necessary strength for restitution, if not of the country or the visage loved and lost, then at least of the text. Language alone is not dissolved in this general dissolution.

For restitution, then, there is only the poem. And yet does it not serve the same esthetic purpose as the former one? The narrator as the subtle perceiver and subtler handler of the text and of his own understanding would have understood that in the dark water only, the true colors are to be found. In the reflection only are the invisible stars to be counted. And in the disappearance of everything around, the text of apparent loss is composed of the self discovered as the setting is decomposed and, with it, is recovered and resolved.

Knowing Edges in Reverdy

Of all French prose poets, there is none more willingly "static" than Pierre Reverdy, as he himself would have had it. The best of his prose poems compose a picture hauntingly conscious of its own composition, obsessed with its own frame, knowing its own limits. To examine these pictures and their edges, setting their scene quite simply by its relation to the reader—in this case the specator—is to see this reading itself absorbed by the spectacle quite as much as by the verbal component of it. Because of the all-enveloping nature of the work, the picture allows no sides to be taken which are not its own; having only its edges and its focus to hold it together in completeness and coherence, the prose poem reinforces itself along those lines.

"Belle Étoile," from Reverdy's earliest collection, makes the revelation of a certain impotence the source of its power, drawn from a succession of images such as the loss of a key, the endless and ubiquitous search in vain for an entry, and the final mockery by others and by the self. The relation of the borders to this psychological focusing on an obsession is poetic in its excruciation of feeling, and prosaic, even classic, in its imagery of mental stress, as the narrator is framed out of whatever inside he is seeking, is relegated continually to the exterior edge of things.

The border state of the stranger in his liminal in-betweenness is initially stressed: the narrator wanders by a river or at the edge of a wood, and later between wood and river, just as in some classic rite of passage, with his intensified consciousness obstructed by the absence of all windows and doors for any sight or entrance:

J'aurai peut-être perdu la clé et tout le monde rit autour de moi et chacun me montre une clé énorme pendue à son cou.

Je suis le seul à ne rien avoir pour entrer quelque part. Ils ont tous disparu et les portes closes laissent la rue plus triste. Personne. Je frapperai partout. (p. 200)

(I shall perhaps have lost the key, and everyone is laughing all around me, each person showing me a great key hung about his neck.

I am the only one to have nothing to let me in somewhere. They have all disappeared and the closed doors leave the street sadder still. No one. I shall knock everywhere.) (p. 201)

In this classic form of paranoid obsession with personal exclusion, the straight line of despair is followed until suddenly a formal change is marked by a tense alteration, as if a change of direction were to be made in the reading of the picture, or a change in the perception of a color. The future perfect of loss ("J'aurai peut-être perdu") initially leads to a future of exasperated continuity ("Je frapperai partout"), with the implication that this loneliness must last forever. But then a sudden switch is made to the past tense:

Alors un peu plus loin que la veille, au bord d'une rivière et d'un bois, j'ai trouvé une porte . . . Je me suis mis derrière et, sous la nuit qui n'a pas de fenêtres mais de larges rideaux, entre la forêt et la rivière qui me protègent, j'ai pu dormir. (p. 200)

(Then a little further than the day before, at the edge of a river and a wood, I found a door . . . I placed myself behind it and, under the night which has no windows but wide curtains, between the forest and the river protecting me, I was able to sleep.) (p. 201)

The tense swerve marks a special occasion, befitting the rite of passage, in which the obsession can be worked out, realized, and experienced all the way to its terrible end. The concluding solution is an ultimate blackout, whose dark curtains protect the voluntary sleeper from any other exclusion, being themselves the solitary and sufficient shutters to edge out of the text.

Here the state of awareness itself is curtained off, and the poem's closure is indeed perfected. The door found held no domestic welcome, so that there is no choice but the absolute barring of sensation for a sleep which serves as a final frame against illumination, even poetic, and continuity, even prosaic. The nightmare has been paradoxically relegated to the world of day, so that the nocturnal curtains may be deliberately pulled, forever, over the painful and liminal scene. This poem is known, like the others discussed here, through its border experience.

"Les Corps ridicules des esprits" in *La Lucarne ovale* is a prose poem with the limited and limiting outlook and the closing curtains which are among Reverdy's preferred motifs; it defines yet again the borders as the knowing parts of the Reverdian poetic experience. Here his customary self-mockery is entwined with a far more potent mockery of the literary "body" in general, in an interior knowledge which cannot help but reflect upon the body of the poem in which it is embodied.

Un cortège de gens plus ou moins honorables. Quelques-uns sourient dans le vide avec sérénité. Ils sont nus. Une auréole à la tête des premiers qui ont su prendre la place. Les plus petits en queue. . . .

On passe devant la maison d'un poète qui n'est pas là. La pluie qui tombait sur son piano, à travers le toit, l'a chassé. . . .

Derrière un monument d'une époque oubliée le soleil se lève en rayons separés et l'ombre des passants lentement s'efface. Les rideaux sont tirés. (p. 226)

(A procession of more or less honorable people. Some of them smile into emptiness serenely. They are naked. A halo around the head of the first ones who managed to take their places. The littlest ones trailing behind. . . .

They are passing by the house of a poet not at home. The rain falling on his piano through the roof sent him away. . . .

Behind a monument to a forgotten time the sun is rising with separate beams and the shadows of the passers-by fade slowly. The curtains are drawn.) (p. 227)

Toward this procession of literary saints, some smiling serenely into emptiness and haloed, Reverdy's bitterness, that of a bystander, is directed, against "ceux qui ont su prendre la place." The pageant passes by like some Flemish procession of the Holy Blood, the sun rises, and the shadows of the passers-by fade in a passage from dark to light, the reverse of the progress from light to dark in the poem previously discussed. Yet the last sentence sums up the scenic procession with a similar final line, shutting off the text with an edge of dark: "Les rideaux sont tirés," after the artificial light of the liminary saints and the natural illumination of the sun on the rise, in contrast to the disappearance of even the shadows of the saints.

"Les Mouvements à l'horizon" from *Étoiles peintes* illustrates from the outset the oblique look the poet directs upon the world, which is never to be seen straight on, never with the regular lines of verse of the "regular" poets, never to be counted exactly in its numbers, but is only to be suggested in the cumulative ignorance and haunting quality of the atmosphere, until the negative final dismissal:

Les cavaliers se tiennent sur la route et de profil. On ne sait plus quel est leur nombre. Contre la nuit qui ferme le chemin, entre la rivière et le pont, une source qui pleure—un arbre qui vous suit. On regarderait la foule qui passe, elle ne vous verrait pas. (p. 234)

(The horsemen are standing on the road in profile. Their number is no longer known. Against the night closing off the path, between the river and the bridge, a weeping spring—a tree following you. You might look at the crowd passing by, it would never see you.) (p. 235)

This typical Reverdy scene is situated between two markers or framing limits: bordered as between river and bridge, in a place of limits, on a blocked path in the darkness, near the "source." The spectator in his ignorance about the scene thus framed ("on ne sait plus") is caught up within the fear, created by the narrator, of the fear itself, by the obsessed I that deforms the ordinary logical and spatial judgments in the poem: whom is the tree following? who is watching, and will not see? Whether this procession does or does not belong to a dream, the uncertainty adds to the fear in the scene, as does the child on its sidelines, unhappy or unconscious in misery or just in the dark: "L'enfant pleure ou dort." Nothing can be said for sure; heavy stress is placed on not knowing, not only by the verbs of ignorance, but also by visual signs, such as the cloud forming a threatening backdrop. The source of rain, it is no less the creator of obscurity, the blocker of the sun, forming a dark but disquietingly vague background for the visible and the artificial scenes: "un fond de tableau sur un nuage" ("a picture backdrop upon a cloud").

The pictorial nature of the text is self-referential; the uncertainty is based in a cloudy matter, a watercolor whose watery being undoes its own form, already threatened by the slippage it suggests, invites, and is powerless to control: "Les chevaux glissent le long de l'eau. Et le cortège glisse aussi dans cette eau qui efface toutes ces couleurs, toutes ces larmes" ("The horses slide the length of the water. And the procession slides also in this water effacing all these colors, all these tears") (pp. 234, 235). The scene in its entirety simply slips away, dissolving in the weeping spring or the flowing river, with these colors and watercolors appearing here for the first and last time, melting also into the grief, whose reality is at once natural—as water and spring are part of nature— and human, as if the child were to have been weeping without any reason being given or sensed as necessary. As the anxiety of the lost narrator transfers itself to the verbal scene, the mist and the motion draw in closer to us: the poem ends, unabashedly, in tears.

The scene whose build-up forms a poem may also be wiped out by a single departure, though less dramatic than Rimbaud's single annihilating ray. When the figures who people the setting, whose projection the scene is, turn their backs upon it, the scene no longer exists for speaker or reader. "Toujours gêné" in *La Lucarne ovale* belongs to the series of haunted poems of definite closure, of psychological disturbance which can only be curtained off, for protection and for control. It shows a tripartite construction like a play in three acts, with three elements once more included within the acts, like a *mise-en-abyme* seen close up. A triple question precedes the description of the scene, and introduces even a revelation as a question: "Qui m'a révélé l'endroit précis? Le ciel où les deux murs se joignent? L'angle où l'on est à l'abri?" ("Who revealed to me the precise place? The sky where the two walls join? The angle where you can take shelter?") (pp. 222, 223). The scene as described reveals not only this exact place but a terrifying and no less precise displacement, the Reverdian self-mockery intense under the sign of its own *vanitas*, with a death's head at its center:

Par-dessus, le vent emporte la terre qui se déplace. . . . L'affreuse tête qui se balance sur le toit en ricanant!
  Ni le mur ni les arbres sont assez grands. (pp. 222)

(Overhead the wind carries off the land which is displaced. . . . The appalling head swinging on the roof and sneering!
  Neither the wall nor the trees are tall enough.) (p. 223)

Nothing in the setting is large enough to fit the spectacle, tall enough to defy the universal sneer: when the departure is made, it has a double effect, for the reader too will desert the text, closed in upon itself, curtained off. He too, like the poet, like the narrator, has been spied upon, waited for, found out—and all that in a place marked as precise, awful, and final in its exact enclosure: "C'est là qu'on attend. C'est de là qu'on regarde et qu'on nous surprend" ("That is where we wait. That is where we look from and are come upon by surprise") (pp. 222, 223). The matter is above all textual. From the shame of such enclosure and revelation there is no final shelter, save in absence and in exile: "Et déjà vous commencez à rougir plus que moi-même. Allons-nous-en" ("And already you've begun to blush more than I do. Let's leave") (pp. 222, 223). The builder's mind has framed the construction with an imperative of fear and a hope of refuge that cannot be dismissed, as we can be, from the poem. When the concerned spectator deserts the page, accused as he is of blushing and of implied shame, mortified into running from the declamatory horror of the sniggering head, he is made to take a paranoid flight.

For Reverdy's enlistment is efficacious, his suggestions are entrapments, and the frame-up is complete, inclusive of the spectator. The poet is rendered incapable of escape from a forced procession (in the poem "Encore marcher"), and is all the more gravely fenced in since the reader is no less forced into contemplation of the pitiful scene: "Et seul je suis perdu là devant vous, devant vous tous et je ne peux plus m'en aller" ("And alone I am lost there before you, before you all and I can no longer leave") (pp. 228, 229). Here the narrator has found the ultimate suggestion of an end, an entrapment terrible exactly because it is continually incomplete. The static form Reverdy chooses to give to his pictures compounds, finally, the sense of closure inherent in that immobility, insofar as it depends upon unwilling and indefinable development and exposure of each picture as it is framed and we with it. Our knowledge of his willing self-observation, however deep its psychological obsessions, can take off none of the edge.

Notes

1. Pierre Reverdy, *Main d'oeuvre* (Paris: Mercure de France, 1964).
2. Paul Claudel, *Introduction à la peinture hollandaise*, in *L'Oeil écoute* (Paris: Gallimard, 1946).

3. Claudel, *Introduction*, p. 26.

4. Unless otherwise noted, all quotations from Claudel are taken from *Connaissance de l'Est, suivi de L'Oiseau noir dans le soleil levant* (Paris: *Poésie*/Gallimard, 1974).

5. The discovering foot has perhaps a source in a preceding text, as Hermine Riffaterre points out. The third stanza of Nerval's "Myrtho" reads: "Je sais pourquoi là-bas le volcan s'est rouvert . . . / C'est qu'hier tu l'avais touché d'un pied agile, / Et de cendres soudain l'horizon s'est couvert" ("I know why the volcano reopened over there . . . It's because yesterday you touched it with an agile foot, and suddenly the horizon was clouded by ash"). The clouding of the horizon by ash or by mist produces the same effect, and the distance between this "pied agile" and that other "pied étonné" is less important than the correlation of attitude—the foot serving as the extremity of human consciousness, entering into primary contact with the natural world, whose order is somehow rendered extraordinary or at least perceived as extraordinary because of that contact. Thus, in Nerval, the horizon is clouded by the action of the foot, so that a small gesture makes a great difference, conferring retrospectively upon the maker of that gesture an undisguised power. Whereas in Claudel, the normally flowing river bearing its normal riches is suddenly seen as the Bearer of the Riches of the West toward the Poet: an ordinary event is transformed into an almost mythological happening, by what can best be described as poetic aggrandizement. The poem pours forth as if from a cornucopia, the form and sign of profusion; the liquid engulfs the speaker/poet and the reader with him, so that the "vers moi" takes on a still larger sense.

6. All quotations from Reverdy are taken from Mary Ann Caws and Patricia Terry, trs. and eds., *Roof Slates and Other Poems of Pierre Reverdy* (Boston: Northeastern University Press, 1981).

11. L'Adieu suprême and Ultimate Composure: The Boundaries of the Prose Poem

Albert Sonnenfeld

> Décor
>
> De l'absence, sinon que sur la glace encor
> De scintillation le septuor se fixe.[1]
>
> —Stéphane Mallarmé

Stéphane Mallarmé's allegorical sonnet of the self as creator of a setting of absence in which poetic being exists only as a vestigial flickering in a mirror of ice coincides with his septimal definition of *L'Oeuvre* in the hour of synthesis: "Three poems in verse, of which *l'Hérodiade* is the overture . . . and four poems in prose, on the spiritual conception of Nothingness."[2] It was a synthesis possible only in conditional futurity, since Mallarmé's inexorable *via dolorosa* was toward minimal signs, "comprehensive brief pieces, like immediate rhythms of thought, commanding a prosody" (*Oeuvres complètes*, p. 1569), which in turn are reducible still further: "Really, there is no prose. There is the alphabet" (p. 867). Yet on one occasion, the two forms of poetic organization are joined in typographical contrariety, when within the precincts of the prose paragraphs of "La Déclaration foraine," the hero-narrator recites the Shakespearean sonnet, "La Chevelure vol d'une flamme," to his lady and to the assembled public, describing his creation apologetically as "rien que le lieu commun d'une esthétique . . ." (p. 283; "nothing but the commonplace of an esthetic . . ."), one which

198

in its rhymed closure suffers from an excess of formal perfection and explicitness: "sa réduplication sur une rime du trait final, mon boniment d'après un mode primitif du sonnet" (p. 281; "its reduplication on a rhyme of the final stroke, my spiel according to a primitive mode of the sonnet"). What is implied is that the arcanal closure of the prose poem, introduced by the expletive "peut-être!" is of a deliberately imprecise and therefore superior construction, an impression confirmed by the poet's own footnote on the sonnet form: "Usité à la Renaissance anglaise" ("In use during the English Renaissance").

From its very origins, the prose poem has responded to the impulse for freedom from traditional prosody: "une partie de dominos" was Cocteau's term for the old rules of the game of versification. Baudelaire justified the *Petits Poèmes en prose* as the miraculous fulfillment of a dream of "a poetic prose, musical without rhyme or rhythm, supple and jerky enough to adapt to the lyric movements of the soul, to the undulations of reverie, to the somersaults of conscience."[3] And if on the one hand the prose poem marks the acceptance of the urbanized industrial age into a *materia poetica* that in Whitman's vision of the poetry of the future will "soar to the freer, vast, diviner, heaven of prose,"[4] its continuing and necessary justification for the symbolists, the surrealists, and their respective heirs was as a translation of a profoundly antimechanistic conception of consciousness: to immobilize, as Mallarmé puts it, "around an idea the diverse glimmerings of the mind" (p. 1570); or as Jacob defined this second aspect in his *Art poétique*, "déclenchements inattendus, l'air de rêve, les conclusions imprévues, les associations de mots et d'idées, voilà l'esprit nouveau"[5] ("unexpected liberations, with an air of dream, unforeseen conclusions, associations of words and ideas, all this is the modern attitude"). From the definition of Des Esseintes's favorite form ("pulsations of a sensitive soul"), through Saint Pol Roux's quest for "forms adequate to the emotions traversed"[6] and Edmond Jaloux's remarks on the centenary of the prose poem about its infinite suggestiveness, to Jacques Rivière's praise of the Claudelian respiratory verset ("It dilates and contracts alternately; it knows the contours of intimate feeling"[7]), the *alleged simulation of incoherence* of the prose poem of consciousness always terrified the Monsieur Homais who make up the unsilent majority, as Huysmans wrote to Mallarmé in 1882. Witness Émile Henriot in 1954: "To write in a beautiful style and to say nothing is worthless: it's just making a prose poem."[8]

Any advocacy of *le poème en prose* would therefore appear to be predicated on a progressive or evolutionary view of poetic form. When André Breton proclaims that freedom in surrealism was revered "in the pure state," it follows inevitably that he denounces those apostates who, in returning to fixed forms in poetry, have lost the benefit of "la volonté d'affranchissement de formes caduques"[9] ("the will to be liberated of decrepit forms"). As Mallarmé foresaw, moreover, in "La Déclaration foraine," the conflict between the *formes caduques* and the *esprit nouveau* is nowhere more dramatically joined than in the final farewell, the restoration of ultimate composure which marks the terms of poetry. Rational thought processes may be organized by topical beginnings and epigrammatic summary conclusions, but surely the transcription of the "état profond de celui qui parle" must not be enclosed, should not, in William Carlos Williams' words, "click like a box." To I. A. Richards' query "How does a poem know when it's finished?" no one has forged a more cogent and far-reaching reply than Barbara Herrnstein Smith in her book *Poetic Closure*.[10] Yet, revealingly, as she approaches the corpus of modernist poetry, her tone is appropriately conjectural. She speaks of the newly positive value of openness, the anticlosural, or (in Leonard B. Meyer's terms) "the antiteleological [which] directs us toward no points of culmination—establishes no goals toward which to move. It arouses no expectation, except presumably that it will stop."[11] She rightly refuses to accept as an axiom a historical schema predicating the progressive weakening of closure from the Renaissance to the minimal songs of uncertainty of our modern age of anxiety.

It would be plausible and tempting to deduce that the prose poem would, as the enactment of freedom from the formal constraints of prosody, aver itself as resolutely antiteleological or anticlosural, engage in a continuous refutation of what Eliot (in *East Coker*) called "the value of the long looked forward to, / Long hoped for calm / the autumnal serenity / And the wisdom" of the formal resources of closure natural to a less suspicious age. But it is my contention here that the *prose poem*, though it may have thrown off the shackles of a caducous tradition of rhyme and meter, is formally a profoundly conservative and traditional structure in its ceremonials of entrance and exit; that no matter how radical its content, how relentless its striving for apparent or real incoherence, the prose poem undergoes the secondary elaboration of syntactical coherence and its boundaries most often are clearly defined and marked.

In his famous, and supposedly revolutionary, ars poetica, Tristan Tzara defined the ideal aleatory process "Pour faire un poème dadaiste" by a series of edicts for action:

Pour faire un poème dadaiste
> Prenez un journal
> Prenez des ciseaux
> Choisissez dans ce journal un article ayant la longeur
> que vous comptez donner à votre poème
> Découpez l'article
> Découpez ensuite avec soin chacun des mots qui forment cet
> article et mettez-les dans un sac
> Agitez doucement
> Sortez ensuite chaque coupure l'une après l'autre dans
> l'ordre où elles ont quitté le sac
> Copiez consciencieusement
> Le poème vous ressemblera.[12]

To make a Dadaist poem
> Take a newspaper / take some scissors / choose in this paper an article of the length you want for your poem / cut up the article / cut out carefully each of the words of the article and put them in a bag / shake gently / then take out each clipping one after the next in the order they left the bag / copy it all carefully / the poem will resemble you.

What is immediately apparent here is that the manifesto violates its own principles: it is typographically traditional (and the prose poem will not achieve the freedom from the tyranny of the conventionally set line exploited by, say, the picture poems of Apollinaire, Tzara himself, or even e. e. cummings). But more pertinent to my thesis here, instead of presenting us with the sought-for-chaos of words pulled from a hat, the manifesto moves inexorably to an aphoristic and memorable closure prepared rhythmically by a highly alliterative, heptasyllabic word: *co ɪ-sci-en-sci-eu-se-ment*. The title "Pour faire un poème dadaiste" functions as topic sentence, and the frame is closed by the repetition and *quod erat demonstrandum* of "Le poème vous ressemblera."

Of course, the example is unfair since it is a prose poem about poetry, a statement of imperatives, but it should be clear that even a self-proclaimed demolitions expert will, in the process of listing the shattered fragments in words, be forced by the processes of language itself to copy consciously and conscientiously; and enslaved as we all are by the despotism of secondary elaboration, he will become a builder of thought-directed word structures. A pulverised poem is no less a poem.

I need not demonstrate the obviously traditional boundaries of the essentially narrative or descriptive *Petits poèmes* of Baudelaire, but surely the meteoric hero of the surrealists, Arthur Rimbaud, offers a standard for visionary incoherence in his *Illuminations*.[13] The meaning of a particular vision may be indecipherable, yet the formal ceremony of entrance and exit, expressed in prose of paradigmatic syntaxicalism, is hardly antiteleological. The reader's eye moves horizontally along the printed line detecting parts of speech in their ordained functions; even the most casual observer will find a preponderance of closures in single lines isolated typographically from the body of the poem, like the closing couplet of the English sonnet. Among the most frequent, and consecrated, closural devices of language itself are aphoristic final declarative sentences, whose stark simplicity has the finality of a tonic cadence. The familiarity of the following examples will attest to the power of Rimbaud's closures: "La musique savante manque à notre désir" ("Learned music is lacking for our desire") ("Conte"); "J'ai seul la clef de cette parade sauvage" ("I alone have the key for this wild show") ("Parade"); "Au réveil il était midi" ("At waking, it was noon") ("Aube"); "Un souffle disperse les limites du foyer" ("One breath disperses the limits of the hearth") ("Nocturne vulgaire"); "C'est aussi simple qu'une phrase musicale" ("It's as simple as a musical phrase") ("Guerre"); "Voici le temps des *Assassins*" ("This is the time of the *Assassins*") ("Matinée d'ivresse").

When there is a final full paragraph, it will often be inaugu-
rated by an expression of summation: "Car depuis qu'ils se sont
dissipés" "For since they have vanished" ("Après le déluge"); "En
effet, ils furent rois toute une matinée" ("In fact, they were kings
a whole morning") ("Royauté"); "Tels qu'un dieu aux énormes
yeux bleus" ("Like a god with enormous blue eyes") ("Fleurs");
"Tout se fit ombre et aquarium ardent" ("Everything became
shadow and ardent aquarium") ("Bottom"); "Au revoir ici, n'importe où" ("Goodbye here, no matter where") ("Démocratie"). In
order to indicate a distancing from involvement with the subject
as a preliminary gesture toward closure, Rimbaud's Illumination
sometimes dims into receding apostrophe: "Ô la face cendrée,
l'écusson de crin" ("Oh the ashen face, the shield of hair") ("Being
Beauteous"); "Ô terrible frisson des amours novices" ("Oh terrible
shudder of novice loves") ("H"). Syntactical changes, particularly
in verb tenses, similarly alert the reader to impending closure.
Thus, the imperfects of "Royauté" are summarized in a preterite:
"En effet, ils furent rois toute une matinée." The present-tense
evocation of the "Génie"—"Il est l'affection. . . . Il est l'a-
mour. . . ."—in passing moves through a future tense—"Il ne s'en
ira pas," ("It will not go away")—then yields to apostrophe—"Ô
lui et nous! . . . Ô monde!" ("Oh he and we! . . . Oh world!")—
before a summation: "Il nous a connus tous" ("He has known us
all"). Many of the prose poems are enclosed within a linguistic
frame established through repetition of a sentence or a single word:
"Un souffle *ouvre* des brèches opéradiques" ("A breath *opens* op-
eratic gaps") opens "Nocturne vulgaire," which closes with "Un
souffle *disperse* les limites du foyer" (italics mine). Often, too, the
linear movement of thought streams or of time leads to the traditional closures defined with such acuity by Barbara Smith: thus,
the embracing of "Aube" in dream ends with awakening: "il était
midi." Only one Illumination seems to me to be anticlosural: "Barbare" ends with elipses after the solitary noun "Le pavillon . . . ";
but here, too, further scrutiny reveals a form that while not teleo-
logical is tautological or circular, the assumption being that the
ultimate word will be followed by "en viande saignante sur la soie
des mers et des fleurs antiques" ("of bleeding flesh on the silk of
the seas and of ancient flowers"), as in its two prior occurrences

in the nine-sentence poem. Despite its title, Rimbaud's very civilized form here hardly answers Charles-Louis Philippe's enjoining battle cry: "Maintenant, il faut des barbares!" ("Now we must have barbarians!"). "Without head or tail. All head and tail."[14] Baudelaire's words justifying the incoherence as *book* of the collected *petits poèmes* might also be an ideal of freedom for the individual prose poem, were it nor for the *linear sight trajectory* of the prose line that makes diachronic perception inevitable. And beyond that, the prose poem has, in this very linearity, a greater commitment to syntactical relationships than the picture poem, say, where the individual word or even letter reigns in solitary supremacy. The prose poem is therefore a far more docile victim to the psychic censor or its equivalent in the translation of vision, to the secondary elaboration which accommodates free vision to the exigencies of language.

The acknowledged masters of *le poème en prose* may proclaim themselves to be visionaries, but as in the case of their own mentor, Rimbaud, their forms of closure belie their content (and their manifestos). Claudel will answer "the celestial interrogation" with "C'en est fait est répondue"[15] ("That is done, it is answered"), whereas René Char often prefers the rhetorical, but nonetheless conclusive, question: "Saurons-nous, sous le pied de la mort, si le coeur, ce gerbeur, ne doit pas précéder mais suivre?"[16] ("Shall we know, under the foot of death, if the heart, gatherer of sheaves, should not precede but follow?"). The still surrealistic Éluard of 1925 will bluntly terminate "Au défaut du silence" with "fini, il n'y a plus de preuves de la nuit"[17] ("finished, there are no more proofs of night"). His sometime mentor and sometime friend André Breton sets up a veritable equation in "Poisson soluble": "Nous y sommes: l'ennui, les belles parallèles, ah! que les parallèles sont belles sous la perpendiculaire de Dieu"[18] ("Here we are: boredom, the lovely parallels, ah, how lovely the parallels are under God's perpendicular"). Saint-John Perse, as any rapid visual examination demonstrates, will resort to the aphoristic topic sentence, isolated typographically as in the following examples: "Que le Poète se fasse entendre, et qu'il dirige le jugement" ("Let the poet be heard, and let him direct the judgement") ("Vents"); "Avis au Maître d'astres et de navigation" ("Warning to the Master of stars and of navigation") ("Amers").[19]

The high rhetorical flourishes of a Perse or a Claudel naturally lend themselves to formal ceremonials of closure: "Telle, un instant, dans le soir, m'apparut une cité solitaire"[20] "Such, a moment in the evening, did a solitary city appear to me"); or "Et nous savons maintenant ce qui nous arrêtait de vivre, au milieu de nos strophes"[21] ("And now we now what was stopping us from living, amid our stanzas"). Adverbs or modulations of verb tenses are traditional closural techniques, of course. And to the Catholic poet's resounding "Ainsi soit-il!" comes the whispered closural reply of the Catholic convert, Max Jacob, on the decline and fall: "Ainsi choient-ils!"[22] (a word play: "So be it!" / "So let them fall!"). If the title of Jacob's collection *Le Cornet à dés* seems to take up the challenge of linguistic and typographical freedom posed by Mallarmé, an examination of his prose poems soon reveals what is old and fearfully symmetrical in his expressions of *l'esprit nouveau*. We find all traditional types of closure, including the most direct—"Adieu! Adieu"—or the frame construction, as in "Avant 1914," which begins "Oh! quelle étrange époque!" ("Oh! what a strange era") and ends with the same exclamation followed by "la scène où le salon était en pente pour faire plage," set off typographically from the body of the poem.[23]

Clearly, I cannot attempt within these precincts a statistical survey of closural patterns, nor am I temperamentally suited to such rigors. I shall therefore limit myself to the problem of closure in "dream poems," since in the very first issue of *La Révolution surréaliste*, Pierre Reverdy confronts the problem in his essay "Le Rêveur parmi les murailles," distinguishing between the form of the poetry of dream-thought and that of an article:

Si je *pensais* en écrivant un poème comme je suis obligé de penser (si faiblement que ce soit) en écrivant un article, ce poème aurait au moins une conclusion. Il y aurait entre ses parties un enchaînement soumis aux règles ordinaires du raisonnement. On y sentirait, pour si obscure qu'elle soit, la volonté de dire quelque chose à quelqu'un. Ne serait-ce que cette idée: Je vous prouve que je suis froidement capable de composer un poème . . .[24]

(If I *thought* in writing a poem as I am obliged to think [however feebly] in writing an article, this poem would at least have a conclusion. There would be between its parts some linkage subordinated to the ordinary rules of reasoning. No matter how obscurely, the will to say something to someone would be felt. Even if it were only this idea: I prove to you that I am coldly capable of composing a poem . . .

Thought moves forward in the mind by words, the dream develops in images. Breton and Éluard, in their "Notes sur la poésie," make the same distinction but more pungently:

À la moindre rature, le principe d'inspiration totale est ruiné. L'imbécillité efface ce que l'oreiller a prudemment créé. Il faut donc ne lui faire aucune part, à peine de produire des monstres. Pas de partage. L'imbécillité ne peut être reine.[25]

(The least thing crossed out, and the principle of total inspiration is ruined. Idiocy wipes out what the pillow has prudently created. So we should never admit it, unless we want to produce monsters. No sharing. Idiocy cannot be queen.)

If rhyme is comparable to "une paire de claques" ("a double slap"), form is bad (form) when it is imitable—that is, predictable and analyzable: "Bad form is essentially linked to repetition."[26]

If we accept their axioms that "a poem is always finished" and "poetry is naturally lazy,"[27] the ideal "lazy" fragment would be the dream transcription, many of which are featured in each issue of *La Révolution surrealiste*. The dream, *dixit* Reverdy, is ("the state in which consciousness is carried to its highest degree of perception,")[28] the only truly noble existence of man where the imagination is "free of any restrictive control," "the limitless extension of thought."[29] In each dream, there are two time streams—that of the dreamer moving from vision to awakening; that, often wildly distorted, of the dream's content. Both, when translated into the compromise of language by secondary elaboration, resort to traditional means of poetic closure. The ten-year-old Collombet narrates a dream of a skeleton who wants to bear him away to the devil, who in turn initiates the dream content's closure with an adverb of recapitulation: "Et maintenant, va-t-en sur la terre" ("And now, go off to earth"). The time stream of a dream concludes with the reappearance of the skeleton (forming a frame), who says that it is time to wake up. The narration had begun with "Un squelette vint me dire. . . ." ("A skeleton came to tell me. . . ."); it closes with "Le squelette revint me dire. . . ."[30] ("The skeleton came back to tell me. . . .").

The same pattern holds for the dream narrations of the much more repressed adult poets. Queneau's famous London dream ends with a *mot de la fin* or curtain line, "Matrice hypercomplexe."[31] One of Michel Leiris' dreams in "Le Pays de mes rêves" contains both a closural adverb and a movement to sculpturesque immobilization: "Mais *finalement* ceux-ci me dépassèrent" ("But *finally* these went beyond me") (italics mine); and "dissolution rapide et pétrification des rois." Another, haunted by the words "Zénith, Porphyre, Péage," resolves itself into an enigmatic adieu with an aphorism, "le porphyre de Zénith n'est pas notre péage" ("the porphyry of Zenith is not our toll"), after the preparation for closure, introduced by an adverb: "Puis les trois mots se formèrent" ("Then the three words were formed").[32]

An examination of surrealistic texts predicated on free association generally sustains this pattern of necessary teleology imposed by the secondary elaboration of language. Jean Arp's symmetrically restrictive opening, "la médaille se lève tandis que le soleil . . . se retire," ("the medal rises while the sun . . . withdraws"), moves with aleatory freedom but is resolutely closural in its postpositive adverb:

vous voyez donc qu'on ne consume monsieur son père que tranche par tranche, impossible d'en finir en un seul déjeuner sur l'herbe et le citron même tombe à genoux devant la beauté de la nature.[33]

(so you see that one only consumes one's father sir slice by slice, it being impossible to finish with it in one single lunch on the grass and even the lemon falls on its knees before the beauty of nature.)

The syntax is regular, and one notices such closural signals as the restrictive *ne . . . que* and the verb *finir*. The sentence strikes one as a kind of summation. Breton's purportedly automatic "Sale nuit, nuit de fleurs, nuit de râles" ("Filthy night, night of flowers, night of death rattles") from "Poisson soluble" gives signals of closure that are anything but automatic. Generated by incantatory repetitions, the poem arises (to use Breton-Éluard's image) from the pillow of free-flowing fantasy, only to yield to reason even in the midst of wilfully maintained confusion:

C'est fini, je ne cacherai plus ma honte, je ne serai plus calmé par rien, par moins que rien. Et si les volants sont grands comme des maisons, comment voulez-vous que nous jouissions, que nous entretenions notre vermine, que nous placions nos mains sur les lèvres des coquilles qui parlent sans cesse (ces coquilles, qui les fera taire enfin?). Plus de souffles, plus de sang, plus d'âme, mais des mains pour pétrir l'air, pour dorer une seule fois le pain de l'air, pour faire claquer la grande gomme des drapeaux qui dorment, des mains solaires, enfin, des mains gelées![34]

(It is finished, I shall no longer hide my shame, I shall not be calmed by anything, by less than anything. And if shuttlecocks are as tall as houses, how do you expect us to enjoy, to keep up our vermin, to place our hands on the lips of shells which ceaselessly speak [these seashells, who will silence them at last?]. No more breath, no more blood, no more soul, but hands to shape the air with, to make the bread of the air golden one single time, to have the great eraser of the dormant banners snap, solar hands, at last, frozen hands!)

Amid the apparent spontaneity of images generated largely through syntax (each *comment voulez-vous que, plus de* construction generates serially discontinuous images linked syntactically), expressions of closure surface. They refer to disappearance, that is, to the end of vision—"ne . . . plus," "rien," "taire," "plus de"—with "mains solaires" becoming "mains gelées." If we look back to the poem's opening, we find, after the serial apostrophe to night, signals of a verbal "frame" linking the opening to the closure: "Nuit sourde dont la main est un cerf-volant abject retenu par des fils de tous côtés, des fils noirs, des fils honteux" ("Deaf night whose hand is an abject kite held back on all sides by black strings/sons, shameful ones"). The image of the hand will conclude the poem, and surely too there is a verbal relationship between those "fils de tous côtés" and the ropes retaining the flapping flags.

"Poetry is the contrary of literature," Breton and Éluard confidently asserted. Yet most dream poetry written in the form of the *poème en prose* strikes one as resolutely literary, especially in its dogged reliance on closure. Jacob's "Charlot au bord de la mer" fades cinematographically: "Je le bouscule et le décor disparaît"[35] ("I push him [the child], and the scene disappears"). The first "Examen de conscience sous forme de rêve nocturne" shifts from present to past tense in its final and typographically isolated summation: "On a repeint en clair tout un appentis de la ferme" ("They have brightly repainted a whole annex of the farm")—the word *ferme* was in the opening sentence as well, and let us not forget that homophonically it is the very sound of closure. The second "Examen" features a concluding word game, almost in the baroque manner: "ma chambre est pleine de Soeurs de Charité. . . . J'achète vos oeuvres à cause du foie de veau. Sans doute! la Soeur est Anglaise"[36] ("my room is full of Sisters of Charity. . . . I am buying your works because of calf liver/faith in you. Of course: the Sister is English"). Into the dazzling enumeration in "Au hasard" of *Capitale de la douleur*, Éluard cannot resist inserting a repetition and the following signal of conclusion: "de parfums, de promesses, de pitié, de vengeances, de délivrances—*dis-je*—de délivrances comme au son des clairons"[37] ("perfumes, promises, pity, vengeance, deliverances, I say, deliverances as at the clarion sound"). The *dis-je* is almost a false note of rhetorical discourse. The beautiful prose poem "Dors" where Éluard illuminates "l'espèce de réussite que sont mes rêves" ("the species of success that my dreams are") hints at continuity—"Sans hier ni lendemain. Ce visage pur recommence" ("Without yesterday or tomorrow. This pure face begins anew"), a superb open ending—but *littérature* usurps the role of *poésie*, appending a single, isolated line of summation: "Le plus grand jour de ma vie, toujours"[38] ("The greatest day of my life, always"). Henri Michaux's oneiric vision of Honfleur in "Projection" has an interesting variation on the two time levels of dream poetry; within the dream, brilliant day yields to night, and the poet awakens to draw gloomy enlightenment from the irrevocable shift from imperfect to preterite: "Au milieu de la nuit, il a disparu tout d'un coup, faisant si subitement place au néant que je le regrettai presque"[39] ("In the middle of the night, it disappeared all at once, so suddenly giving way to nothingness that I almost missed it"). That final qualifying adverb is doubtless an attempt to reactivate uncertainty in the face of such closural negations as "nuit," "dis-

paru," "néant," "regrettai." "A transforming oneiric inspiration
is then tempered by poetic work," Mary Ann Caws has said of
Char's "Le Marteau sans maître." So, indeed, do the visionary
evocations—in the present and imperfect—of "Artine" yield to
action as conclusion in the only active past tense of a poem dom-
inated by passive verbs: "Le poète a tué son modèle" ("The poet
has killed his model").[40]

L. Meyer, in "The Radical Empiricism of the Avant-Garde,"
defined the antiteleological in music as "arousing no expectations,
except presumably that it will stop." The *poème en prose* does more
than merely stop. Despite its origins as an expression of the striving
for poetic freedom in form and language of the post-romantic era,
it remains largely faithful to typographical linearity, to accepted
syntax, and, above all, to clearly marked boundaries. It retains its
composure, in other words. Picabia's memorable esthetic, "tous
mes poèmes sont des poèmes en forme d'errata" ("all my poems
are poems in the form of errata"), may apply to "L'Antitête" of a
Tzara, but the great tradition of the *poème en prose* is, in its formal
expression of the ceremonial of closure, anything but avant-garde.
Poetry is not, as Breton and Éluard proclaimed, the opposite of
literature. What was prose for Des Esseintes remains Literature for
us.

Notes

1. Stéphane Mallarmé, *Oeuvres complètes* (Paris: Bibliothèque de la Pléiade, 1951), p. 1488. Unless otherwise noted, all quotations from Mallarmé are taken from this edition.

2. Stéphane Mallarmé, *Correspondance (1862–1871)* (Paris: Gallimard 1959), p. 242.

3. Charles Baudelaire, "À Arsène Houssaye," *Petits Poèmes en prose* (Paris: Garnier, 1962), p. 7.

4. Quoted by Suzanne Bernard, *Le Poème en prose de Baudelaire jusqu'à nos jours* (Paris: Nizet, 1959), p. 616. Bernard's thesis remains the basic source book for all studies of the prose poem, and my debt to her can only partially be expressed by the indispensable quotations I have derived from her own enormously wide-ranging readings.

5. Quoted by Bernard, *Le Poème en prose*, p. 627.

6. See Bernard, *Le Poème en prose*, p. 411.

7. Quoted by Bernard, *Le Poème en prose*, p. 598.

8. Émile Henriot in *Comoedia*, March 2, 1954.

9. See Bernard, *Le Poème en prose*, p. 689.

10. Barbara Herrnstein Smith, *Poetic Closure: A Study of How Poems End* (Chicago: University of Chicago Press, 1968).

11. Smith, *Poetic Closure*, p. 239.

12. Quoted by Bernard, *Le Poème en prose*, p. 655.

13. I shall limit myself to giving the titles of the *Illuminations* quoted, since listing pagination would be superfluous for these short and easily available pieces.

14. Baudelaire, *Petits Poèmes en prose*, p. 3.

15. Paul Claudel, *Oeuvre poétique* (Paris: Bibliothèque de la Pléiade, 1957), p. 53.

16. René Char, *Poems of René Char*, M. A. Caws and J. Griffin, trs., (Princeton: Princeton University Press, 1976), p. 192.

17. Paul Éluard, *Oeuvres complètes* (Paris: Bibliothèque de la Pléiade, 1968), 1:169.

18. André Breton, *Poèmes* (Paris: Gallimard, 1948), p. 56.

19. Saint-John Perse, *Oeuvres complètes* (Paris: Bibliothèque de la Pléiade, 1972), pp. 126, 277.

20. Claudel, *Oeuvre poétique*, p. 69.

21. Perse, *Oeuvres complètes*, p. 290.

22. Max Jacob, *Le Cornet à dés* (Paris: Gallimard, 1955), 2:71.

23. *Ibid.*, 2:101, 40.

24. Pierre Reverdy, "Le Rêveur parmi les murailles," *La Révolution surréaliste* (December 1924), 1:20

25. André Breton and Paul Éluard, "Notes sur la poésie," *La Révolution surréaliste* (December 1929) 12:54.

26. *Ibid.*, p. 55.

27. *Ibid.*, p. 54.

28. Reverdy, "Le Rêveur," p. 19.

29. *Ibid.*, p. 20.

30. Collombet, in Rêves," *La Révolution surréaliste* (April 1925), 3:3.

31. Raymond Queneau, in "Rêves," *La Révolution surréaliste* (April 1925), 3:5.

32. Michel Leiris, "Le Pays de mes rêves," *La Révolution surréaliste* (January 1925), 2:26, 29.

33. Jean Arp, "Textes surréalistes," *La Révolution surréaliste* (June 1926), 7:23.

34. Breton, *Poèmes*, p. 58.

35. Jacob, *Cornet à dés*, 2:65.

36. *Ibid.*, 2:146, 149.

37. Éluard, *Oeuvres complètes*, 1:190.

38. *Ibid.*, 1:360.

39. Henri Michaux, "Projection," in *Poètes d'aujourd'hui* (Paris: 1957), p. 114.

40. *Poems of René Char*, p. 12.

PART IV

Two Prose Poems

12. Poème en prose, prose en poème

MICHEL DEGUY

Je

me propose de fournir ici à la fois des exemples et des réflexions à leur sujet. La différence du poème-en-prose et du poème-poème, j'en fais l'expérience, et j'y reviens; ce qui peut passer soit pour banal (retour ordinaire d'un écrivain sur son procédé), soit pour insolite: un même sujet s'expose en écrivain et en critique de sa facture, dans un type de publication (une revue) où il est d'usage que le soussigné prenne pour objet d'autres échantillons que de son oeuvre. Ceci est donc une amorce d'auto-poiético-graphie.

Impudemment, je vous fais lire deux textes, que je choisis récemment écrits, et américains—et par là je veux dire en relation avec (et de) tel moment de ma vie aux USA—tout simplement pour prendre la chance d'intéresser un peu plus que d'habitude un lecteur américain. Et par "impudence" j'entends le risque couru que le manque d'appétence d'un lecteur pour les poèmes specimens entraîne sa dépréciation des remarques faites à leur propos.

La Fin d'après-midi près d'Annapolis est pour moi un poème en prose; *Étude avancée,* un poème en vers libres. Les deux furent écrits en 1980 après des voyages aux USA. Réflexion faite, je les rejette en appendice.

Entre

Le mot de *prose* se trouve, on le sait, doublement conjugué: avec celui de *poésie* et avec celui de *poème*. En tant qu'il s'oppose à poème comme d'une espèce à l'autre, il se laisse subsumer à *poésie*, qui dit le genre. "Poésie" est pris dans trois usages: virtuellement majusculé, le terme désigne un langage total de la langue; au singulier et minusculé, il dénotera l'oeuvre de X ou Y, et par allusion, sa tonalité singulière ("la poésie d'Apollinaire est ceci, ou cela, etc."); au pluriel, il fait double emploi avec poèmes ("Avez-vous appris vos poésies?"). Il y a la poésie, il y a le poème, il y a le poète; leur relation complexe, compliquée du fait qu'ils se prêtent souvent leur nom l'un aux autres, peut être évoquée comme "pratique poétique."

Mon rapport à la poésie est celui d'une *hésitation prolongée entre poème et prose.* Le poème est "entre nous deux . . ." Qui donc, ces deux? La "poésie" qui vient de redisparaître là-bas, qui hante; et "moi," ici, l'écrivain, cette personne, comme on l'appelle, qui est à tout instant multiplement autre que "poète," et qui espère le moment de synthèse, le bref court-circuit, où par la médiation du poème en train, *poète* redevient un prédicat possible pour *je.* Quand je suis *lecteur* de poésie, le poème est aussi "entre nous." La poésie est passée par ici, elle repassera par là, dit la chanson, *attachée* (c'est aussi le sens de *haerere*, qui fait étymologie pour "hésitation") à ces séquences de langue française que ma diction fait réentendre.

Le poème en prose, dans mon expérience d'écrivain, désire ceci: faire parler la poésie en parlant de poésie dans ce langage de *prose du poème* de "ma" langue (la française). Ces formules nouées—"parler la prose de la poésie, m'entendre faire parler la prose de mon poème"—aimeraient suggérer qu'il y a, pour le poète comme agent de change, une relation entre prose et poésie telle qu'il existe "un langage de prose du poème de ma langue."

Partition

Je suis en alerte, la main au stylo, et il y a cette possibilité indécise, jusqu'au dernier moment, où le geste d'écrire se suspend aux prises avec le *dicendum* qui cherche à faire sens en prenant langue; cette option pour la phrase de se faire *prose* ou *vers*. De sorte que j'imagine une double page, une page pliée, et de chaque côté du pli pendant l'alerte (c'est-à-dire, selon l'étymologie, la *mise en ligne*) certaine formule tombe d'un côté en "prose" ou de l'autre en "vers," comme dans les *juxtalinéaires* de notre adolescence laborieusement traductrice des "Anciens." Sujet de la langue, sujet à parler, j'*exerce* cette double possibilité, éduqué (élevé, érigé: en alerte) dans le double langage de la langue, pas moins surpris que le locuteur ordinaire entendant le retour de sa phrase à la source et disant, "Tiens? Ça rime!" ou quelque chose de ce genre; mais distinct, par la *réflexion*, du moment où Monsieur Jourdain ne se savait pas encore prosateur, autant que Malherbe de son crocheteur.

La *poésie* est alors ici—pour le moment—ce qui nomme la langue en tant qu'elle hésite entre les deux, et le "poète," celui qui prend une décision de partage plus ou moins tranché, entre poème en vers et poème en prose, dans la responsabilité à l'égard des phrases de la tribu—sa langue. Ecrire, c'est entrer plus complexement, plus retorsement, dans l'intraductibilité de sa langue, la rendre hermétique, la refermer sur soi: faire jouer le rapport de soi à soi de sa langue selon ces deux registres, selon le pli intime de la langue en "prose et poésie," son inter- ou intra-traductibilité de soi à soi, le jeu de cette différence.

La *poésie* est ce que nous appelons quand nous nous rapportons à la langue; nous attendons d'elle qu'elle nous assujettisse à notre langue et, par là, à ce qui parle dans une langue (et d'autant mieux que la langue nous possède davantage, "maternellement et naturellement"), c'est-à-dire aux choses, au langage des choses, comme on dit parfois, par exemple en évoquant la fable de Siegfried entendant "le langage des oiseaux."

De quoi un poème cherche à chaque fois à s'acquitter, *pris en défaut* d'une manière déterminée.

En

La poésie peut passer en prose; le poème peut être en prose, comme la table en bois et le portrait de l'artiste en jeune singe.

Le dictionnaire détaille les valences prépositionnelles de *en*:
(a) locative, au sens du *dans*, et avec la nuance de l'aboutissement
d'un mouvement (correspondant au *in* latin suivi de l'accusatif);
(b) durative, au sens du *pendant*: poème durant la prose, en même
temps que sa prose; (c) de disposition et d'occupation; (d) géron-
dive, ou de moyen, poème en prosant; (e) qualitative et comparative: prose en qualité de poème; (f) de métamorphose: le poème
s'est changé en prose, la prose en poésie; la prose donne le change
. . .

En quoi est la poésie? Elle peut être en poème, et celui-ci en
prose. Reversiblement, la prose peut être en poème: il s'agit d'é-
change entre ces deux; et la *prose*, comme toute chose (un amour,
un élément linguistique, un motif), cherche à entrer dans le poème,
à intéresser la poésie. La prose peut faire contenance pour un contenu poétique, c'est-à-dire un rapport poétique avec la langue et
ce qui est. La langue, nous le savons, peut véhiculer superficielle-
ment, légèrement, du "contenu," dont elle se décharge aussitôt,
en actions, en gestes, en autres choses, les mots ayant fonctionné
comme signes pour des choses qu'il s'agissait de faire, de modifier,
etc.; valeur d'échange, comparée par Mallarmé à de la monnaie.
Mais elle peut aussi réfléchir sa propre contenance, se comporter
elle-même, c'est-à-dire inscrire dans sa *hylê*—sa signifiance comme
on dit volontiers aujourd'hui, (phonétique, morphologique, syn-
taxique, etc.) *ce* qu'elle contient: faire ce qu'elle dit.

Métamorphose

Et je voudrais raconter la temporalité d'un poème en cours
comme celle d'une métamorphose: sur-le-champ quelque chose qui
n'est pas livresque se fait ligne, honore la langue, se fait livre. *Une
obscurité se déclare*; la langue lapide le silence, une image se dessine
sous les coups, une figure apparaît. Comme un orage qui peut
passer par l'arbre, par la pointe d'acier, par Sémélê, ou se dissiper
plus loin, ainsi la chose qui se précipite fait tenir à la langue un
langage, "poème," qui est en même temps (*cum, simul*) un (se) dire
de la langue et un dit (dict, dictée) de quelque chose.

En colonne par deux

Cependant il faut marquer, descriptivement, quelques traits de l'opposition "en prose" vs. "en vers," à laquelle je réfère depuis le début comme à la différence intrinsèque à la langue dans son rapport à la poésie (et, derechef, dans "mon" usage).

	En prose vs.	*En vers*
Composition	L'unité est la strophe, de pleine "justification" (pris ici dans le sens typographique, qu'il a pour le prote); le poème peut courir sur plusieurs pages	Le *vers* est inférieur à la "justification"; son autonomie est marquée par la majuscule initiale à la ligne; le "compte totale" du poème lyrique est, en fait, le plus souvent $\leq$ à la page
Orthographie	Ponctué	Déponctué (les espacements et les majuscules assument la scansion des pauses)
Itérations	Irrégularité, "anisométrique," des intervalles entre ce qui se ressemble paronomastiquement; "hypogrammatisme"	Rimes, ou assonances; et en général cadence; régularité des intervalles entre ce qui est marqué comme *revenant*
Segmentation	Désegmentation, ou brouillage des segments (métrique, phrastique, sémantique . . .) en recouvrement et désarticulation partiels; pas de composants métriques indentifiables en versîfication	Parallélisme des segments plus *ou moins* coextensifs mètre phrase sens la relative autonomie du parallélisme faisant jouer l'*enjambement* comme tel, saillir les "rejets," etc.; hantise des mètres traditionnels déréglés
Ton	Enchainement; "élastique ondulation"	Chaque ligne est un *incipit* possible
Grammaticalité	Discursivité, syntax-	Paratactisme, ou lignes en ap-

Grammaticalité
(cont.)

En Prose	vs.	En vers
isme, conjonctions et subordinations "grammaticales"		positions (juxtaposition, superposition); le blanc assume des valeurs de subordination indéterminée; pauses de silence, syncopes grammaticales
Logique	Rhétorique; persuasive; raisonneuse—récitatif de pensée; tissu conjonctif	Oraculaire, énigmatique; tresses d'isotopies/isotropies non "peignées"; peu de recours aux "temps passés" du verbe; fait sauter le disjoncteur
Psychologie de l'auteur	Temps "ramassé," volontaire, de composition	Ramassage en constellation d'éléments épars et arbitrairement apparentés; temps "réel" de composition—des jours, des semaines, des mois . . .

Le tiers

Quel serait le *tiers*, le ni l'un ni l'autre de ces deux? N'y a-t-il pas, récemment développée, une formule graphique qui ne ressemble ni au poème en vers ni au poème en prose; où le rapport, d'antagonisme, entre le quantum de signifiance, ce paquet de vocables, et le blanc, ce milieu de silence, soit plus tendu, plus déchirant, plus harcelé, presque "à une autre échelle," comme les griffes du lynx ("bonds de la bête féroce"—Rimbaud) par rapport aux prestesses des rongeurs; une sorte de texte webernien qui se jette aux yeux d'abord comme ni strophique ni versimorphe; une disposition plus intense (cf. André du Bouchet)?

L'un

Prose et poème, ce sont deux formules d'alliage distinctes; comme deux possibilités différentes de la composition de l'un et du multiple, de la retenue de la diversité dans l'unification, de la lutte du sens avec les significations.

Qu'est devenue la *règle des unités* en général?

De même que chaque jour, pour un adolescent, doit faire sens par lui-même, *vase communicant* d'un début à une fin, du dedans (la maison, par exemple) au dehors (la *sortie*) avant le tombeau de la nuit qui permettra la répétition, l'écrivain en est un qui se demande quelle *unité* il veut faire, défaire et refaire, et comment perdre l'unité dans un divers qui soit sa diversification. Il s'agit de faire des économies, et il y en a deux régimes distincts (voir plus haut). L'unité de *la page* correspond à une certaine mesure de l'unité de temps; l'unité d'un sens intégrant des significations, à une certaine mesure de l'*unité d'action* dramatique, destinale, narrable; l'unité de la scène figurale, à l'*unité du lieu* d'exister; l'unité de la phrase, quelque disloquée qu'en soit la récurrence, à l'unité de la pensée maintenant son désir de se penser . . .

Poem in Prose in Poem

I

propose to give some examples of and reflections about the poem as prose, and prose as poem. The difference between the prose-poem and the poem-as-poem. I am trying it out, turning it over. A process both banal—the same old turning back of a writer on his craft—and odd—the same subject exposes himself as a writer and as a critic of his production, and in the sort of publication in which the author usually takes examples from other writers' work; this is, then, a sketch of an auto-poetic writing.

Two texts accompany this one, concerning a specific moment of a specific passage, both written in 1980 after some trips to the United States. For this reason the American reader may find them interesting. This is, however, taking a risk, for the reader put off by the sample poems might tend to denigrate the remarks made about the genre to which they belong.

"End of Afternoon near Annapolis" I consider a prose poem, "Advanced Study," a poem in free verse. You will find them at the end.

Between

The word *prose* is coupled both with *poetry* and *poem*. Insofar as it is set against the word *poem*, as one species is distinguished from another, it may be subsumed in the term *poetry*, which tells us the genus. *Poetry* can be understood in three ways: in essence with a capital *P* it denotes the total expressive range of our language; with a small *p* it can designate the work of a particular poet, and further his distinctive tone ("Apollinaire's poetry is this or it's that"); it can also be used in the same sense as poem in the plural ("Have you learned your poetry?"). Poetry, poem, poet; let's call their complex relation, complicated by the fact that each of them often refers to the others, "poetic practice."

My relation to poetry is a *long hesitation between poem and prose*. The poem is "between ourselves, between us two . . ." Who are they, these two? "Poetry," which has again just disappeared out there, haunting; and "me," here, the writer, a person, as they say, having at every instant innumerable identities other than "poet," and hoping for the moment of synthesis, the brief short-circuit that through the poem in progress will again make *poet* a possible predicate for *I*. When I am reading poetry, the poem is also "between ourselves." Poetry passes by here, it will pass by again there, as the song says, *fastened* (that's also the meaning of *haerere*, which is the root of "hesitation") to those sequences of French which my speech lets me hear again.

The prose poem, in my experience as a writer, wants to give poetry a voice by speaking of poetry in this *prose language of the poem* in "my" language, French. These intertwined formulas—"to speak the prose of poetry, to hear myself give voice to my poem's prose"—would like to suggest that for the poet as broker, the relation between prose and poetry implies "a prose language of the poem in my tongue."

Score

The alert has sounded, I've taken up my pen, and up to the last minute there is an undetermined possibility while the act of writing is in suspense, grappling with the *dicendum* that must make itself understood in language; the sentence can become *prose* or *verse*. I imagine a double page, a page folded in two, and on each side of the fold during the alert (according to its etymology, the *lining up*), a formula falls on the side in "prose" or on the other in "verse," as in the line-by-line bilingual versions we ploughed through as adolescents translating the Ancients. As a subject of language, a speaking subject, I *use* this dual possibility, educated (raised, erected: on the alert) in the dual modes of language, no less suprised then the ordinary speaker hearing his sentence return to its source and saying, "Why, that rhymes!" or something like that; yet different, because of my *thought*, from the moment when Mr. Jourdain discovers he's talking prose, just as Malherbe was different from the workmen whose French usage he found instructive.

Poetry in this connection at this moment is what designates language insofar as it hesitates between the two, and the "poet" is he who takes a more or less firm decision between verse poem and prose poem, mindful of his responsibility to the words/phrases of the tribe—his language. The writer gets into the untranslatability of his language in a more complex, more artful fashion, making it hermetic, closing himself up in it: there is an interplay of selves within this language in these two registers according to the essential bent of the language in "prose and poetry," its inter- or intra-translatability from self to self, the play of this difference.

Poetry is what we call upon when we relate ourselves to language; we expect it to subject us to our language and, in this way, to what speaks in a language (and it will do this better the more thoroughly our language possesses us, "maternally and naturally"), that is, to things, the language of things. Telling the story of Siegfried, for example, we say he understood the "language of the birds."

And a poem always tries to fulfill this obligation, *inadequate* though it be on certain scores.

In

Poetry can turn into prose; a poem can be in prose, as a table can be in wood and the portrait of the artist in the form of a young monkey.

The dictionary explains in detail the prepositional valences of *in*: (a) locative, in the sense of *into*, and with the nuance of the goal of a movement (as when Latin *in* is followed by the accusative); (b) durative, in the sense *during*: poem during prose, at the same time as its prose; (c) pertaining to disposition or occupation; (d) gerundive or denoting means, poem in prosing; (e) qualitative and comparative: prose in the form of poem; (f) pertaining to metamorphosis: the poem changed into prose, prose into poetry; prose sidetracks us . . .

Of what does poetry consist? Perhaps of a poem, and the poem can be in prose. Conversely, prose can be in the form of a poem: there is an exchange between these two; and *prose*, like everything else (a love, a linguistic element, a design theme), tries to come into the poem, to involve poetry. Prose can serve as a container for a poetic content, that is, a poetic relationship with language and reality. We know that language can move superficially, lightly, from the content it immediately sloughs off, into actions, gestures, other things, words having served as signs for things to be done, changed, etc; they have an exchange value, which Mallarmé compared to currency. But it can also reflect its own content, include itself, inscribe in its *hyle*—its significance, as we say these days (phonetic, morphological, syntactic, etc.)—*what* it contains: do what it says.

Metamorphosis

I'd like to tell about the time lived as a poem takes shape as one recounts a metamorphosis: something not bookish immediately becomes a line, honors language, becomes a book. *Darkness descends*; language stones silence, an image takes form under the blows, a figure appears. Like a storm that can *pass* through the tree, through the steel tip of the spear, through Semele, or vanish further on, what is rushing upon us gives speech a language, the "poem," which is at the same time (*cum, simul*) something language is saying (about itself) and something said (dict, dictée) about something.

Two-by-Two

I shall now describe some features of the contrast between "in prose" and "in verse," which from the outset I have called the difference intrinsic to language in its relation to poetry. (And, I repeat, as *I* use these terms).

	In prose	*vs.*	*In verse*
Composition	The unit is the stanza with the lines extending from margin to margin; the poem may fill several pages		The line of verse is shorter than the space between the margins; its autonomy is denoted by the initial capital letter; the total length of the lyric poem is very often less than a page
Orthography	Punctuated		Not punctuated (spacing and capital letters mark the rhythmic pauses)
Repetitions	"Anisometric" irregularity of intervals between paronomasias or puns; "hypogramatism"		Rhyme, or assonance; in general, cadence; regularity of intervals between elements that *re*appear

Segmentation	Desegmentation, or mingling of segments (metric, semantic, sentence elements . . .) partially overlapping and disarticulated; no identifiable metric components		Parallelism of more or less coextensive segments
			    meter
			    sentence
			    meaning
			the relative autonomy of parallelism results in *enjambement*, emphasizes the "rejets", etc.; obsession with traditional regular metres

	In Prose	*vs.*	*In verse*
Tone	Linking of ideas; "elastic undulation"		Each line is a possible new beginning
Grammar	Discursiveness, logical syntax, "grammatical" conjunctions and sub-ordinations		Parataxis or lines in apposition (juxtaposition, superposition); spaces have the force of indeterminate subordinations; pauses of silence, grammatical breaks
Logic	Rhetorical; persuasive; reasoning—recitative of thought; connective tissue in the texture		Oracular, enigmatic; strands of "uncombed" isotopies/isotropies; little recourse to "past tenses" of the verb; destroys the circuit-breaker
Author's Psychology	Time deliberately set aside for composition		Gathering of scattered and arbitrarily related elements in a constellation; "real" time for composition—days, weeks, months . . .

The Third

What might be the *third* possibility, the one that is neither of these two? Hasn't a type of writing developed recently that is unlike either the verse poem or the prose poem; in which the antagonism between the quantity of meaning, that package of vocables, and the blank spaces, refuge of silence, is tenser, more painful, more tormented, almost "on another scale," like a lynx's claws (Rimbaud's "bonds de la bête féroce") in comparison with a rodent's agile speed; texts recalling Webern's music, which at first glance are neither in stanza or verse form; a more intense pattern (André du Bouchet, for example)?

The One

Prose and poem are two different formulas for an alloy; like two possible ways of composing the one and the many, of gathering diversity into unity, of the struggle between meaning and individual words.

In general what has become of *the rule of the unities*?

Just as each day, for an adolescent, must have a meaning in itself, a *vessel communicating* from a beginning to an end, from inside (the house, for instance) to outside (the *exit*) before the tomb of night that leads to repeating the cycle, the writer wonders what *unity* he wants to make, unmake, and remake, and how to lose that unity in a diversity that is its own. Energies must be saved, and there are two different means of doing that (see above). The unity of *the page* corresponds in some degree with the unity of time; the unity of a meaning that integrates individual meanings, in some degree with the *unity of action*, dramatic, destined, capable of being recounted; the unity of the visual scene corresponds to the *unity of place*; the unity of the sentence, no matter how displaced its recurrence, to the unity of thought maintaining its desire to think itself . . .

Translated by Sylvia Goldfrank

Étude avancée

A ton nom qui précède un nom que je ne connaissais pas
Ton nom commun sans nom propre à quelques unes
(d'Anna Magnani neuve dentelée prête à l'Annonciation)
Et ta voix pour laquelle il faut chercher d'autres comparants

Avec ces traits grossis qui me rendent invisible
Avariés plus encore sous les loupes de la pluie
Je me hais jusque dans les chambres
Les guillottines lacérèrent la nuit

L'averse nous siamoisa tu disais
(Elle dit): la Grèce à Princeton
Une course sans vainqueur sur la piste aux pelouses
Nous attelait jusqu'à la gare où
La permission des yeux fut suspendue

     Amants qui vous aimez
Je ne connaissais pas le jeune héros de la course
     là-bas   ici
J'ai déja oublié ce qui va commencer

Advanced Study
> At your name preceding a name I used not to know
> Your common name without a name proper to some
> (of Anna Magnani newly teethed ready for the Annunciation)
> And your voice for which you would have to find a comparable one

> With these coarsened traits making me invisible
> Spoiled still more under the lenses of the rain
> I hate myself even in the rooms
> The guillotines lacerated at night

> The downpour Siamesed us, you were saying
> (She says): Greece in Princeton
> A race victorless on the lawn track
> Yoked us as far as the station where
> The eyes' leave was suspended

> Lovers who love each other
> I did not know the young hero of the race
> over there   here
> I have already forgotten what is about to begin

Translated by Mary Ann Caws

La Fin d'après-midi près d'Annapolis
> Ce qui reste d'un voyage; ce en vue de quoi, à contre-prévoyance,
> le voyage avait lieu, frisant ses catastrophes et qu'il aura perdu sur
> la route du retour, jusqu'au retour de ce qui ne fut pas refoulé mais
> perdu, dans aucun inconscient ni par aucun intérêt à la perte, et qui,
> revenant, sera donc, pour l'attente de rien, cadeau; ce qui reste d'un
> voyage est souvenir, mais de quoi, de la douceur de l'impasse, ou,
> plus équivoquement, du don que se faisaient l'un de l'autre l'im-
> passe et la douceur, le bord et le rebroussement.

> Quand l'après-midi eut cherché sa fin dans Annapolis, le ciel prenait
> des ris dans la lumière, il y eut avec l'amorce du retour un goût de
> finition que ce génitif: fin-de-la-fin, suggère et que le bout d'An-
> napolis n'avait pas encore offert: d'une baie de la baie, d'une boucle
> où se boutonne la baie aux abords retroussés où le monde du voyage
> fît une fin, qui pouvait bien encore ne pas avoir lieu.

> L'après-midi finissait près d'Annapolis aux bords où le détour cher-
> chait son rebroussement, longeant la baie avec M. et S. L'égarement
> inventait un abord jusqu'où ne pas pouvoir aller plus loin, le point

d'inflexion du voyage enfin équivalent aux autres. Nous avons trouvé enfin une impasse, enfin nous nous sommes perdus doucement au hasard par un chemin de la route redondant, qui annonçait à la fin une place où ici ou ailleurs revinssent au même, à être ici, à être bien ici, et ainsi au repos sans comparaison. ''Une nuée lumineuse les prit sous son ombre; Rabbi, il est heureux que nous soyons ici, faisons donc trois tentes . . .''

On pouvait rester ou ne pas rester, la coïncidence des opposés faisait un nid où dans l'herbe haute et prostrée les corps se couchèrent sur leurs ombres, tandis que le soir abattait le ciel. La mer octroyée par l'énorme Bay-Bridge guéant l'horizon et par les cargos qui croisaient, la mer qui passait là émoussait cette langue de lande, dans la fin, les confins, la douceur, l'indifférence de l'impasse, la stance de notre retour. ''Relevez-vous, et n'ayez pas peur . . .''

Une photo en témoigne, mais le montre-t-elle? Pour l'exhaustion de ce qu'un ''souvenir'' augure, s'il est vrai que l'oublié qui revient est *le vrai*—non pas tant deux morceaux de temps arrachés à la succession que son *image* arrimant spacieusement un site à lui-même—il est besoin de redescendre à terre les mots de l'arche encyclopédique: étambots ou laiches. Tels ils veillaient dans les scabieuses sages et leurs paroles entendirent le vent.

Ce qui donne contenance à l'hospitalité de poème, disons qu'il est le Rapprochant. L'image est l'oisiveté qui accueille les choses par leurs noms dans le Rapprochant, que notre système métrique tient éloignées comme de la rizière à la rimaye, mais dont la proximité allitérative est l'aspect chanceux le plus simple. Ce qui possibilise la traduction n'est pas une machine ni une compétence; dont la courtoisie est le figurant. Le poème tient à ce qui tient dans le poème et qui tient au poème.

End of Afternoon near Annapolis
What remains of a trip; the reason for which, unexpectedly, you made the trip, just avoiding its catastrophes and what it loses on the way home, until the return of what was not suppressed but lost, not in any part of your unconscious mind or because you wanted to lose it, and which, when it comes back, because you expected nothing, is a gift; what remains of a trip is memory, but of what, of the sweetness of the dead end, or, more equivocally, of the gift that one made of the other, the road's end and sweetness, the edge of the bay and the road retraced.

As afternoon drew to a close in Annapolis, the sky took in reefs in the light; in the beginning of the return there was a taste of ending which the genitive end-of-the-end suggests, and which the end of Annapolis hadn't yet offered: of a bay of the bay, of a curl where the bay with its turned-up edges buttons itself up where the world of the trip might come to an end that might still not take place.

The afternoon was coming to an end near Annapolis where the detour was turning back, as I walked along the bay shore with M. and S. Having lost our way, we found a turn that led to a spot where we couldn't go any farther, the turning point of the trip finally equivalent to the others. We finally found the dead end, finally we got quietly lost following a path parallel to the road, which eventually led to a place where here or elsewhere came to the same thing, to being here, to feeling fine here, and so to a matchless rest. "A luminous cloud enveloped them in its shadow; Rabbi, it is fortunate that we are here, let us pitch three tents . . ."

We could stay or not stay, the coming together of opposites made a nest where our bodies lay down on their shadows in the high, flattened grass, while evening lowered the sky. The sea granted to us by the huge Bay Bridge fording the horizon and by the freighters crossing the bay, the sea passing by wore down that tongue of moorland in the end, the boundaries, the gentleness, the indifference of the dead end, the stanza of our return. "Arise and fear not . . ."

A photo records it but does it show it? To absorb all that a "souvenir" promises, if it is true that the forgotten element which comes back is *true*—not so much two bits of time torn from the succession of moments as its *image* comfortably arranging a space for itself—one must bring back to earth the words of the encyclopedic ark: sternposts or sedge. So they watched amid the healing scabious, and their words heard the wind.

What gives volume to the poem's hospitality we might call what relates. The image is leisure which receives things by their names within what relates, things which our metrical system keeps as far from each other as the rice paddy from the mountain glacier but whose alliterative proximity is the simplest effect of chance. What makes translation into poetry possible is not a machine or competence in which courtesy figures. The poem depends upon what the poem holds and what holds to the poem.

Translated by Sylvia Goldfrank

13. The Way We Walk Now:
A Theory of the Prose Poem

JOHN HOLLANDER

*I*t was not that there were only the old ways of going from one chamber to another: we had learned to imitate the noble walk of those who had built, and dwelt in, the Great Palaces, moving gravely through the interconnecting rooms; aware of the painted ceilings and the import of the images there for their lives, but never needing to look up at them; free among their footmen; roaming their spaces and yet by no means imprisoned in the fragile grandeur to which, in the afternoon light, the rooms had fallen. We had learned thereafter to mock that stiff way of walking, and after that, to replace it with our own little dances and gallops; we roller-skated from room to room, or occasionally bicycled. Being confined by the layout was not the point, nor was it what may or may not have happened to the houses—whether they were indeed in ruins or merely in need of repair. We had all gone away somewhere: off to war, or to the city, or had shipped out for the East. And those of us who returned, or who had stayed wherever it was, came quite naturally to go about in the field, or among the hills or through the streets. At first, it was almost with memorized maps of the ways rooms opened off each other, and of just what courts it was on which the various windows gave; after that, with no recollected plan, but always moving the better for having started out in one of the great houses.

But then it almost ceased to matter where we were. What had become necessary that we do by way of amble, or of hop, skip, and jump, had so taken over power from mere place that it generated the shapes of space through which it moved, like a lost, late arrival at the start of a quest who had set out nonetheless, dreaming each new region into which he landed. Pictures of the old palaces still had a certain pathos; but they were not of ourselves or of our lives. The distance that had been put between us and the houses crammed full of chambers was utter, like that between the starry heavens above and the text below us, on the opened page.

Index

N.B. Names of authors participating in this volume are not indexed, nor are fictitious characters, nor the titles of individual works. Last names only are given in the obvious cases (e.g. Aragon, Bataille, Matisse, Renoir, Saussure).